BIOGRAPHICAL SUPPLEMENT AND INDEX

THE YOUNG OXFORD HISTORY OF WOMEN IN THE UNITED STATES

Nancy F. Cott, *General Editor*

BIOGRAPHICAL SUPPLEMENT AND INDEX

Harriet Sigerman

OXFORD UNIVERSITY PRESS

New York • Oxford

For Thea and her generation, who will carry on the fight

Oxford University Press

Oxford   New York
Athens Auckland Bangkok Bombay
Calcutta Cape Town Dar es Salaam Delhi
Florence Hong Kong Istanbul Karachi
Kuala Lumpur Madras Madrid Melbourne
Mexico City Nairobi Paris Singapore
Taipei Tokyo Toronto
and associated companies in
Berlin   Ibadan

Library of Congress Cataloging-in-Publication Data
Biographical Supplement and Index / Harriet Sigerman
p. cm. — (The young Oxford history of women in the United States; v.11)
Includes bibliographical references and index
1. Women—United States—History—Juvenile literature.
2. Women—United States—Social conditions—Juvenile literature.
3. Women—History. 4. Women—Social conditions. 5. United States—Social conditions.
I. Cott, Nancy F.
HQ 1410.Y68   1994
305.4'0973   94-222524
ISBN 0-19-508829-8
ISBN 0-19-508830-1 (series)

1 3 5 7 9 8 6 4 2
Printed in the United States of America
on acid-free paper

Listing of Museums and Historic Sites compiled by Ann T. Keene
Design: Leonard Levitsky

On the cover: Top row, left to right, Abigail Adams, Pocahontas, Clara Barton; middle row, Harriet Beecher Stowe, Eleanor Roosevelt, Amelia Earhart; bottom row, Elizabeth Ann Seton, Jessie Fauset, Barbara Jordan.
Frontispiece: An engraving from *The History of the World's Columbian Exposition* (1892).

CONTENTS

A Note from the Author
The women whose biographies are presented in this volume appear in volumes 1 through 10 of *The Young Oxford History of Women in the United States*. They each have played a role in shaping this nation's history, but they by no means represent all of the unique and talented women who have contributed to the sweep of American history.

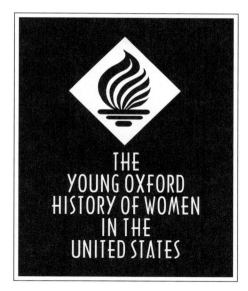

THE YOUNG OXFORD HISTORY OF WOMEN IN THE UNITED STATES

On February 15, 1921, this memorial to the pioneers of the woman suffrage movement—(from left) Elizabeth Cady Stanton, Susan B. Anthony, and Lucretia Mott—was presented to the U.S. Capitol by the National Woman's Party.

BIOGRAPHICAL SUPPLEMENT

Abbott, Edith

SOCIAL WORKER, EDUCATOR,
SOCIALREFORMER

Born: September 26, 1876
Grand Island, Nebraska

Died: July 28, 1957
Grand Island, Nebraska

Along with her sister Grace Abbott, Edith Abbott was a forceful advocate for economic rights for women, immigrants, and low-income workers. In addition, she helped to shape a new, more comprehensive and scientific approach to training in social work and human services.

Both sisters received their first exposure to new ideas from their mother, a high school principal and champion of progressive ideas about women's rights and social reform. Edith Abbott attended public schools in Grand Island and Brownell Hall, a boarding school for girls in Omaha, Nebraska. After a brief teaching career, she entered college and, in 1905, received a Ph.D. with honors in economics from the

University of Chicago, where she studied under some of the most distinguished economists of the day.

She pursued postgraduate study in London and returned to the United States convinced of the need for new ways to combat poverty. She taught at Wellesley College for one year, then joined the visionary and talented staff at Jane Addams's Hull House. There, along with her sister Grace, she worked for woman suffrage, a 10-hour day for working women, immigrants' rights, better tenement housing, and child labor laws. To document her efforts, Abbott produced several studies, such as *Women in Industry* (1910) and *The Real Jail Problem* (1915).

In 1920, Abbott joined the faculty of the University of Chicago. There, she helped to establish the nation's first graduate school of social work. She wanted students to receive a firm intellectual grasp of social issues rather than perfunctory on-the-job training. Four years later, she became dean of the social work program and together with her longtime mentor, Sophonisba Breckinridge, devised a cross-disciplinary curriculum that focused on ways to change inadequate social conditions rather than merely distribute charity.

Abbott continued to launch programs and projects in social work at the university and helped devise social policy on issues affecting the poor. She attacked corrupt practices in existing welfare programs, urged the establishment of a network of public social services, and during the depression called on the federal government to assume responsibility for providing these services. Many of her ideas found a niche in President Franklin Delano Roosevelt's New Deal programs. Abbott's contribution to the development of more effective social welfare policies is immeasurable.

MAJOR PUBLICATIONS
Report on Crime and the Foreign Born (1931)
Social Welfare and Professional Education (1931; 2nd ed., 1942)

FURTHER READING
Costin, Lela B. *Two Sisters for Social Justice: A Biography of Grace and Edith Abbott*. Urbana: University of Illinois Press, 1983.

Abbott, Grace

SOCIAL WORKER

Born: November 17, 1878
Grand Island, Nebraska

Died: June 19, 1939
Chicago, Illinois

Grace Abbott, along with her older sister Edith, left a lasting imprint on the field of social work. From their parents, advocates of the abolition of slavery and of woman suffrage, they both developed a reformer's yearning to improve public life. Grace Abbott attended Brownell Hall, a girls' boarding school in Omaha, Nebraska, then returned home to Grand Island to graduate from high school. In 1898, she received a Ph.B. degree from Grand Island College, then taught for several years in the local high school.

In 1907, she moved to Chicago and embarked

upon a master's degree in political science, which she completed two years later. She also joined the staff of Hull House, under Jane Addams's dynamic leadership, and became immersed in an exciting new world of ideas and social reform. At Hull House, she participated in the Chicago garment workers' strike of 1910, campaigned for Theodore Roosevelt's Bull Moose Presidential ticket, and worked for woman suffrage.

But her true contribution to social reform lay in her work for the Immigrants' Protection League, of which she was director from its beginning in 1908. In this capacity, she worked to end exploitation of immigrants by employers, lawyers, prostitution rings, and others who preyed upon the unsuspecting newcomers. She initiated reforms in the treatment of immigrants and fought against literacy tests and other measures to restrict immigration.

In 1917, she shifted her focus from immigration to child welfare by directing the child welfare division of the newly established Children's Bureau. Although she failed to secure a constitutional amendment to ban child labor, she managed to ensure the regulation of child labor in wartime manufacturing industries. In 1921, she became director of the Children's Bureau, presiding over the establishment of 3,000 child health and prenatal clinics around the country. She also helped to create a system of federal-state cooperation for social welfare, which served as a model for future welfare programs.

From 1922 to 1934, she served as a U.S. delegate to the League of Nations' Advisory Committee on Traffic in Women and Children, and during the New Deal she helped write the nation's first Social Security Act. In later years, she taught public welfare at the University of Chicago and defended progressive social change against its conservative critics. She was, in the words of a colleague, "the hero and the pride of women who were just beginning to find a place in public affairs."

MAJOR PUBLICATIONS
The Immigrant and the Community (1917)
The Child and the State (1938)

FURTHER READING
Costin, Lela B. *Two Sisters for Social Justice: A Biography of Grace and Edith Abbott.* Urbana: University of Illinois Press, 1983.

Abzug, Bella Savitzky

FEMINIST LEADER, CONGRESSWOMAN

Born: July 24, 1920
New York, New York

The daughter of Russian Jewish immigrants, Bella Abzug has enjoyed a long and controversial career as an activist and politician. Her flamboyant style has earned her the nickname "Bellicosa Bella" and the distinction of being the namesake for Hurricane Bella.

Abzug attended public schools in the Bronx, New York City, and graduated from Hunter College in 1942. During her student days, she protested against fascism and supported the Republicans fighting in the Spanish Civil War. In 1944, she married Martin Abzug and a year later earned her law degree at Columbia University. She was admitted to the New York bar in 1947 and practiced law in New York until 1970, taking on controversial and often unpopular cases. During the 1950s, she defended civil rights workers in the South and writers accused of harboring communist sympathies. Over the next decade, she shifted her attention to the peace, antinuclear, and women's movements. She was founder and, from 1961 to 1970, national legislative director of Women Strike for Peace, as well as founder and chairwoman of the National Women's Political Caucus.

In 1971, Abzug was elected to the United States House of Representatives. For the next six years, she worked diligently for welfare rights, public works programs that created jobs, consumer and environmental protection, and aid to Israel. She ran for the U.S. Senate in 1976 but lost that race as well as the mayoral race in New York City the following year.

Since the late 1970s, Abzug has continued to work for women's rights and social welfare concerns. She is a member of the National Organization of Women (NOW), the American Civil Liberties Union (ACLU), and other liberal political organizations. Never one to shy from embracing unpopular causes, she loyally supports programs and candidates who speak out for the least empowered in American society.

PUBLICATIONS
Bella: Ms. Abzug Goes to Washington (1972)
Gender Gap: Bella Abzug's Guide to Political Power for Women (1984)

FURTHER READING
Faber, Doris. *Bella Abzug.* New York: Lothrop, Lee and Shepard, 1976.

Adams, Abigail

FIRST LADY

Born: November 11, 1744
Weymouth, Massachusetts

Died: October 28, 1818
Braintree, Massachusetts

While her husband, John, was off in Philadelphia helping to foment a revolution against Britain, Abigail Adams declared revolt against another form of tyranny—that of men's social and political power over women. She wrote to her husband that "if perticuliar care and attention is not paid to the Laidies we are determined to foment a Rebellion, and will not hold ourselves bound by any Laws in which we have no voice, or Representation." Few women of her time dared to voice such sentiments. But from her early years as a colonial farmer's daughter, Adams was accustomed to speaking her mind.

Although she had no formal education, she was highly literate. In October 1764, she married John Adams, an ambitious young man preparing for a law career. She fully expected to live quietly as the wife of a country lawyer, but events dictated otherwise. As her husband became more immersed in revolutionary activities against Great Britain, she, too, was swept up into political turmoil.

During the first decade of their marriage, the Adamses had four children, then spent most of the next decade apart as John's revolutionary activities took him to Philadelphia and Europe. Abigail stayed behind in Braintree, supervising the family farm and organizing local women to sew clothing for the Continental army.

In 1796, John Adams became the second President of the United States, and Abigail Adams became the first First Lady to preside over the White House, the new Presidential home in Washington, D.C. Later, her son, John Quincy Adams, also served as U.S. President. Thus Abigail Adams is the only woman in American history to be the wife and mother of U.S. Presidents.

After her husband lost his bid for reelection, she and John returned to their beloved farm in Braintree, Massachusetts, where she died in 1818.

FURTHER READING

Gelles, Edith Belle. *Portia: The World of Abigail Adams.* Bloomington: Indiana University Press, 1992.

Kline, Mary Jo, ed. *The Book of Abigail and John: Selected Letters of the Adams Family, 1762–1784.* Cambridge: Harvard University Press, 1975.

Withey, Lynne. *Dearest Friend: The Life of Abigail Adams.* New York: Free Press, 1981.

Addams, Jane

SOCIAL REFORMER, FOUNDER OF HULL HOUSE

Born: September 6, 1860
Cedarville, Illinois

Died: May 21, 1935
Chicago, Illinois

Neighborhood health care, abolition of child labor, world peace, and free speech—Jane

Addams championed these causes and more. She was born in a small town in north central Illinois, and as a child was greatly influenced by the moral fervor of the antislavery movement. She attended Rockford Female Seminary, a religious school, where she met Ellen Gates Starr, her future partner in settlement work. After graduating in 1881, she entered medical school but decided she was not suited for a career in medicine.

For the next eight years, she drifted about, traveling in Europe and doing charity work, uncertain of what her life's work should be. Finally, during a trip to Spain with Starr, she confided that she would like to open a settlement house in a poor neighborhood in Chicago. Starr reacted with eager enthusiasm, and upon returning to the United States they searched for a suitable building.

In September 1889, they moved into the Hull mansion in Chicago's immigrant district, and Hull House soon became the hub of the neighborhood. It included a day-care center, gymnasium, playground, courses in cooking and sewing, a cooperative boardinghouse for young women, and space for some 40 clubs to meet. For her staff, Jane Addams attracted a remarkable group of talented women and college students who yearned, in her words, "to construct the world anew." Under her leadership, they spearheaded an array of reforms, including a campaign to abolish child labor and create better living and working conditions for all factory workers. In 1893, they achieved passage of Illinois's first factory inspection act. They also initiated the establishment of the nation's first juvenile court in Chicago in 1899.

Addams soon earned a reputation as one of the premier women reformers of the day. She lectured and wrote for several publications, and received numerous awards—culminating in sharing the Nobel Peace Prize in 1931 for her long-standing efforts on behalf of world peace.

Addams also championed woman suffrage because she believed that women's "moral energy" was needed to combat social ills, and she helped found the American Civil Liberties Union to defend free speech. She devoted her last years to Hull House and to the many causes that she espoused. She was a remarkable woman who possessed the vision and passion needed to effect broad social reforms.

MAJOR PUBLICATIONS

Twenty Years at Hull-House (autobiography, 1910)
The Second Twenty Years at Hull-House (autobiography, 1930)
The Long Road of Woman's Memory (1916)
The Excellent Becomes the Permanent (1932)

FURTHER READING

Davis, Allen Freeman. *American Heroine: The Life and Legend of Jane Addams.* New York: Oxford University Press, 1973.
Kittredge, Mary. *Jane Addams.* New York: Chelsea House, 1988.

Alcott, Louisa May

AUTHOR

Born: November 29, 1832
Germantown, Pennsylvania

Died: March 6, 1888
Boston, Massachusetts

Although Alcott's name is forever entwined with *Little Women,* her classic children's story about four sisters, she also wrote many other stories and novels, mostly for children. Her father, Amos Bronson Alcott, was an educator and patron saint of the most unusual and idealistic reform movements of the day. Unfortunately, his gentle, visionary new ideas about educating children did not translate into economic security for his family, and Louisa and her three sisters endured periods of extreme hardship—because of poverty and their father's belief in the curative values of ice-cold baths and meager diets.

But if the girls lived on a pallid diet, their intellectual menu was far richer. Their father tutored them personally and introduced them to such intellectual giants of the day as Henry David Thoreau, Ralph Waldo Emerson, Nathaniel Hawthorne, and Margaret Fuller.

By her 18th birthday, Louisa May Alcott felt obligated to support her family. At one time or another, she worked as a seamstress, domestic servant, governess, teacher, and companion. During the Civil War, she also worked briefly as a Union army nurse. In 1863, she published *Hospital Sketches,* a series of articles about her nursing adventures. The success of this first book launched her writing career. Over the next 25 years, she wrote 270 articles, short stories, and novels. While most of these writings were directed to a juvenile audience, including the sentimental *Little Women,* she also tried her hand at thrillers, romances, and travel pieces.

Like *Little Women,* published in two parts in 1868, most of Alcott's children's books instilled moral lessons and middle-class values, such as diligence, thrift, love of family, and hard work. Her readers loved her books and demanded more. By the end of her life, Alcott had achieved economic security and international acclaim. Besides writing, she supported woman suffrage and helped organize a temperance society in Concord, Massachusetts. Her last years, however, were plagued by constant health problems and family illness. Indeed, she died two days after her father, the man whose high-flown speculations and bedeviling mildness had repeatedly clashed with her own volatile and practical temperament.

MAJOR PUBLICATIONS

Hospital Sketches (1863)
Little Women (1868)
An Old-Fashioned Girl (1870)
Little Men (1871)
Work (a pointed novel portraying the indignities suffered by a young female domestic servant as she must contend with exploitive working conditions and a lecherous employer, 1873)
Eight Cousins (1875)
Jo's Boys (1886)

FURTHER READING

Bedell, Madelon. *The Alcotts: Biography of a Family.* New York: Clarkson N. Potter, 1980.
Johnston, Norma. *Louisa May: The World and Works of Louisa May Alcott.* New York: Four Winds Press, 1991.

Anderson, Mary

LABOR LEADER, GOVERNMENT OFFICIAL

Born: August 27, 1872
Sweden

Died: January 29, 1964
Washington, D.C.

Mary Anderson, first director of the Women's Bureau, a federal agency established in 1920 within the Department of Labor, was a committed advocate of working women. Born in Sweden, she attended a Lutheran school and graduated at the top of her class. At 16, she journeyed by steerage to America and worked first as a dishwasher in a lumberjacks' boardinghouse and later in a shoe factory in Chicago.

She joined the International Boot and Shoe Workers Union and quickly worked her way up the ranks to president of her local. In 1911, after several years of participating in the Chicago sector of the Women's Trade Union League (WTUL), she became one of its paid organizers. During World War I, she was hired to be assistant director of a wartime government bureau, the Women in Industry Service. A year later, when the bureau was reorganized as the Women's Bureau and converted into a permanent government agency, Anderson was promoted to director.

For 25 years, she was a tireless advocate for working women. Anderson commanded the loyalty of her subordinates as well as that of thousands of women workers, whose interests she represented. She supported woman suffrage and protective legislation for wage-earning women. During World War II, she strove to ensure women's access to jobs and training. Through her long tenure as first director of the Women's Bureau, she made working women's needs a part of government policy.

PUBLICATION
Women at Work (1951)

Angelou, Maya

WRITER, POET

Born: April 4, 1928
St. Louis, Missouri

From an impoverished childhood in the dusty town of Stamps, Arkansas, where she was raised by her paternal grandmother, to poet laureate at the inauguration of a U.S. President—Maya Angelou has followed a remarkable odyssey that has brought her recognition as one of America's most acclaimed poets. After a difficult childhood, including being raped when she was seven, the young girl learned to fend for herself. She graduated from high school and took drama and dance lessons at the California Labor School in San Francisco.

For the next several years, she worked variously as a streetcar collector in San Francisco—the first woman to do so—a cook, cocktail waitress, and nightclub dancer. She soon discovered a desire to perform, and in 1954 she traveled through Europe and Africa with a touring opera company of *Porgy and Bess.*

She also pledged her support to the fledgling civil rights movement. From 1960 to 1961, she served as northern coordinator for the Southern Christian Leadership Conference (SCLC), the civil rights organization headed by Dr. Martin Luther King, Jr. During this period as well, she realized a desire to write, and through disciplined study and practice she developed her astounding gift for language.

During the early 1960s, Angelou lived in Ghana, where she worked as a broadcast and newspaper journalist. Back in the United States, she wrote songs as well as a television script and was the first black woman to have a screenplay, *Georgia, Georgia,* produced. She also performed on stage and television.

Since 1981, she has been the Reynolds Professor of American Studies at Wake Forest University in Winston-Salem, North Carolina. She also lectures around the country. Her poem "On the Pulse of a New Morning" stirred the hopes of Americans across the nation as they celebrated the inauguration of President William Jefferson Clinton in January 1993. In both her poetry and prose, luminous with vivid, rich imagery, Angelou mines her personal past as well as America's collective past to express the struggle for identity and self-acceptance in a racist society.

MAJOR PUBLICATIONS
I Know Why the Caged Bird Sings (1970)
Just Give Me a Cool Drink of Water 'fore I Diiie (1971)
The Heart of a Woman (1982)
I Shall Not Be Moved (1990)
Wouldn't Take Nothing for My Journey Now (1993)

Anthony, Susan Brownell

WOMEN'S RIGHTS LEADER

Born: February 15, 1820
Adams, Massachusetts

Died: March 13, 1906
Rochester, New York

For more than half a century, Susan B. Anthony and Elizabeth Cady Stanton led the organized women's rights movement in America. Anthony's dedication to the cause and her prodigious energy for the work were legendary. Her progressive upbringing prepared her for this fierce battle. Raised in the Quaker faith, which emphasized the equality of women before God, she was accustomed to seeing women in leadership positions within the church. Anthony's father, moreover, was a staunch opponent of slavery, and advocates of the leading reform movements of the day—temperance, antislavery, and the nascent women's rights movement—were welcomed in the Anthony home.

Young Susan B. Anthony was educated in a district school and also a home school established by her father. In addition, she briefly attended a Quaker Friends' Seminary near Philadelphia. From 1839 to 1849, she taught school in various academies throughout upstate New York.

Anthony did not meet Stanton until 1850, nearly two years after the Seneca Falls Convention. At that time, her chief interest was temperance, not women's rights. By 1853, however, she had shifted her allegiance to women's rights because she realized that women who had no political or economic power also had no power to achieve any other reform.

In the early years of the women's rights movement, Anthony helped organize state and national conventions, rallied recruits, and researched the facts and ideas that Stanton used in her fiery speeches. During the Civil War, she, Stanton, and others established the Women's Loyal National League, which instigated a petition campaign to abolish slavery.

After the war, she and Stanton resumed their women's rights work. They launched the *Revolution,* a newspaper calling for such visionary reforms as equal education and pay, new occupations for women, more liberal divorce laws, and the vote for women. For twenty years, from 1869 to 1890, they led the National Woman Suffrage Association, one branch of the suffrage movement, and then presided over a reunited national movement.

Called the "Napoleon of the woman's rights movement" by contemporaries, Anthony, on her own, helped organize a Working Women's Association in 1868 to encourage working women to organize for better wages and working hours. In later years, she lectured around the country for women's rights and, in 1892, succeeded Stanton as president of the National American Woman Suffrage Association, a post she held until 1900. As Stanton retired from organized women's rights activity, Anthony became the symbol of the movement and remained dedicated to the cause until her death. "Failure is impossible," she proclaimed at the last suffrage convention she attended. She was peerless in her energy, organizational powers, and devotion to the cause of equality for women.

PUBLICATIONS

History of Woman Suffrage (with Elizabeth Cady Stanton et al.; 6 volumes, 1881–1922)
DuBois, Ellen, ed. *Correspondence Between Elizabeth Cady Stanton and Susan B. Anthony* (1981)

FURTHER READING

Barry, Kathleen. *A Singular Feminist*. New York: New York University Press, 1988.
Weisberg, Barbara. *Susan B. Anthony: Woman Suffragist*. New York: Chelsea House, 1988.

Atkinson, Ti-Grace

RADICAL FEMINIST

Born: 1939 (exact date not known)

During a vibrant and fractious period in the American women's movement, Ti-Grace Atkinson presided over the New York chapter of the National Organization of Women (NOW) and went on to join the vanguard of a new and radical feminist movement. The daughter of an affluent Louisiana family, she married at seventeen and was divorced five years later. She earned a B.A. in fine arts at the University of Pennsylvania and helped found the Institute of Contemporary Art in Philadelphia.

She was a graduate student in philosophy at Columbia University when she was elected president of NOW–New York in 1967. With her "Main Line accent and ladylike blond good looks," as Betty Friedan described her, she seemed hardly the type to promote militant political activism.

But Atkinson, who had taken to heart the spirit of equality and democracy that inspired the student antiwar movement, found the governing structure of NOW to be too rigid. She urged the organization to rotate leadership positions among all members rather than elect officers for a designated period of time. In 1968, when both the national board and the New York chapter of NOW rejected her proposal, she resigned and founded The Feminists, one of the first radical feminist groups.

Acting on Atkinson's proposal, The Feminists rotated leadership positions so that all members had an opportunity to chair meetings and hold other positions. In this way, all members developed new skills and shared power equally. In addition, The Feminists rejected the institution of marriage and instead suggested raising children in all-women communes. Atkinson called romantic love "the psychological pivot in the persecution of women."

The Feminists was one of several early radical feminist groups that rejected the values and structure of American middle-class society. Rather than try to modify those values, they chose to break away from what they considered to be a sexist society and to create an alternative community based on complete equality and power sharing. They infused the women's movement with vitality, quirkiness, and provocative new ideas.

PUBLICATION

Amazon Odyssey (1974)

Baker, Ella

CIVIL RIGHTS AND COMMUNITY ACTIVIST

Born: December 13, 1903
Norfolk, Virginia

Died: December 13, 1986

Ella Baker was the guiding spirit behind the civil rights movement of the 1950s and 1960s. She helped organize the key groups and activities that defined those fervent years. After graduating as valedictorian of her class from Shaw University in Raleigh, North Carolina, Baker moved to New York City, where she promptly encountered radical ideas and numerous outlets for her desire to promote social justice. During the Depression, she helped organize consumer cooperatives among blacks to protect them from exploitive white merchants.

In the early 1940s, she moved up to become national field secretary in the National Association for the Advancement of Colored People (NAACP), crisscrossing the South to organize NAACP branches and develop membership drives. As leader of the New York City branch, she spearheaded community protests against segregation in New York City's public schools.

After the 1955 Montgomery, Alabama, bus boycott, organized by Rosa Parks and others, achieved its goal of integrating Montgomery's public facilities, the civil rights movement came to a temporary halt; no one had figured out the next stage of protest. Baker stepped in to suggest new targets of racial injustice, and in 1957 she helped organize the Southern Christian Leadership Conference (SCLC) to coordinate a comprehensive assault on racial discrimination throughout the South. Although the Reverend Martin Luther King, Jr., became leader of the SCLC, Baker ran its central office in Atlanta, Georgia, and coordinated the activities of its 65 branch offices.

In 1960, she helped student leaders at Shaw University, her alma mater, organize the Student Nonviolent Coordinating Committee (SNCC). This group became the student-led branch of the civil rights movement—as well as the most effective student activist movement in American history—and Baker's influence could be seen in the sit-ins, boycotts, and free-speech protests that SNCC launched. Later she said, "The kind of role that I tried to play was to pick up pieces or put together pieces out of which I hoped organization might come. My theory is, strong people don't need strong leaders."

Baker tirelessly recruited grassroots support for the civil rights movement. Credit came late for her key role in the movement, but that was of little consequence to her. For over half a century, she dedicated herself to achieving equality and justice for American blacks.

FURTHER READING

Branch, Taylor. *Parting the Waters: America in the King Years, 1954–63.* New York: Simon & Schuster, 1988.

Canterow, Ellen, et al. *Moving Mountains: Women Working for Social Change.* New York: Feminist Press, 1979.

Wiley, Jean. "On the Front Lines: Four Women Activists Whose Work Touched Millions of Lives," *Essence* 20 (February 1990): 45.

Barton, Clara

NURSE, FOUNDER OF THE AMERICAN RED CROSS

Born: December 25, 1821
North Oxford, Massachusetts

Died: April 12, 1912
Glen Echo, Maryland

Few women in American history are as well known and revered as Clara Barton. For more than 50 years, she dedicated her life to easing suffering. Her childhood in a loving, compassionate, and patriotic home prepared her for a life of public service. After attending local schools, she became a schoolteacher and proved to be highly skilled and respected in the classroom.

In 1854, she left teaching and moved to Washington, D.C., where she secured a clerkship in the Patent Office; she was perhaps the first woman to become a regularly appointed civil servant.

With the outbreak of the Civil War, she found her own way to serve the Union cause—by becoming a one-woman relief agency, collecting supplies from northern women's relief societies and distributing them to army camps.

Within a year, she was nursing as well, right on the battlefield or in the wretched field hospitals near the front lines. She chose not to enlist in Dorothea Dix's Department of Female Nurses and instead overcame the initial resistance of military officers, doctors, and male assistants to perform her vital function. She called the soldiers "my boys" and did everything from holding the hands of dying soldiers to removing bullets and assisting in surgery.

After the war, Barton took on the formidable task of seeking out missing Union soldiers. From

1866 to 1868, she and her small staff located the remains of more than 30,000 soldiers.

Though she could have retired to private life, secure in the public's gratitude for her wartime service, she assisted the International Red Cross Committee during the Franco-Prussian War of 1870 to 1871. She also campaigned for American affiliation with the International Red Cross.

In 1881, she organized the American Red Cross and served as president for the next two decades. Under her leadership, the organization, relying only on contributions from the public, provided relief and rebuilding materials in 21 foreign and domestic disasters. At age 75, during the Spanish-American War of 1898, she was right there on the battlefield, leading Red Cross supply convoys.

Barton supported the women's rights movement. But, more important, by her own example she demonstrated that women, no less than men, can wield tough, decisive, and accomplished leadership.

PUBLICATIONS
The Red Cross (1898)
A Story of the Red Cross (1904)
The Story of My Childhood (autobiography, 1907)

FURTHER READING
Hamilton, Leni. *Clara Barton: Founder, American Red Cross.* New York: Chelsea House, 1988.
Oates, Stephen B. *Clara Barton.* New York: Free Press, 1994.
Pryor, Elizabeth Brown. *Clara Barton: Professional Angel.* Philadelphia: University of Pennsylvania Press, 1987.

Beecher, Catharine Esther

AUTHOR, EDUCATOR

Born: September 6, 1800
East Hampton, New York

Died: May 12, 1878
Elmira, New York

Daughter of Lyman Beecher, a famous Presbyterian minister deeply involved in moral re-

form, Catharine Beecher devoted her life to two causes: educating the nation's children and elevating women's domestic status. As a child, she briefly attended a private girls' school in Litchfield, Connecticut, but her real education took place in the family home, where she met interesting boarders and took part in lively discussions.

In 1823, she and her sister Mary opened a girls' school, later to be incorporated as the Hartford Female Seminary. Unlike many female seminaries, their school offered calisthenics and courses that required students to think for themselves. Gradually, Beecher became convinced of the need to train and dispatch teachers to frontier communities where no schools yet existed. By her efforts, more than 400 New England schoolteachers were sent west to open schools in newly settled regions of the country.

But Beecher wielded her greatest influence as an author of domestic tracts. Her *Treatise on Domestic Economy* (1841) and a revised edition, *The American Woman's Home* (1869)—on which she collaborated with her sister Harriet Beecher Stowe—offered advice and instruction on cooking, family health and child care, household management, and even interior design. Beecher wished to elevate and dignify women's domestic role. For her, the ideal woman was a healthy, energetic, devoted homemaker rather than an exploited factory worker or a spoiled lady of leisure. Beecher opposed female suffrage; instead, she urged women to seek greater power within the home.

In later years, she returned to the Hartford Female Seminary as principal. She also wrote, lectured at other female seminaries, and raised money for new colleges for women.

MAJOR PUBLICATIONS
A Treatise on Domestic Economy (1841)
The Duty of American Women to Their Country (1845)
The Domestic Receipt Book (1846)
The Evils Suffered by American Women and American Children: The Causes and the Remedy (1846)
The American Woman's Home (1869)

FURTHER READING

Boydston, Jeanne et al., eds. *The Limits of Sisterhood: The Beecher Sisters on Women's Rights and Women's Sphere.* Chapel Hill: University of North Carolina Press, 1989.

Rugoff, Milton. *The Beechers: An American Family in the Nineteenth Century.* New York: Harper and Row, 1981.

Sklar, Kathryn Kish. *Catharine Beecher: A Study in American Domesticity.* New York: W. W. Norton, 1976.

Belknap, Ruth

COLONIAL POET

Born: date and location unknown

Died: date and location unknown

R uth Belknap was a minister's wife in Dover, New Hampshire, and a member of a highly influential New England family. As such, she was hardly among the poorest New Englanders. But in her poem "The Pleasures of a Country Life," she ruefully offers a portrayal of the typical goodwife's laborious existence:

> All summer long I toil & sweat,
> Blister my hands, and scold & fret.
> And when the summer's work is o'er,
> New toils arise from Autumn's store.
> Corn must be husk'd, and pork be kill'd.
> The house with all confusion fill'd.
> O could you see the grand display
> Upon our annual butchering day,—
> See me look like ten thousand sluts,
> My kitchen spread with grease & guts.

In the poem, Belknap also took aim at the "starch'd up folks that live in town/That lounge upon your beds till noon/That never tire yourselves with work/Unless with handling knife & fork." She revealed an acute awareness of the geographical and class differences that determine people's lives. Witty and outspoken, Belknap was among the New World's earliest female poets.

FURTHER READING

Ulrich, Laurel. *Good Wives: Image and Reality in the Lives of Women in Northern New England, 1650–1750.* New York: Knopf, 1982.

Belmont, Alva Erskine Smith Vanderbilt

SOCIALITE AND SUFFRAGIST

Born: January 17, 1853
Mobile, Alabama

Died: January 26, 1933
Paris, France

A lva Belmont traveled a curious path from high-society socialite to militant suffrage fighter—though she never shed her upper-class pedigree. Educated in private schools in France, she moved with her wealthy parents to New York City in the post–Civil War era, forming part of a newly rich class that horrified New York's established families. She married twice, first to a member of the Vanderbilt dynasty and then to O. H. P. Belmont, another heir to family wealth.

After the death of her second husband in 1908, Belmont joined the suffrage movement, devoting the rest of her life and much of her wealth to the cause. Later, she said that she had become convinced that women had to "take this world muddle that men have created and . . . turn it into an ordered, peaceful, happy abiding place for humanity."

To this end, she published articles advocating suffrage in *Harper's Bazaar, Good Housekeeping, Collier's,* and other popular magazines; rented an entire floor of a Fifth Avenue office building to serve as headquarters for the suffrage movement; and helped found the Political Equality League, a New York suffrage organization. She also brought the militant English suffragist Christabel Pankhurst to the United States and arranged her lecture tour around the country. During the great New York City shirtwaist makers' strike of 1909—the Uprising of the 20,000—she helped to pay the bail of arrested strikers and even walked the picket line herself. And in 1912, she contributed $2,000 to prevent the socialist magazine *The Masses* from going bankrupt. She served on the executive board of the Congressional Union, the militant organization founded by Alice Paul and Lucy Burns to secure a federal women's suffrage amendment, and joined its successor, the National Woman's Party. In 1921, she was elected president of the National Woman's Party and supported its innovative strategy to achieve an Equal Rights Amendment. She also joined the international suffrage movement. Belmont put the power of her social position and pocketbook behind the cause of women's rights.

FURTHER READING
Rector, Margaret Hayden. *Alva: That Vanderbilt Woman*. Wickford, R.I.: Dutch Island Press, 1992.

Bethune, Mary McLeod

EDUCATOR, CIVIL RIGHTS ACTIVIST,
FEDERAL GOVERNMENT OFFICIAL

Born: July 10, 1875
Mayesville, South Carolina

Died: May 18, 1955
Daytona Beach, Florida

Born to former slaves, Bethune became one of the most influential African-American women in 20th-century America. After attending a local school and then a seminary for young black women, she embarked upon a teaching career to help her people. She believed that education was vital for their advancement in American society.

In 1904, Bethune established a school for young African-American women in Daytona Beach, Florida. Over the years, the school grew from six students studying in a rented room to a 20-acre campus serving 300 students. The curriculum offered vocational training as well as academic subjects. Bethune exhorted her students—and indeed all black women—to rise above racial discrimination and achieve, in her words, "Self-Control, Self-Respect, Self-Reliance and Race Pride." In 1923, the school became coeducational and was later accredited as a junior college.

Meanwhile, Bethune, who had become a prominent black clubwoman, traveled widely throughout the United States to investigate the social and economic needs of America's blacks. Through her organizational work, she met Eleanor Roosevelt, wife of U.S. President Franklin Delano Roosevelt, and quickly educated the First Lady on African-American concerns.

During the 1930s, Bethune directed the division of African-American affairs within the National Youth Administration (NYA), a New Deal government agency. In this position, she strove to create more educational and employment opportunities for young blacks and to combat discrimination in government programs and agencies. In 1935, she established the National Council of Negro Women (NCNW), a network of the major national black women's associations. She represented the NCNW in 1945 at the founding conference of the United Nations. Through these and other activities, she became a tireless fighter for civil rights.

In later years, Bethune relinquished most of her organizational responsibilities but continued to crusade for equal rights. She was a powerful and eloquent voice for all African Americans.

PUBLICATIONS
"I'll Never Turn Back No More," *Opportunity* (November 1938)
"My Last Will and Testament," *Ebony* (August 1955)

FURTHER READING
Halasa, Malu. *Mary McLeod Bethune*. New York: Chelsea House, 1989.

Bishop, Bridget Oliver

ACCUSED WITCH

Born: ca. 1640
England

Died: June 10, 1692
Salem, Massachusetts

Bridget Bishop was the first accused witch to be executed in the Salem witch-hunt of 1692. Little is known about her early life except that around age 20 she was married and widowed in England. She made her way to New England and in 1666 married widower Thomas Oliver in Salem. Several years later, she was widowed once more.

In 1680, she was charged with witchcraft but was declared to be innocent. Four years later, she married Edward Bishop, a widower. Her upper-class standing in Salem aroused the envy of her less-affluent neighbors and made her an easy mark for the hysteria sweeping the region during the Salem witch-hunt.

To make matters worse, she gave late-night entertainments in her house, where the cider flowed freely and young people could play shuffleboard until the ungodly early-morning hours—practices frowned upon by the starched and straitlaced Puritan community.

On April 18, 1692, Bishop was once again formally accused of practicing witchcraft. The charges against her described how she destroyed her neighbors' pigs and poultry and caused their carts to be overturned. She was also accused of killing two children, causing the illness of a third child, and sending forth a spectral image of herself to taunt her next-door neighbor. The court in Salem assembled a formidable array of accusers against her, even though Bishop had never set foot in Salem Village, a separate town from Salem, where her witchly deeds supposedly took place. She was even accused of practicing witchcraft while in prison.

On June 4, 1692, the jury found her guilty, and Bishop was sentenced to die. To her death, she refused to disavow her innocence. On the day of her execution, she was forced to ride standing up in a horse-drawn cart to the gallows overlooking Salem.

FURTHER READING
Boyer, Paul and Stephen Nissenbaum. *Salem Possessed: The Social Origins of Witchcraft.* Cambridge: Harvard University Press, 1974.
Demos, John. *Entertaining Satan: Witchcraft and the Culture of Early New England.* New York: Oxford University Press, 1982.
Robinson, Enders A. *The Devil Discovered: Salem Witchcraft, 1692.* New York: Hippocrene, 1991.

Blackwell, Alice Stone

FEMINIST, SOCIAL ACTIVIST

Born: September 14, 1857
Orange, New Jersey

Died: March 15, 1950
Cambridge, Massachusetts

Alice Stone Blackwell was born to be a feminist and a fighter. Her parents, Lucy Stone and Henry Blackwell, were movers and shakers in the American antislavery movement and the fight for women's rights. One of her aunts, Elizabeth Blackwell, was the first American woman to receive a medical degree, and another aunt, Antoinette Brown Blackwell, was the first American woman to be ordained a minister in a major religious denomination.

After a childhood spent moving from one place to another, because of her parents' reform work and her father's itinerant business dealings, she settled with her family in Boston. She attended local elementary and high schools and, in 1881, entered Boston University, where she graduated Phi Beta Kappa. For the next 30 years, she edited the *Woman's Journal,* the suffrage newspaper launched by her mother. In 1887, she also edited the "Woman's Column," a feature about national suffrage news carried in newspapers around the country.

In 1890, Blackwell helped merge once-competing suffrage organizations—the National Woman Suffrage Association (NWSA) and the American Woman Suffrage Association (AWSA)—into the National American Woman Suffrage Association (NAWSA). She served as recording secretary of the new organization.

Beyond suffrage, however, she developed a host of other interests. In the 1910s and 1920s, she supported freedom fighters and revolutionaries throughout Europe, and translated and published poetry by immigrant poets. She also joined organizations that promoted trade unionism, civil rights, and international peace. She decried the suppression of free speech and the deportation of American radicals after World War I, and became an active socialist. She died at age 96, after carrying her family's social reform legacy to brave new heights.

PUBLICATION
Lucy Stone (1930)

FURTHER READING
Merrill, Marlene Deahl, ed. *Growing Up in Boston's Gilded Age: The Journal of Alice Stone Blackwell, 1872–1874.* New Haven, Conn.: Yale University Press, 1990.

Blackwell, Antoinette Brown
CONGREGATIONAL AND UNITARIAN MINISTER,
AUTHOR, LECTURER

Born: May 20, 1825
Henrietta, New York

Died: November 5, 1921
Elizabeth, New Jersey

Antoinette Brown Blackwell was the first American woman to be ordained a minister in a major religious denomination. She came from a devoutly religious family and revealed an intense spiritual bent early on. At age nine, after making a public confession of faith, she became a member of her local Congregational church. She attended local district schools and a pri-

vate academy before becoming a schoolteacher.

In 1846, with her father's assistance, she enrolled at Oberlin College, the only coeducational college in the country and also the only school to accept black students. There she met Lucy Stone, a future women's rights leader, and together they challenged Oberlin's unequal treatment of female students. Despite her parents' and teachers' objections, Blackwell decided to attend divinity school at Oberlin. The faculty grudgingly admitted her but prevented her from graduating after she completed the program in 1850, though she had already served as an itinerant preacher.

In 1853, she was ordained a minister of a Congregational church in Wayne County, New York. But the Congregationalists' conservative views did not suit her searching spiritual nature, and she eventually converted to the Unitarian faith.

She married Samuel Charles Blackwell, whose brother Henry would soon marry her dear friend Lucy Stone. Blackwell eagerly supported his wife's religious calling. Though she was no longer affiliated with a congregation she continued to study, write, and lecture about spiritual and political matters. In 1873, at the first congress of the Association for the Advancement of Women, she urged women to seek work outside the home and encourage their husbands to share household responsibilities. She continued to lecture and preach around the country, and in later years she helped to found a Unitarian church in Elizabeth, New Jersey. Shortly before her death, she voted for the first time, after the 19th Amendment to the Constitution, granting women the right to vote, was ratified.

PUBLICATIONS
Studies in General Science (1869)
The Island Neighbors (novel, 1871)
The Sexes Throughout Nature (1875)
The Philosophy of Individuality (1893)
The Social Side of Mind and Action (1915)

FURTHER READING
Cazden, Elizabeth. *Antoinette Brown Blackwell: A Biography.* Old Westbury, N.Y.: Feminist Press, 1983.

Lasser, Carol and Marlene Deahl Merrill, eds. *Friends and Sisters: Letters Between Lucy Stone and Antoinette Brown Blackwell, 1846–1893*. Urbana: University of Illinois Press, 1987.

Blackwell, Elizabeth

PHYSICIAN

Born: February 3, 1821
Bristol, England

Died: May 31, 1910
Hastings, England

Elizabeth Blackwell paved the way for women physicians and for better health care for all women. She was educated by tutor, in a family that supported women's rights, temperance, and abolition—the three major reform causes of the era. In 1832, her family emigrated to America. Her father died a few years later, leaving the family penniless, and young Elizabeth and her mother and sisters opened a private school.

But her real interest was medicine. She studied privately with two physicians, and after being turned down by several medical schools because she was a woman, she was finally accepted by Geneva College in west central New York State. Enduring the scorn of fellow students and townspeople who believed that women were not suited for a medical career, she quietly completed her studies and graduated in 1849. She then pursued postgraduate work in England and France, and returned to New York in 1851.

After being barred from practicing in hospitals throughout New York City, she opened a one-room clinic in a tenement neighborhood. In her first year, she treated 200 poor women. Within a few years, she had expanded the clinic into a hospital, the New York Infirmary for Women and Children: her sister, Emily Blackwell, also a physician, helped her run the facility.

During the Civil War, Blackwell helped organize the Woman's Central Association of Relief (WCAR) to collect and distribute supplies for the troops. This group, in turn, helped inspire the formation of the United States Sanitary Commission, a comprehensive volunteer organization that raised money for the Union war effort, outfitted Union military hospitals with staff and supplies, and prepared clothing and food baskets for the soldiers. Both Elizabeth and Emily Blackwell helped hire and train nurses for the commission.

In 1868, Elizabeth Blackwell realized another dream, one deferred by the war—to establish a medical school affiliated with her hospital. This school, the Woman's Medical College of the New York Infirmary, offered the most rigorous and comprehensive training then available to either male or female students.

A year later, Blackwell turned the operation of the school and hospital over to her sister and moved back to England. She opened a private practice, taught and assisted other women doctors, and campaigned for better hygiene, preventive medicine, and sex education. Her contribution to improving medical education and care is immeasurable.

PUBLICATIONS
Pioneer Work in Opening the Medical Profession to Women (autobiography, 1895)
Essays in Medical Sociology (1902)

FURTHER READING
Abram, Ruth. *Send Us a Lady Physician: Women Doctors in America, 1835–1920*. New York: Norton, 1986.
Brown, Jordan. *Elizabeth Blackwell: Physician*. New York: Chelsea House, 1989.

Blackwell, Emily

PHYSICIAN

Born: October 8, 1826
Bristol, England

Died: September 7, 1910
York Cliffs, Maine

Though less well known than her sister, Elizabeth Blackwell, Emily Blackwell also played a vital role in opening the medical profession to women. As a child, she loved nature and science and performed scientific experiments at home. Her sister inspired her to go into medicine, but Emily, like Elizabeth, had great difficulty finding a medical school that accepted women. Finally, in 1853, she was admitted to the medical school of Western Reserve University in Cleveland, Ohio.

After graduating with honors, she pursued additional training in England, where she studied with a physician who pioneered the use of chloroform in childbirth, and in Paris and Germany.

In 1856, she returned to the United States and helped Elizabeth convert her dispensary for poor women into a fully equipped hospital, chartered as the New York Infirmary for Women and Children. The hospital offered women physicians the clinical experience denied them by other hospitals and enabled female patients to consult with women doctors.

Emily Blackwell proved to be a superb hospital administrator. Besides supervising the surgery unit, she took charge of nursing, housekeeping, and fundraising. Through her efforts, the hospital flourished and expanded. In 1868, her sister established a medical school for women, and Emily served as dean and professor of obstetrics and gynecology. Because of its outstanding facilities, rigorous curriculum, and affiliation with the infirmary, the school soon became one of the best medical colleges in the United States.

In 1898, believing that coeducational medical training was more desirable, she closed the school and arranged for her students to attend the newly established Cornell University Medical College in New York City, which accepted both men and women. She devoted her energies to the infirmary and retired in 1900, leaving a lasting imprint on women's medical education and health care.

FURTHER READING
Abram, Ruth. *Send Us a Lady Physician: Women Doctors in America, 1835–1920.* New York: Norton, 1986.

Blair, Emily Jane Newell

SUFFRAGE FIGHTER, FEMINIST,
DEMOCRATIC PARTY OFFICIAL

Born: January 9, 1877
Joplin, Missouri

Died: August 3, 1951
Alexandria, Virginia

From middle-class wife and mother to Democratic party official—as her feminist consciousness deepened, so did Emily Newell Blair's commitment to political reform. Born into a middle-class family, she attended elementary and high schools in Missouri and entered the Woman's College of Baltimore (later Goucher). After one year, however, she was forced to drop out and teach school to help support her family.

After marrying Harry Wallace Blair, a lawyer, she settled into middle-class domesticity. But she felt restless and began to write. She soon sold short stories to *Cosmopolitan, Harper's Magazine, Woman's Home Companion,* and other magazines. She also joined the woman suffrage movement around 1910, and during World War I she served on a wartime preparedness agency for women.

After American women secured the vote, Blair helped found the League of Women Voters, a nonpartisan organization committed to educating women about their rights and responsibilities as citizens. Believing that women must gain power within national political groups, she joined the Democratic party in 1920 and soon became national vice chairwoman with a mandate to recruit women's support. Over the next several years, she traveled around the country organizing more than 2,000 Democratic women's clubs and strengthening regional training programs for women workers.

Nevertheless, she felt that she had pursued the wrong strategy to gain political power for women and argued that women must run for office themselves rather than work to elect men. She resumed writing, served as an associate editor of *Good Housekeeping* from 1925 to 1933, and served in two federal government agencies during the Depression and World War II.

PUBLICATIONS
"Are Women a Failure in Politics?" *Harper's Magazine* (October 1925)
"Putting Women Into Politics," *Woman's Journal* (March 1931)
Letters of a Contented Wife (1931)
A Woman of Courage (novel, 1933)

Blatch, Harriot Stanton

WOMAN SUFFRAGE LEADER

Born: January 20, 1856
Seneca Falls, New York

Died: November 20, 1940
Greenwich, Connecticut

Harriot Stanton Blatch, like her famous mother, Elizabeth Cady Stanton, was a trailblazer for women's rights. Born and educated in Seneca Falls, site of the first American women's rights convention, she graduated with honors from Vassar College in 1878 and, after living in Germany, assisted her mother and Susan B. Anthony in writing their massive *History of Woman Suffrage*. To her fell the difficult task of including information about the American Woman Suffrage Association (AWSA), the rival group to Stanton and Anthony's National Woman Suffrage Association (NWSA). Her favorable account of AWSA helped bring about renewed harmony between the two groups and their merger into the National American Woman Suffrage Association (NAWSA) in 1890.

After living in England for several years, where she married William Henry Blatch and gave birth

to a daughter, Blatch returned to the United States and threw herself into the work of reviving the sluggish American women's rights movement. In 1907, she organized the Equality League of Self-Supporting Women, a group of professional and working-class women. This group, with a growing membership, devised such new and bold strategies as open-air meetings, suffrage parades, and the use of women as poll watchers and witnesses at state legislative hearings. Blatch's innovative efforts breathed new life into the suffrage movement, and she became one of its chief strategists.

After touring war-torn Europe at the end of World War I, she worked for international peace. She supported the League of Nations, condemned the hysteria against political radicals sweeping the United States, and remained a vigorous advocate for working women.

PUBLICATIONS
A Woman's Point of View (1920)
Challenging Years (autobiography, 1940)

Bloomer, Amelia Jenks

TEMPERANCE REFORMER, EDITOR,
WOMEN'S RIGHTS ACTIVIST

Born: May 27, 1818
Cortland County, New York

Died: December 30, 1894
Council Bluffs, Iowa

Amelia Jenks Bloomer is perhaps the only woman in American history to be the namesake for a pair of pants. She grew up in a small town in upstate New York and, after attending a district school, became a teacher and then a governess.

In 1840, she married Dexter Chamberlain Bloomer, soon to become a prominent lawyer, anti-slavery reformer, and editor. They moved to

Seneca Falls, New York, future site of the first American women's rights convention, and Bloomer began to write articles for her husband's newspaper on social, political, and moral questions.

In 1848, she became an officer of a newly organized Ladies' Temperance Society, and the following year she founded the *Lily,* a temperance journal. Soon, however, the *Lily* gave as much coverage to women's rights as to temperance.

In 1850, Bloomer introduced Elizabeth Cady Stanton and Susan B. Anthony, launching their illustrious 50-year partnership as the chief architects of the women's rights movement. Bloomer also publicized the famous pantaloon costume in the *Lily.* This new garment—pantaloons worn underneath a short skirt—was infinitely more comfortable than the tight corsets and heavy layers of petticoats that women of that time wore. Within days, she was flooded with requests for patterns and information about bloomers, as the costume came to be called. But Bloomer and other women stopped wearing the costume in public because of all the controversy it aroused; ministers, in particular, thundered that bloomers defied the biblical injunction that women should not dress like men.

Throughout the 1850s, Bloomer remained active in temperance and women's rights, even after she and her husband moved to the Midwest. During the Civil War, she organized a soldiers' aid society in her hometown of Council Bluffs, and in 1871 she became president of the Iowa Woman Suffrage Society. She also wrote articles and letters to newspapers and other journals to promote her ideas on women's rights.

FURTHER READING

Bloomer, Dexter C. *Life and Writings of Amelia Bloomer.* Reprint. New York: Schocken Books, 1975.

Blumberg, Rhoda. *Bloomers!* New York: Bradbury Press, 1993.

Bradstreet, Anne
POET

*Born: 1612 (exact date unknown)
near Northampton, England*

*Died: September 16, 1672
North Andover, Massachusetts*

Anne Bradstreet, America's first known woman poet, grew up in the palatial surroundings of an English castle, where her father was first steward to the Earl of Lincoln. She enjoyed many privileges, such as private tutors, access to the earl's vast library, and exposure to the cultural benefits of aristocratic life.

In 1628, at age 16, she was married to Simon Bradstreet, also a member of the earl's royal staff. Two years later, she and her husband and parents sailed for New England aboard the *Arbella,* the flagship of John Winthrop's fleet. The shock of their new and rustic surroundings, away from all that had been familiar, deeply distressed her, but she later said, "After I was convinced it was the way of God, I submitted to it and joined to the church at Boston." She briefly lived in Cambridge, Massachusetts, then moved to Ipswich and, later, North Andover.

While raising eight children and helping to establish a home and community in the wilderness, she somehow found time to commit her thoughts to poetry. With no intention of publishing them, she wrote her poems for her own creative satisfaction as well as for her family. But unbeknownst to her, a volume of her poetry was published in 1650 by her brother-in-law, who had obtained a manuscript copy and sent it to a publisher in London. The poems dealt not with her migration to the New World but with the grand themes of history and philosophy that she had earlier studied in the earl's library in England. In this volume of poetry, she had not yet found her own voice.

In 1678, six years after she died, a second volume was published in Boston, and these poems reflected her growth as a poet and a woman. She had absorbed the contemplative rhythms of the New England landscape, and her poems bespoke both her Puritan outlook of life as a journey to spiritual grace and her abiding love for her family. "If ever two were one, then surely we," she addressed her husband in one poem. "If ever man were loved by wife, then thee."

PUBLICATION
The Complete Works of Anne Bradstreet. Edited by Joseph R. McElrath, Jr., and Allan B. Robb. Boston: Twayne Publishers, 1981

FURTHER READING
Dunham, Montrew et al. *Anne Bradstreet: Young Puritan Poet.* Indianapolis: Bobbs-Merrill, 1969.

Bradwell, Myra Colby

LAWYER, JOURNALIST

Born: February 12, 1831
Manchester, Vermont

Died: February 14, 1894
Chicago, Illinois

Myra Colby Bradwell dedicated her life to improving the standards of the legal profession and guaranteeing women's right to practice law. Raised in an abolitionist family, she attended the Ladies' Seminary in Elgin, Illinois, and taught school.

In 1852, she married James Bolesworth Bradwell, a future lawyer and county judge. He tutored his wife in the law, but the Civil War interrupted her studies. She joined the Northwestern Sanitary Commission and other volunteer organizations and did not resume her interest in the law until 1868, when she began publishing a weekly legal newspaper called the *Chicago Legal News.* She supervised the content, production, and financial operation of the paper. For the next 25 years, this journal was the most influential legal publication in the Midwest. In its pages, Bradwell commented on current legal opinions, called for laws regulating railroads and other corporations, and proposed standards to improve the practice of law. She also advocated women's rights and prison reform.

Bradwell served on the executive committee of the Illinois Woman Suffrage Association, and she and her husband drafted bills protecting married women's economic rights and calling for more employment opportunities for women in Illinois.

Meanwhile, in 1869, she applied for admission to the Illinois bar. After the state supreme court denied her petition, she took her case to the U.S. Supreme Court, which upheld the lower court ruling. But in 1872, a new state law enabled her to practice law. Bradwell soon gained the reputation of being the nation's most distinguished woman lawyer. She served four terms as vice president of the Illinois State Bar Association, while continuing to publish the *Chicago Legal News.*

FURTHER READING
Friedman, Jane M. *America's First Woman Lawyer: The Biography of Myra Bradwell.* Buffalo, N.Y.: Prometheus Books, 1993.

Breckinridge, Sophonisba Preston

SOCIAL WORKER

Born: April 1, 1866
Lexington, Kentucky

Died: July 30, 1948
Chicago, Illinois

Sophonisba Breckinridge had a profound impact on the field of social welfare and reform during the Progressive Era. As a young woman, she took to heart her father's urging to get an education and uphold the family tradition of "good intellectual work." After graduating from Wellesley College in 1888, she taught high school math in Washington, D.C., and then—despite her father's objections—returned to Kentucky and studied law on her own. She passed the Kentucky bar exam—the first woman to do so—but her law practice did not succeed.

In despair, she began to study for a Ph.D. in political science at the University of Chicago. In 1901, she received her degree, the first woman to do so in that field, and joined the university as an instructor in the economic and legal aspects of family life.

Still unsure of her professional goals, she joined the newly formed Women's Trade Union League (WTUL) and the talented staff of Jane Addams's Hull House. In addition, she began to teach at the Chicago School of Civics and Philanthropy and sought new ways to reform urban working-class life. She had found her life's work.

Her wide-ranging interests reflect the close connection between new ideas and concrete reform efforts during the Progressive Era. Besides writing about urban conditions, she investigated those conditions as a city health inspector, reported on Chicago's pioneering juvenile court movement, served on the executive committee of the state Consumers' League, campaigned for child labor laws, and joined the National Association for the Advancement of Colored People (NAACP). In addition, she was a vice president of the National American Woman Suffrage Association (NAWSA) and helped draft legislation to regulate the wages and hours of women's employment.

But she exerted her greatest influence in improving the training of social workers. At the University of Chicago, she helped devise a curriculum that required rigorous course work as well as better on-the-job training. She wanted to bridge the gap between ivory-tower ideas and the real needs of low-income citizens, and she urged the federal government to play a larger role in delivering social welfare services.

Her ideas found support during the New Deal, and her students easily obtained employment in a growing public welfare system. In 1934, she was elected president of the American Association of Schools of Social Work in recognition of her vital contribution to the field. Breckinridge's impressive, multifaceted career reflects the rich opportunities available to women who wished to reform American society during the Progressive Era.

PUBLICATIONS

The Delinquent Child and the Home (with Edith Abbott, 1912)
New Homes for Old (1921)
Public Welfare Administration (1927)
Marriage and the Civic Right of Women (1931)
The Family and the State (1934)

Brent, Margaret

COLONIAL LANDOWNER AND ADMINISTRATOR

Born: ca. 1601
England

Died: ca. 1671
Virginia

Margaret Brent played an important role in quelling unrest in the royal colony of Maryland. She was born in England and reared a Roman Catholic, but, beyond these two facts, her early life remains a mystery.

On November 22, 1638—four years after the colony was founded—she and her sister, Mary, and their two brothers left England and migrated to Maryland. They carried with them a letter from the proprietor of the colony urging that they be granted land. Over the next several years, Margaret Brent apparently amassed some wealth, because court records indicate that she filed several lawsuits to collect debts due her.

She and her siblings played an important role in Maryland's affairs. Indeed, in May 1647, the royal governor of Maryland, on his deathbed, chose Margaret Brent to be the executor of his estate. He also charged her to "Take all, pay all," thereby giving her the power and authority to resolve any crises within the colony.

Margaret Brent proved to be a capable trustee of the colony's welfare, guiding it through a difficult period of internal dissension. With shrewd financial skill, she found the funds necessary to pay English soldiers whom the royal governor had dispatched from nearby Virginia to put down a revolt—thus preventing them from fomenting their own rebellion.

But Brent was later remembered for another unorthodox act: On January 21, 1647 (or 1648—the records are unclear), she demanded two votes for herself in the colonial assembly—one because she was a landowner, and all landowners were granted voting rights; and the second because she had served as the former governor's attorney. The assembly denied her both votes because she was a woman—though its members expressed their gratitude for her capable service during the colony's troubled times.

In 1651, Brent and her sister moved to Virginia, where they once again acquired land and contributed to the colony's economic development. Margaret Brent named her plantation in Virginia "Peace" and apparently lived her final years in that manner. She remains known for her skillful leadership in guiding Maryland through a difficult time. Few other women of her day wielded such power.

Bullock, Carrie E.

NURSING ADMINISTRATOR AND PRESIDENT OF
THE NATIONAL ASSOCIATION OF COLORED
GRADUATE NURSES

Born: date and location unknown

Died: ca. 1961

Carrie E. Bullock made a vital contribution to expanding the professional stature of African-American nurses. Very little is known about her early life. She graduated from Scotia Seminary Normal

Department in Concord, North Carolina, and, after completing her nurse's training, joined the staff of Provident Hospital of Chicago in 1909; she worked there for 19 years. She also served as assistant supervisor and then supervisor of the Chicago Visiting Nurse Association, endeavoring to expand the agency's services to Chicago's black residents.

In 1923, Bullock was elected vice president of the National Association of Colored Graduate Nurses (NACGN) and served as managing editor of its official publication, the *National News Bulletin*. In 1927, she ascended to the presidency of the organization, and for the rest of her tenure dedicated herself to promoting its goals. She played a major role as an organizer and advocate for black nurses, a commitment that was captured by her motto: "I try to practice the golden rule; I believe we get out of the world what we put into it. I wish sincerely to be just to others."

FURTHER READING

Hine, Darlene Clark. *Black Women in White: Racial Conflict and Cooperation in the Nursing Profession, 1890–1950*. Bloomington: University of Indiana Press, 1989.

Bunch, Charlotte

FEMINIST WRITER, ACTIVIST

Born: ca. 1944

Activist, editor, teacher, and lecturer, Charlotte Bunch is part of a vanguard of women who have contributed vital new ideas to the women's movement. She majored in history at Duke University, where she worked for antipoverty programs and the civil rights movement of the 1960s. Like many other feminist activists, she found her way to feminism through her work on behalf of civil rights.

As the feminist movement was gaining ground in the late 1960s, she became a founding editor of *The Furies,* a lesbian feminist newspaper, and of

Quest: A Feminist Quarterly, a scholarly journal of feminist thought. In addition, she has edited numerous anthologies on feminist ideas and strategies. Bunch defines feminism as "transformational politics . . . a perspective on life that can transform the next century . . . a perspective on the world that grows out of women's oppression." She calls feminism "an entire world view, not just a laundry list of 'women's issues.'"

During the late 1980s, Bunch served as a consultant to the United Nations Secretariat for the World Conference of the United Nations Decade for Women. She has also worked with the New York City Commission on the Status of Women, the National Gay Task Force, and the American Friends Service Committee.

PUBLICATIONS
By Degrees: Essays on Feminist Education. Edited by Charlotte Bunch (1979)
Passionate Politics (1992)

Burns, Lucy

SUFFRAGIST

Born: July 28, 1879
Brooklyn, New York

Died: December 22, 1966
Brooklyn, New York

Lucy Burns and Alice Paul, like Elizabeth Cady Stanton and Susan B. Anthony before them, forged a powerful partnership to work for passage of the constitutional amendment granting American women the right to vote. Together, Paul and Burns spearheaded the militant branch of the American woman suffrage movement before and during World War I. By 1919, Burns had spent more time in jail than any other American suffragist.

Raised by parents who encouraged their daughters to get an education, Lucy and her sisters attended the Packer (Collegiate) Institute in Brooklyn, New York. After graduating in 1899, she enrolled at Vassar College, where she distinguished herself as an outstanding student. After graduating in 1902, she taught English in a New York City high school before embarking on graduate work in languages at two German universities.

In England, she started work on her doctorate, but the British woman suffrage movement soon captured her full attention. She led street-corner rallies, went to jail, and joined prison hunger strikes on behalf of suffrage.

In 1912, Burns returned to the United States, and she and Paul, whom she had met in England, headed a newly formed committee within the National American Woman Suffrage Association (NAWSA) to work for a woman suffrage constitutional amendment. Strategy differences with NAWSA forced them to break away and organize a new group, the Congressional Union (CU).

In 1916, the CU evolved into the National Woman's Party (NWP), with Paul and Burns serving as chief strategist and organizer, respectively. In this role, Burns conducted suffrage schools to educate followers, campaigned against candidates unsympathetic to women's suffrage, and edited *The Suffragist*, the organization's journal. She also led demonstrations against President Woodrow Wilson and went to jail, where she led a 19-day hunger strike. After the 19th Amendment, granting woman suffrage, was ratified, she retired from public life and lived quietly in Brooklyn.

Carson, Rachel Louise

ENVIRONMENTAL WRITER, SCIENTIST

Born: May 27, 1907
Springdale, Pennsylvania

Died: April 14, 1964
Silver Spring, Maryland

By her deep love of the natural world and fears for its survival, Rachel Carson helped create and give inspiration to the present-day environmental movement. As a child, she came by her love of nature from her mother, who taught her to appreciate its wonders.

After attending public elementary and high schools, Carson entered Pennsylvania College for Women (later Chatham College). She wanted to write, but she was also interested in science and decided to combine the two interests. She went on to complete a master's degree in zoology at Johns Hopkins University.

In 1935, she joined the United States Bureau of Fisheries in Washington, D.C., as a junior biologist. She was one of the first two women whom the bureau hired for a professional-level position. In her spare time, she wrote feature articles about fisheries.

Over the next 15 years, she rose steadily in the ranks to biologist and chief editor of publications at the United States Fish and Wildlife Service. She also wrote and went on bird-watching expeditions. Carson published three books that established her as a pioneer environmentalist: *The Sea Around Us* (1951), *The Edge of the Sea* (1955), and *Silent Spring* (1962), her most influential book. With a poet's gift for language, she exposed the dangers of DDT, an insecticide, on bird and plant life and described the potentially disastrous global impact of other toxic chemicals on the natural world. Carson urged readers to stop the indiscriminate plundering of the environment by unchecked industrial and technological growth.

Silent Spring prompted the creation of a presidential panel to study the effects of pesticides on the environment; the commission's findings corroborated Carson's conclusions. Despite her book's success in arousing public concern, Carson did not view herself as a crusader. She simply wanted to use her gift of language to make readers aware of the beauty, mystery, and fragility of the natural world.

MAJOR PUBLICATIONS
Under the Sea-Wind (1941)
The Sea Around Us (1951)
The Edge of the Sea (1955)
Silent Spring (1962)

FURTHER READING
Gartner, Carol B. *Rachel Carson.* New York: Ungar Publishing Company, 1983.
Jezer, Marty. *Rachel Carson: Biologist and Author.* New York: Chelsea House, 1988.

Cary, Alice
AUTHOR, CLUBWOMAN

Born: April 26, 1820
Hamilton County, Ohio

Died: February 12, 1871
New York, New York

Alice Cary, poet and novelist, was the first president of Sorosis, the professional women's club, which launched the women's club movement in the United States. She and her younger sister, Phoebe, grew up on a farm with few books, but their parents' ardent encouragement inspired them to achieve literary distinction. Alice attended a district school, but the natural beauty surrounding her family's farm was the true inspiration for her writing. At an early age, she submitted verses to various publications and soon counted poet John Greenleaf Whittier and author Edgar Allan Poe among her fans. In 1849, poems by both sisters appeared in the volume *The Female Poets of America,* and a year later the sisters published their own volume, *Poems of Alice and Phoebe Carey* [sic].

In 1850, Alice moved to New York City and Phoebe followed shortly after. On Sunday evenings, their home became a literary salon, drawing a wide range of talented people for stimulating and convivial conversation. Alice continued to write poetry as well as three volumes of sketches and short stories about life in rural Ohio. She also wrote three novels, each of which bleakly portrayed a society in which women had little power or independence.

In 1868, she became president of the newly organized Sorosis. In her inaugural address, she proclaimed, "We have, then, to begin at the beginning . . . to teach [women] to think for themselves . . . because it is their duty." Though she had played no significant role in the American women's rights movement, she believed that women must have greater employment opportunities and a domestic role endowed with greater authority and independence from men's power. She died before she could exert significant impact on Sorosis and the women's club movement in this country.

MAJOR PUBLICATIONS
Hagar, A Story of To-day (1852)
Married, Not Mated (1856)
The Bishop's Son (1867)

Cary, Mary Ann Shadd
JOURNALIST, TEACHER, LAWYER

Born: October 9, 1823
Wilmington, Delaware

Died: June 5, 1893
Washington, D.C.

Mary Ann Shadd Cary acquired her desire to help her people from her father, a free black who was an abolitionist and advocate for the civil and economic rights of free blacks. She graduated from a Quaker-sponsored school for free blacks in 1839, and went on to establish or teach in schools for African Americans in Delaware, Pennsylvania, and New York City.

In 1851, she moved to Windsor, Canada, to assist black refugees escaping from the Fugitive Slave Act of 1850. She opened a school for blacks and, in 1853, helped establish the *Provincial Freeman,* a newspaper for blacks living in Canada. In editorials

and on the lecture circuit, Shadd urged American blacks to emigrate to Canada, where she believed they would find less discrimination and more economic opportunity.

In 1856, she married Thomas E. Cary, a barber, and during the Civil War she helped recruit black soldiers for the Union army. After the war, she moved to Washington, D.C., where she resumed teaching and also served as principal of a grammar school. She attended law school at Howard University, fitting in her studies between teaching responsibilities, and received her law degree in June 1883. She was the only black woman in her class.

Cary was a committed suffragist. In 1880, she organized the Colored Women's Progressive Association, the first major organization created and led by black women, to work for economic, political, and social equality. The association endorsed female suffrage as a tool to improve the lives of all American blacks. Intelligent, forceful, and outspoken, Cary used her prodigious talents to help her fellow African-American citizens.

FURTHER READING
Giddings, Paula. *When and Where I Enter: The Impact of Black Women on Race and Sex in America.* New York: Morrow, 1984.
Sterling, Dorothy. *We Are Your Sisters.* New York: Norton, 1984.

Cassatt, Mary
ARTIST

Born: May 22, 1844
Allegheny City, Pennsylvania

Died: June 14, 1926
Oise, France

Mary Cassatt was one of the few women artists to join the Impressionist movement, a dramatically new art form originating in France. From her first exposure to the great art museums of France and Germany as a child, she knew she wanted to be an artist. In 1861, she enrolled in the Pennsylvania Academy of Fine Arts, but she was dismayed by the tedious, rigid academic course of study. She returned to France in 1866 for additional study and over the next several years traveled throughout France, Italy, Spain, and Holland to study the work of other artists and to refine her own style.

In the early 1870s, she made her home in Paris—just as the controversial new movement of Impressionism was raising eyebrows and disdain in the art world. This movement rejected the traditional artistic approach of faithfully reproducing a scene in paint, as if the artist were trying to create a photographic image. Instead, Impressionist painters approached their art from a highly subjective, or impressionistic, response. Rather than convey a detailed and accurate rendering of the subject, they played with color and light to create a much freer, more vibrant, and atmospheric effect. Their subjects ranged from busy Parisian streets to tranquil farms and meadows.

Cassatt was the first American artist to exhibit her work in an Impressionist show. Unlike other Impressionists, she chose to portray mostly women and children. Her paintings depict gentle, loving moments between women and young children. She also captured women in a variety of private moments—at tea, enjoying the opera, or simply reading a book or writing a letter. She and Lilla Perry Cabot, another American woman artist, knew the great master of French Impressionism, Claude Monet, and their paintings reflect his artistic influence. A century later, Cassatt's work remains a visual feast.

The French embraced Cassatt's art more eagerly than did Americans. In 1904, she was made a *chevalier* of the Legion of Honor, a singular tribute, especially for a foreigner. By 1914, a serious eye ailment had left her nearly blind and unable to paint. She died 12 years later from diabetes at her country home in France. She was one of the most talented artists of her time, with a vision all her own.

FURTHER READING
Cain, Michael. *Mary Cassatt: Artist*. New York: Chelsea House, 1989.
Mathews, Nancy. *Mary Cassatt: A Life*. New York: Villard Books, 1994.

Cather, Willa Sibert

AUTHOR

Born: December 7, 1873
Back Creek Valley, Virginia

Died: April 24, 1947
New York, New York

Willa Cather was the premier chronicler of the pioneer experience, giving voice in her novels to the hopes and dreams of the last generation of homesteaders to settle the flat, arid lands of the Nebraska plains.

Cather herself spent a bucolic childhood in an old Virginia farmhouse. Her maternal grandmother educated her at home, and she immersed herself in the beauty of nature by exploring the woods and creeks beyond her family's homestead.

She lived the pioneer experience firsthand when her family moved to Red Cloud, Nebraska. In this wilderness region, she encountered pioneers from across the ocean—Swedes, Bohemians, Germans, Russians, and Poles—and absorbed many different cultural traditions. She entered public high school and, in 1891, enrolled in the University of Nebraska at Lincoln. When one of her stories was published in a little magazine, she quickly changed her major from science to literature. After graduating in 1895, she became a journalist and magazine editor.

Finally, in 1912, after her first novel was serialized in *McClure's*, she quit her job to write full time. Over the next 30 years, she published several major novels. In her fiction, she explored the dilemma of strong, ambitious characters who have struggled to achieve success, only to discover how illusory that success can be. Her novels span a range of time periods and settings, including the Southwest, the Great Plains, New York City, and French Canada.

In 1922, Cather won a Pulitzer Prize for a novel, *One of Ours*. But her most famous novels are *O Pioneers!*, published in 1913, and *My Ántonia*, published in 1918. Both novels depict the life she had known in Nebraska, and their strong female protagonists—determined to make the land they loved flourish for them—were drawn from the stalwart immigrant pioneer women of her childhood. Cather gave American literature a panoply of rich, complex characters and unforgettable settings.

MAJOR PUBLICATIONS
O Pioneers! (1913)
The Song of the Lark (1915)
My Ántonia (1918)
Death Comes for the Archbishop (1927)
Shadows on the Rock (1931)

FURTHER READING
Keene, Ann. *Willa Cather*. New York: Simon and Schuster, 1994.
O'Brien, Sharon. *Willa Cather: The Emerging Voice*. New York: Oxford University Press, 1987.

Catt, Carrie Chapman

SUFFRAGIST, PEACE LEADER

Born: January 9, 1859
Ripon, Wisconsin

Died: March 9, 1947
New Rochelle, New York

Following in the footsteps of Elizabeth Cady Stanton and Susan B. Anthony, Carrie Chapman Catt dedicated her life to the struggle to achieve woman suffrage in America. Born on a farm, she attended public schools and taught for a year before entering Iowa State College in 1877 as a sophomore. She graduated in 1880, intending to go to law school.

Instead, she took a position as a high school principal, and two years later became superintendent of schools, a post not commonly offered to women of her day.

In 1885, marriage to Leo Chapman, a newspaper editor, derailed her career as an educator, and she became assistant editor of his newspaper. After he died she began to lecture, and in 1887 she joined the Iowa Woman Suffrage Association. She also married again, and her new husband, George William Catt, urged her to devote all her energies to women's rights. Catt rapidly rose through the leadership ranks of the National American Woman Suffrage Association (NAWSA), occupying a front-line position as a strategist and fund-raiser.

In 1900, she succeeded Susan B. Anthony as president of NAWSA and expanded the organization into a nationwide movement with a healthy treasury and a strong administrative structure. During her two terms in office, interrupted by her husband's illness, she devised a flexible strategy to achieve congressional support for a federal suffrage amendment as well as to increase the number of states in which women could vote. She also helped convert President Woodrow Wilson into a suffrage supporter and managed to keep suffrage activity alive during the bleak days of World War I.

Catt presided over the ratification of the 19th Amendment to the Constitution of the United States, which granted women the right to vote, and went on to campaign for women's suffrage in other countries. She proposed the creation of the League of Women Voters but did not participate in it. Instead, like some other suffragists, she devoted her last years to achieving global peace and disarmament.

PUBLICATION
Woman Suffrage and Politics (with Nettie Rogers Shuler, 1923)

FURTHER READING
Van Voris, Jacqueline. *Carrie Chapman Catt: A Public Life*. New York: Feminist Press, 1987.

Chapman, Maria Weston

ABOLITIONIST

Born: July 25, 1806
Weymouth, Massachusetts

Died: July 12, 1885
Weymouth, Massachusetts

In an era when being an abolitionist, an advocate of the immediate and unconditional end to slavery—and especially a female abolitionist—could lead to harassment and even bodily harm, Maria Weston Chapman proudly upheld her abolitionist beliefs. Raised on a farm in Weymouth, Massachusetts, she attended district schools and then moved to England, where she received a genteel education in the arts. She returned to Boston in 1828 and served as "lady principal" of a girls' high school.

In 1830, she married Henry Grafton Chapman, an affluent Boston merchant and an ardent abolitionist. Through her husband, she joined the cause, and, in 1832, with 12 other women, she organized the Boston Female Antislavery Society. The society circulated petitions to abolish slavery in Washington, D.C., and supported efforts to educate Boston's free blacks. During a mob assault on one of their meetings, Chapman refused to flee, claiming, "If this is the last bulwark of freedom, we may as well die here as anywhere."

William Lloyd Garrison, leader of the radical abolitionists, singled Chapman out as a loyal captain. She helped Garrison edit the *Liberator,* the journal of the Massachusetts Antislavery Society, and also supported abolitionists Sarah and Angelina Grimké against the Massachusetts clergymen who had chastized them for lecturing in public.

Chapman remained a leading figure in the abolitionist movement until the early 1840s, when her husband's illness curtailed her activities. But she continued to support Garrison's staunch opposition to gradual emancipation or to other compromises in abolishing slavery. During the Civil War, she worked in her son's New York City brokerage office, and spent her last years in Weymouth.

PUBLICATION
Right and Wrong in Massachusetts (pamphlet, 1839)

FURTHER READING
Hersh, Blanche Glassman. *The Slavery of Sex: Feminist Abolitionists in America.* Urbana: University of Illinois Press, 1978.

Chesnut, Mary Boykin Miller

DIARIST

Born: March 31, 1823
Camden, South Carolina

Died: November 22, 1886
Camden, South Carolina

During the Civil War, Mary Boykin Chesnut, like scores of other northern and southern women, kept a diary about the dramatic, and also mundane, events of war. Chesnut, the wife of a high-ranking Confederate officer and politician, was ideally positioned to comment on wartime conditions and mischief, and her diary offers a tart, timeless insider's glimpse of daily life in the Civil War South.

After a carefree childhood rudely disrupted by her father's sudden death, she courted James Chesnut, Jr., a law student, while still in her teens. The romantic blush of their courtship ripened into an abiding, loving, and mutually respecting marriage, and Chesnut proudly watched her husband move into the highest ranks of southern leadership.

Although she was no abolitionist, she condemned slavery because of the burdens and humiliations it imposed on white planter women. All this and more she committed to her diary, which she began keeping at the start of the Civil War. But she remained loyal to the Confederacy, and she cried for the ruin of the South in defeat.

Like so many other Southerners, from the planter class to the lowliest yeomen farmers, the Chesnuts were reduced to poverty by the war. Chesnut helped her husband recoup their financial losses, even selling butter to bring in extra money, and worked steadily on her diary to revise it for publication. But she never lived to see the diary published. A volume of excerpts, entitled *A Diary from Dixie*, was published in 1905 and again in 1949, and the entire diary was published in 1981. The diary not only offers a revealing view of southern life during the war; it also reflects the complex, independent mind of a woman who criticized slavery but who remained fiercely loyal to her beloved South.

PUBLICATIONS
Mary Chesnut's Civil War, edited by C. Vann Woodward (1981)
The Private Mary Chesnut: The Unpublished Civil War Diaries, edited by C. Vann Woodward and Elizabeth Muhlenfeld (1984)

FURTHER READING
Muhlenfeld, Elizabeth. *Mary Boykin Chesnut: A Further Reading.* Baton Rouge: Louisiana State University Press, 1981.

Child, Lydia Maria

AUTHOR, ABOLITIONIST

Born: February 11, 1802
Medford, Massachusetts

Died: October 20, 1880
Wayland, Massachusetts

A precocious young woman who read Milton and Homer at 15, Lydia Maria Child became a leading advocate for the antislavery movement. Her own formal education was brief, consisting of instruction at a dame school and a year at a seminary. She studied on her own and taught briefly in Gardiner, Massachusetts.

But her true talent lay in writing, not teaching. At 22, she published her first novel, *Hobomok*, a love story about a Native American man and a white woman. In 1826, she launched the *Juvenile Miscellany*, the first American magazine for children. Versatile in style as well as subject matter, Child wrote both fiction and nonfiction, including the best-selling household manual *The Frugal Housewife*, and she captured the admiration of Boston's literary and intellectual elite.

In 1833, she published *An Appeal in Favor of That Class of Americans Called Africans*, an early antislavery work that traced the history and evils of slavery. The last chapter denounced laws against interracial marriage and condemned inequality toward blacks and segregation in churches, theaters, and stagecoaches. The book aroused the furor of Boston's conservative upper class—as well as much of Child's readership—but it helped to convert leading politicians and writers to the antislavery cause. Child wrote two other antislavery pamphlets, along with other novels and nonfiction.

In 1840, she joined the executive committee of the American Antislavery Society and moved to New York City to edit its weekly *National Antislavery Standard*. She also wrote a regular column for the *Boston Courier*. Although she did not join the women's rights movement, she believed in greater equality for women, declaring to Elizabeth Cady Stanton that women "should go right ahead, and do whatever they can do well, without talking about it."

The eve of the Civil War found her once again writing antislavery tracts, including *The Duty of Disobedience to the Fugitive Slave Act, The Patriarchal Institution,* and *The Right Way, the Safe Way,* which advocated immediate emancipation of all slaves. In 1861, she edited the autobiography of former slave Harriet Jacobs, *Incidents in the Life of a Slave Girl,* a revealing glimpse into the ordeal of bondage for a young slave woman.

Child lived her final years in Wayland, Massachusetts, and published her last book, *Aspirations of the World,* two years before her death. She was one of America's first women of letters, and she used her literary talents to plead the cause of enslaved African Americans and mistreated Native Americans.

MAJOR PUBLICATIONS

The Frugal Housewife (1829)
The Mother's Book (1831)
An Appeal in Favor of That Class of Americans Called Africans (1833)
Autumnal Leaves (1857)
An Appeal for the Indians (1868)

FURTHER READING

Clifford, Deborah Pickman. *Crusader for Freedom: A Life of Lydia Maria Child.* Boston: Beacon Press, 1992.
Meltzer, Milton. *Tongue of Flame: The Story of Lydia Maria Child.* New York: HarperCollins, 1991.

Chisholm, Shirley Anita St. Hill

CONGRESSWOMAN, AUTHOR

Born: November 20, 1924
Brooklyn, New York

Shirley Chisholm, a diminutive woman with crackling energy and presence, has accomplished two firsts: She was the first African-American woman to be elected to Congress and was also the first woman, and first black, to seek the endorsement of a major political party as candidate for U.S. President.

Although she was born in Brooklyn, New York, Chisholm spent her early years in Barbados, where she received a rigorous British-style education. Her parents, though poor, strove to give their daughters many cultural advantages, such as piano lessons and a love of reading.

Chisholm attended Brooklyn College, where she majored in psychology. After graduating, she worked at a child-care center in Harlem and toward a master's degree in early childhood education at Columbia University. Although she planned to teach, she gradually became involved in New York City politics. In 1964, she ran for a seat in the New York State Assembly. She won by a comfortable margin and, among other projects, worked on legislation to enable poor students to attend college.

In 1968, she embarked on a bruising campaign for the U.S. Congress and won easily. She served six terms in Congress, from 1969 to 1982, and focused on issues, such as minimum-wage increases and federal funding for day-care centers, that benefited women and the poor.

In 1972, she decided to run for U.S. President and sought her party's nomination at the Democratic National Convention. Although she lost, she believed that her short-lived campaign had served an important purpose. "What I hope most," she explained later, "is that now there will be others who will feel themselves as capable of running for high political office as any wealthy, good-looking white male."

In 1982, Chisholm retired from Congress but not from public life. Since then, she has taught political science and women's studies at Mount Holyoke College and Spelman College. She also helped establish the National Political Congress of Black Women (NPCBW) to promote civil rights and social reform, and is active in a number of political organizations.

PUBLICATIONS

Unbought and Unbossed (1970)
The Good Fight (1973)

FURTHER READING

Haskins, Jim. *Fighting Shirley Chisholm.* New York: Dial Press, 1975.
Scheader, Catherine. *Shirley Chisholm: Teacher and Congresswoman.* Hillside, N.J.: Enslow, 1990.

Claflin, Tennessee

FEMINIST, POLITICAL ACTIVIST

Born: October 26, 1845
Homer, Ohio

Died: January 18, 1923
London, England

Tennessee Claflin and her sister Victoria Woodhull enjoyed a colorful and controversial life, starting in their childhood as they followed their scoundrel father about as he tried to earn a living—not always by honest means. Such a nomadic life allowed for little schooling, but both sisters acquired their father's genius for devising business schemes. They joined forces with their brother to create a traveling medicine show that featured the sale of a phony elixir of life as well as their services as spiritualists.

In 1869, the two sisters teamed up in New York City as Wall Street speculators. Railroad baron Cornelius Vanderbilt offered helpful advice, and their business thrived. Soon the "Bewitching Brokers," as they were called, shifted their prodigious energies to politics, and both became persuasive—and provocative—spokeswomen for the women's rights movement.

In their journal, *Woodhull & Claflin's Weekly,* which began publication in 1870, they espoused their controversial beliefs on dress reform, free love, legalized prostitution, and world government. They also became early muckrakers by exposing fraud on Wall Street. In 1871, the two sisters published Karl Marx's *Communist Manifesto,* the blueprint of communism, in their journal— the first appearance of this historic document in the United States.

For her part, Claflin regarded dress reform as "one of the most important Humanitarian movements of the age." She condemned current fashions for endangering women's health and for contributing to the image of women as sexual objects who dressed only for men's pleasure. Claflin urged women to cast off these life-threatening garments and dress for their own comfort, health, and pleasure.

By the late 1870s, scandal involving Victoria Woodhull prompted the sisters to resettle in London, where Claflin married Francis Cook, a wealthy businessman, and continued to fight for the causes in which she believed. Merrier in manner, she evoked far less controversy than her brilliant and more combative sister.

FURTHER READING
Brough, James. *The Vixens! A Biography of Victoria and Tennessee Claflin.* New York: Simon & Schuster, 1980.

Cleveland, Emeline Horton

SURGEON, MEDICAL SCHOOL
ADMINISTRATOR

Born: September 22, 1829
Ashford, Connecticut

Died: December 8, 1878
Philadelphia, Pennsylvania

Emeline Cleveland was the first American woman physician to perform major surgery. She developed an expertise in removing ovarian tumors and also launched one of the first training programs in the nation for nurses' aides.

As a child, she received private instruction, then taught school briefly before going to Oberlin College. She graduated in 1853 and entered the Female (later Woman's) Medical College of Pennsylvania in Philadelphia. She received her medical degree two years later and became an instructor of anatomy at the college.

In 1860, several Quaker women financed a trip to Paris for Cleveland to pursue postgraduate training in obstetrics. They hoped to establish a hospital for women and children in Philadelphia. Cleveland completed her training with top honors and returned to Philadelphia, where she served as chief of obstetrics at the newly chartered Woman's Hospital of Philadelphia. She managed to balance a highly demanding job with marriage and motherhood.

More importantly, her impressive medical skills helped break down resistance to female physicians within the male-dominated medical profession. Although she was barred from joining the Philadelphia Obstetrical Society because she was a woman, she braved the way for other women doctors.

From 1872 to 1874, she served as dean of the Woman's Medical College, and in 1878, despite teaching duties and an active private practice, she became a staff gynecologist at the Pennsylvania Hospital—and one of the first female physicians to join the staff of a public hospital. Sadly, she died of tuberculosis at an early age, unable to complete a brilliant career.

Clinton, Hillary Rodham

LAWYER, FIRST LADY

Born: October 26, 1947
Chicago, Illinois

Hillary Rodham Clinton is a pathbreaker: She is the first First Lady to have pursued a high-powered career—law—and to wield unprecedented influence in her husband's Presidential administration. Besides practicing law, Clinton has spent much of her professional life working for educational reform and children's welfare, and she is committed to improving the delivery of health care in the United States, a cornerstone of her husband's domestic program.

Hillary Rodham grew up in a middle-class suburb of Chicago and was the only daughter in a family of three children. She attended public elementary and high schools, where she revealed a keen, inquiring mind and a desire to achieve academic excellence. She joined her high school's debating team and student government and was a National Merit Scholarship finalist and a member of the National Honor Society.

She embarked upon the pathway of social activism in her teen years by organizing baby-sitting services for local migrant workers and participating in local civil-rights activities. Yet, despite her exposure to social problems and to ideas for social reform, she remained a staunch Republican, like her parents, and campaigned for conservative Republican Presidential candidate Barry Goldwater in 1964 while still in high school.

In 1965, Clinton entered Wellesley College, an all-female school near Boston. There she headed the local chapter of the Young Republicans. But the turmoil of the late 1960s—the student protests against the Vietnam War and the assassinations of Dr. Martin Luther King, Jr., and Robert F. Kennedy in 1968—propelled her leftward into the Democratic party. She worked to enroll more black students at Wellesley, organized the school's first teach-ins on the Vietnam War, and wrote her senior thesis on poverty and community development. She graduated from Wellesley in 1969 and was the first student to give a commencement address at the school, which earned her a profile in *Life* magazine.

She enrolled in Yale Law School—after a professor at Harvard informed her that its law school did not need any more female students. At Yale, she tried to wed social activism with a legal career by volunteering to work on a Washington-based project to promote children's welfare and rights. She spent one summer interviewing the families of migrant workers and reported her findings to a U.S. Senate subcommittee. In addition, she worked at the Yale Child Study Center and did legal research for the Carnegie Council on Children, with the goal of improving children's access to education and medical care.

In 1970, she met Bill Clinton, a fellow law student at Yale, who shared her desire to pursue a career in public service. Before graduating from law school in 1973, they both worked on George S. McGovern's Democratic Presidential campaign. While Bill Clinton taught constitutional law at the University of Arkansas, Hillary Rodham worked as a staff attorney for the Children's Defense Fund. In 1974, she joined the legal team of the House Judiciary Committee pursuing impeachment proceedings against President Richard Nixon. When the impeachment staff was disbanded after Nixon's resignation in August 1974, she too joined the faculty of the University of Arkansas law school.

A little more than a year later, on October 11, 1975, she and Clinton were married. While her husband served first as state attorney general and then as governor of Arkansas for four terms, she carved out her own area of expertise in social welfare. In 1977, President Jimmy Carter appointed her to the board of directors of the Legal Services Corporation, an agency that provides legal counsel to poor people. In addition, she founded the Arkansas Advocates for Children and Families, a group that lobbies the state legislature for laws to help low-income children.

Besides pursuing a high-powered career as a corporate lawyer for the Rose Law Firm of Little Rock, Arkansas, Clinton, as First Lady of Arkansas, chaired a task force on ways to deliver health care to isolated areas. In 1980, she gave birth to a daughter, Chelsea, and three years later she spearheaded efforts to improve the quality of public education in Arkansas. Among her most controversial recommendations was a suggestion to institute teacher-competency testing. She continued to promote access to education and health care for the state's children, and also garnered acclaim for her legal skills. In 1988 and 1991, she was named one of the most influential lawyers in the United States by the *National Law Journal*.

In 1992, Hillary Rodham Clinton received national scrutiny when her husband announced his candidacy for the U.S. Presidency. During a bruising campaign, marred by rumors of his marital infidelity and intense public concern about how much power she would wield as Presidential spouse, she was the focus of more media attention than any previous Presidential candidate's wife. She handled the scrutiny with dignity and grace.

Only a few days after Clinton took office, he appointed his wife leader of the Task Force on National Health Care. To her and a staff of some 500 fell the task of restructuring the nation's health care system. The challenge was formidable—to control costs while expanding coverage and services. On February 4, 1993, she held the first series of meet-

ings with congressional leaders—an unprecedented act for a First Lady. She has impressed even opposition leaders with her command of the most minute facts and complex ideas. Clearly, Hillary Rodham Clinton has set a new standard for the role of First Lady.

FURTHER READING
Guernsey, Jo Ann Bren. *Hillary Rodham Clinton: A New Kind of First Lady*. Minneapolis: Lerner, 1993.

Cole, Rebecca J.

PHYSICIAN

Born: March 16, 1846
Philadelphia, Pennsylvania

Died: August 14, 1922
Philadelphia, Pennsylvania

The daughter of free blacks, Rebecca Cole received an education that enabled her to achieve a career in medicine—a field that welcomed neither African Americans nor women.

Cole graduated in 1863 from the Institute for Colored Youth in Philadelphia, where she excelled in math and the classics. She taught school briefly, then entered the Female Medical College of Pennsylvania (later the Medical College of Pennsylvania) in 1864. She graduated three years later, becoming the second black woman physician in America.

Cole moved to New York City and joined the medical staff of the New York Infirmary for Women and Children, the hospital established by Elizabeth Blackwell. Blackwell, who had started a neighborhood hygiene program at the hospital, assigned Cole to this position because of her previous work with patients in tenement districts. In this role, she taught poor mothers how to care for their infants and protect their families' health. She was thus a pioneer in two areas of medicine—pediatrics and preventive health care.

In later years, Cole served as superintendent of the Government House for Children and Old Women in Washington, D.C. She then returned to Philadelphia, where she established a practice, ran a shelter for the homeless, and opened a Woman's Directory, an agency that gave medical and legal aid to women. When she died in 1922, she had been a physician for more than half a century.

FURTHER READING
Sterling, Dorothy, ed. *We Are Your Sisters: Black Women in Nineteenth-Century America.* New York: Norton, 1984.

Cooper, Anna "Annie" Julia

EDUCATOR, SCHOLAR, WRITER, ACTIVIST

Born: August 10, 1858 or 1859
Raleigh, North Carolina

Died: February 27, 1964
Washington, D.C.

Born a slave, Anna Julia Cooper gained renown as a scholar and teacher. Her impressive life and career spanned slavery and the Civil War, Reconstruction, two world wars, the Great Depression, and the civil rights movement. During Reconstruction, she attended Saint Augustine's Normal School and Collegiate Institute (now Saint Augustine's College) in Raleigh, North Carolina, then joined the faculty there. In 1877, she married George A. C. Cooper, a fellow teacher.

In 1881, she entered Oberlin College, receiving her A.B. degree in 1884 and her M.A. in math three years later. For the next two decades, she taught and also served as principal of the M Street High School in Washington, D.C. During this time, she lectured around the country against racism and helped to launch the African-American women's club movement. She spoke and wrote about women's rights and the betterment of her people and vigorously defended every woman's right to an equal

education because, as she wrote, "the world needs to hear her voice." In articles and speeches, she eloquently articulated a new leadership role for black women in their communities.

In 1925, after many years of study at Columbia University and at the Sorbonne in Paris, Cooper received her Ph.D. Her dissertation, a study of French racial attitudes, revealed a penetrating understanding of the root causes of slavery and chronicled the struggles of blacks to overthrow their enslavement. At age 66, she was only the fourth known African-American woman to receive a doctorate—having done so while working full-time and rearing several foster children. Cooper was a towering figure among African-American educators and reformers.

PUBLICATIONS
The Third Step (autobiography, ca. 1950, unpublished)
A Voice from the South. By a Black Woman from the South (1892; reprinted 1988)

FURTHER READING
Giddings, Paula. *When and Where I Enter: The Impact of Black Women on Race and Sex in America.* New York: Morrow, 1984.

Coppin, Fanny Marion Jackson

EDUCATOR, FOREIGN MISSIONARY

Born: 1837 (exact date unknown)
Washington, D.C.

Died: January 21, 1913
Philadelphia, Pennsylvania

Like many other outstanding African-American women of her era, Fanny Jackson was born a slave, but through determination and hard work she achieved her goals in life. When she was a child, an aunt, Sarah Clark, secured her freedom for $125 and sent her to live in New Bedford, Massachusetts. There the young girl hired herself out as a domestic and received a modicum of schooling. She was determined, she said later, to "get an education and become a teacher to my people."

To that end, she attended the Rhode Island State Normal School, then enrolled at Oberlin College in Ohio, the only college in the nation to accept both African-American and women students. Once again, her aunt helped her by financing her tuition. Fanny Jackson quickly excelled, and by her junior year she was one of the most skillful junior teachers at Oberlin.

After graduating in 1865, she joined the faculty of the Institute for Colored Youth in Philadelphia as a classics and math teacher. She was also principal of the girls' high school department. In 1869, she became head principal—the first black woman to rise to that position.

Jackson, who married in 1881, was fiercely devoted to her students. She believed that education was the chief tool for advancement among American blacks. During her long tenure at the institute, she developed a teacher-training curriculum and an industrial arts program in 10 different trades. But Coppin did not want her students only to be carpenters and factory workers. She also urged them to become doctors, lawyers, engineers, and above all, teachers. With her help, scores of students went on to become accomplished professionals.

In later years, Coppin joined the foreign missionary movement. She became president of the Women's Home and Foreign Missionary Society of the African Methodist Episcopal church and, in 1902, accompanied her husband, a minister, to Cape Town, South Africa. For the next several years, she traveled throughout South Africa, organizing female missionary societies. Fannie Jackson Coppin left an indelible imprint on the quality of African Americans' lives in the late 19th century.

PUBLICATION
Reminiscences of School Life (1913)

FURTHER READING
Giddings, Paula. *When and Where I Enter: The Impact of Black Women on Race and Sex in America.* New York: Morrow, 1984.

Cotten, Sallie Sims Southall

SOUTHERN CLUBWOMAN

Born: June 13, 1846
Lawrenceville, Virginia

Died: May 4, 1929
Winchester, Massachusetts

Daughter of a Virginia planter, Sallie Southall Cotten attended Wesleyan Female College in Murfreesboro, North Carolina, and graduated in 1863 from the Greensboro (North Carolina) Female College. She taught school for two years before marrying Robert Randolph Cotten, a penniless Confederate veteran. For the next 30 years, Cotten lived the private domestic life of a southern homemaker, overseeing her growing family and thriving plantation. She also organized a school on the plantation and tried to pursue a program of self-education.

In 1893, she underwent a sea change of interests when she became one of North Carolina's "lady managers" for the Chicago World's Columbian Exposition. At the exposition, she met women from across the country who were active in women's clubs and the women's rights movement. She returned home eager to help organize the women of her state to improve their lives and communities. To this end, Cotten helped establish clubs throughout North Carolina and was a founding leader of the North Carolina Federation of Women's Clubs.

Cotten was convinced that "the new force in modern civilization . . . is educated, Christianized, organized womanhood." Under her leadership, North Carolina women undertook a wide-ranging campaign of civic reform. They promoted adult literacy, worked for prison reform and laws regulating child labor, and secured passage of a law enabling women to serve on school boards. For her energy and leadership, Cotten earned the reputation of being the "Julia Ward Howe of the South" after the famous creator of the "Battle Hymn of the Republic" who galvanized the New England women's club movement.

PUBLICATION
*The History of the North Carolina Federation of
Women's Clubs, 1901–1925* (1925)

Craft, Ellen

FUGITIVE SLAVE, TEACHER

*Born: ca. 1826 (exact date unknown)
Clinton, Georgia*

*Died: ca. 1897 (exact date unknown)
Charleston, South Carolina*

On December 21, 1848, Ellen Craft and her husband, William, both slaves, boarded a steamer in Savannah, Georgia, and—unbeknownst to anyone else—traveled first class to freedom. They had contrived an elaborate escape plan by which Ellen, pretending she was an ailing young man, wrapped herself in bandages to disguise her true identity and William played the role of her servant. Journeying by steamer and train, they went first to Philadelphia and then to New England.

News of their ingenious escape spread, but they were safe in New England until 1850, when Congress passed the Fugitive Slave Law. That law granted southern slave owners more power than any previous law to retrieve runaway slaves from the North and return them to slavery. Abolitionists helped the Crafts escape first to Maine and then to Canada. From there, they sailed for England, where they attended school and learned how to read and write. They also taught their fellow students manual skills.

After the Civil War, they returned to the United States and used their savings to purchase a planta-

tion in Georgia. They also opened an industrial school for former slaves. Ellen, who had been sold away from her mother as a child and had escaped from bondage because she feared the same fate awaited any children she bore, gave birth to five children and experienced the pleasures of family life denied to her as a child.

FURTHER READING
Craft, William. *Running a Thousand Miles for
Freedom.* 1860. Reprint. New York: Arno Press,
1969.
Lerner, Gerda, ed. *Black Women in White America: A
Documentary History.* New York: Vintage, 1973.
New edition, 1993.

Crandall, Prudence

TEACHER, ABOLITIONIST

*Born: September 3, 1803
Hopkinton, Rhode Island*

*Died: January 28, 1890
Elk Falls, Kansas*

Reared in a Quaker family, Prudence Crandall attended the New England Friends' Boarding School in Providence, Rhode Island, and then taught school in Plainfield, Connecticut. When her family moved to the lovely, quiet town of Canterbury, Connecticut, in 1831, the citizens of that small town beseeched her to open a school for their daughters.

Crandall quietly conducted the Canterbury Female Boarding School—until she decided to admit a young black female student. Her students' parents threatened to withdraw their daughters and close the school. The more opposition she encountered, the more determined Crandall was to keep the school open and dedicate her efforts to educating people of color. She had become an abolitionist and urged the immediate end of American slavery.

In the spring of 1833, she reopened the school as a teacher-training school for African-American women. Outraged, the town elders passed a law barring the establishment of any school that taught black students from out of state—who were the majority of Crandall's students—and Crandall was arrested and spent the night in jail. Her case went to trial and she was eventually cleared of all charges. But this did not deter Canterbury's prejudiced citizens. They smashed the school's windows, polluted its well, and set fire to the building. After a mob rampaged through the school—with Crandall and her students barely escaping unharmed—she gave up the good fight and closed the school in September 1834.

She and her husband, Calvin Philleo, an abolitionist and Baptist minister, left Canterbury and resettled in Illinois, where Crandall opened a school in her home and supported the women's rights movement. After her husband died, she moved to a farm in Elk Falls, Kansas, and continued to support women's rights and temperance.

FURTHER READING

Strane, Susan. *A Whole-Souled Woman: Prudence Crandall and the Education of Black Women.* New York: Norton, 1990.

Crawford, Joan

ACTRESS

Born: ca. March 23, 1908 (exact date unknown)
San Antonio, Texas

Died: May 10, 1977
New York, New York

From a blithe shop girl on the silent screen in *Our Dancing Daughters* (1928) to an embittered old actress in the horror movie *Whatever Happened to Baby Jane?* (1962)—Joan Crawford played these and other unforgettable roles in a film career that spanned almost half a century. Like Bette Davis and other high-profile Hollywood actresses, she was tough, disciplined, and willing to fight for the best roles. At the peak of her popularity in the 1930s, she epitomized the glamour and fairy-tale magic of Hollywood.

Crawford's own story is a Cinderella tale of childhood misery ending in a burst of professional success. Born Lucille Lesueur, she worked from an early age to help her divorced mother. While going to private schools she worked to pay her tuition, and she often felt more like a slave than a student as she cooked, washed dishes, waited tables, and made beds for the other students.

She enrolled in Stephens College in Columbia, Missouri, but soon dropped out and worked first as a salesgirl and then as a singer and dancer. In 1924, she was plucked from a nightclub chorus line to dance on Broadway. A talent scout discovered her and she was off to Hollywood, the film-making capital.

She began her film career as a chorus girl before moving on to more dramatic roles. Over the years, she starred opposite such leading men as Lon Chaney, Clark Gable, and Fred Astaire. In 1945, she won an Academy Award for her role in *Mildred Pierce,* a movie about an ambitious waitress who aspires to be a wealthy restaurateur. In this and other movies, she played roles that appealed especially to female moviegoers—portraying the struggle to achieve love or professional success against great odds. Crawford was also willing to play less flattering roles, such as a prostitute, blackmailer, and schizophrenic, as long as the parts were dramatic and interesting. In later years, she appeared occasionally on television.

Married four times, she adopted four children. She was as tough and steely in private life as she was on the screen. For millions of Americans her name is synonymous with the golden glamour of Hollywood.

FURTHER READING

Considine, Shaun. *Bette and Joan: The Divine Feud.* New York: Dutton, 1989.
Crawford, Christina. *Mommie Dearest.* New York: Morrow, 1978.

Croly, Jane Cunningham

JOURNALIST, CLUB LEADER

Born: December 19, 1829
Leicestershire, England

Died: December 23, 1901
New York, New York

Jane Cunningham Croly launched the American women's club movement. An immigrant from England, she received her early education at home by reading in her father's library. She taught school briefly and in 1855 went to New York City hoping to become a journalist. Soon she was writing for the *New York Tribune,* the Sunday *Times,* and other newspapers, and in 1857 she became the first woman journalist to syndicate her material to other publications.

From 1862 to 1872, she managed the woman's department of the *New York World* and also wrote for several women's magazines. Although Croly believed that women's true roles lay in being "the caretakers, the home-makers, the educators of children," she also believed that women must have paid work and financial independence—rights that, to her, were more important than the right to vote. She did not actively participate in the women's rights movement, but she made a lasting contribution to American women's social and economic advancement by inspiring the club movement.

In 1868, after being barred from a reception sponsored by the New York Press Club because she was a woman, she founded Sorosis, a club for self-supporting women to advance their mutual interests and "create a bond of fellowship between them," as she wrote. Her idea caught fire, and soon women across the country were organizing clubs for social, educational, and civic purposes. Through their club work American women improved their communities and also gained the confidence and leadership skills to demand greater equality.

In 1889, Croly organized a convention of women's clubs, and out of this meeting emerged the General Federation of Women's Clubs, a national network of women's clubs. She launched the *Woman's Cycle,* the federation's journal, and wrote a comprehensive history of the club movement. A successful journalist and dedicated clubwoman, as well as a wife and mother, she proved that women's realm was indeed the world.

PUBLICATION
History of the Woman's Club Movement in America (1898)

FURTHER READING
Blair, Karen. *The Clubwoman as Feminist: True Womanhood Redefined, 1868–1914.* New York: Holmes and Meier, 1980.

Davis, Bette

ACTRESS

Born: April 5, 1908
Lowell, Massachusetts

Died: October 6, 1989
Paris, France

Bette Davis played a flamboyant southern belle, a stoic heiress facing death, a slatternly waitress, a deranged woman, and scores of other roles on stage and screen. With her enormous doelike eyes and unforgettable voice, she was a Hollywood legend—a woman who created strong, stubborn, volatile characters out of her own complex personality. She once opined, "I suppose I'm larger than life."

She was born Ruth Elizabeth Davis and attended exclusive private schools in western Massachusetts. Deciding that she wanted to be an actress, she enrolled in a dramatic school in New York City but dropped out at the age of 20 to do stock theater in

Rochester, New York. Within a year, she had made her Broadway debut and was soon on her way to Hollywood to star in a new form of motion picture called the "talkies."

Despite an Academy Award nomination in 1934 for her role as a cruel, coarse waitress in *Of Human Bondage,* Davis did not hit her stride until the late 1930s and early 1940s, when she made a string of films that showcased her astonishing range of talents. Among these was *Jezebel* (1938), in which she played a tempestuous southern belle, and *The Little Foxes* (1941), a movie based on the play of the same name by Lillian Hellman. Other stunning performances followed on stage and in film.

Davis was nominated 10 times for an Academy Award—the most nominations that any actress has ever received—and won the award twice, for film roles in *Dangerous* (1935) and *Jezebel* (1938). In 1987, at the age of 79, she appeared in her hundredth film, *The Whales of August.*

PUBLICATIONS
The Lonely Life: An Autobiography (1962)
This 'n That (1987)
Mother Goddam: The Story of the Career of Bette Davis (1974)

FURTHER READING
Higham, Charles. *Bette: The Life of Bette Davis.* New York: Macmillan, 1981.

Davis, Paulina Kellogg Wright

FEMINIST, REFORMER

Born: August 7, 1813
Bloomfield, New York

Died: August 24, 1876
Providence, Rhode Island

Paulina Wright Davis was an ardent advocate of women's rights. Largely self-educated, she overcame a strict, unhappy childhood to devote her life to social reform. Later she said she was not happy until "I outgrew my early religious faith [in the Presbyterian church], and felt free to think and act from my own convictions." She rejected the church's view of women as inferior beings.

In 1833, she married Francis Wright, an affluent merchant, and together they plunged into antislavery work, temperance, and women's rights. In the late 1830s, Paulina Wright, along with Ernestine Rose, petitioned the New York legislature for a law to enable married women to retain possession of their own property, rather than ceding it to their husbands as the common-law tradition had prescribed. Their efforts were not successful until 1848, when the New York legislature passed such a law.

But Wright's most important early contribution to women's rights was health reform. She studied anatomy and physiology, then toured the East and Midwest to educate women about their bodies. She used a female mannequin imported from Paris, and though some in her audience fainted from the "indelicate" sight of a model of the female body, other listeners went on to join the first generation of female physicians.

After her first husband died, Wright married Thomas Davis, who also shared her commitment to women's rights. In 1850, she helped organize the first National Woman's Rights Convention in Worcester, Massachusetts, and in 1853 Wright launched *Una,* one of the first women's rights journals.

After the women's rights movement split into two camps in the late 1860s, she aligned herself with Elizabeth Cady Stanton and Susan B. Anthony, and was a lively contributor to their journal, *Revolution.* In later years, she traveled to Europe and studied painting. She remained an unwavering supporter of women's rights.

PUBLICATION
A History of the National Woman's Rights Movement (pamphlet, 1871)

Day, Dorothy

AMERICAN COFOUNDER OF THE CATHOLIC
WORKER MOVEMENT

Born: November 8, 1897
New York, New York

Died: November 29, 1980
New York, New York

A journalist by training, Dorothy Day sought inspiration in Catholicism to champion many causes that offended the Catholic church. After growing up in California and the Midwest, she graduated from Urbana College in Illinois and found her calling in journalism.

Very liberal in her political thinking, she joined the Industrial Workers of the World and worked for newspapers with a socialist or Marxist perspective, including the *New York Call, Liberator,* and the *Masses.* She also immersed herself in the bohemian spirit of Greenwich Village. Pulled by a strong sympathy for the downtrodden, she moved to a New York City tenement to be closer to the urban poor.

After traveling in Europe during the late 1920s, where she converted to Catholicism, she joined the editorial staff of *Commonweal,* a Catholic newspaper. In 1932, she met Peter Maurin, a priest and professor of French. He inspired her to wed her Catholic beliefs to her left-wing politics, and together they founded the Catholic Workers Movement, a pacifist organization for social justice inspired by religious precepts. During the Great Depression, they opened St. Joseph's House of Hospitality in New York City to feed and shelter the poor and homeless. Soon other hospitality houses and farms sprung up around the United States.

Day carried on the work of the movement after Maurin died, and became an outspoken supporter of causes that offended the Catholic church, such as nuclear disarmament, opposition to the Vietnam War, and support for migrant farm workers who tried to unionize. She was a devout but maverick Catholic, an irritant to church authorities for her unstinting commitment to social justice.

PUBLICATIONS
From Union Square to Rome (1938)
On Pilgrimage (1948)
The Long Loneliness (1952)
Loaves and Fishes (1963)
On Pilgrimage: The Sixties (1972)

FURTHER READING
Coles, Robert. *Dorothy Day: A Radical Devotion.* Reading, Mass.: Addison-Wesley, 1987.
Forest, James H. *Love is the Measure. A Biography of Dorothy Day.* New York: Paulist Press, 1986.

de Kooning, Elaine Fried

ARTIST

Born: March 12, 1920
New York, New York

Died: February 1, 1989
Southampton, New York

Elaine de Kooning was a prominent 20th-century American artist. She splashed her canvases with bold strokes of color in the manner of abstract expressionism, a style of art that spurned depictions of people, places, or objects for less realistic designs. But de Kooning also pursued a distinguished career as a portrait painter, and she received her most important commission when she was asked to paint a portrait of President John F. Kennedy. She did numerous sketches but never completed a final portrait because of Kennedy's assassination.

Elaine de Kooning knew from early childhood that she wanted to be an artist. At age six, she decided that she could draw better than her mother, who had instilled in her a love of art. She attended the American Artists School and the Leonardo da

Vinci School in New York City. There she met Willem de Kooning, an instructor who gave her private lessons, and they were married in 1943. Like other abstract expressionist artists whose innovative work was not yet popularly accepted, the de Koonings struggled financially until their work commanded greater respect.

During the late 1950s, Elaine de Kooning moved to New Mexico to teach at the University of New Mexico in Albuquerque. Like Georgia O'Keeffe, another famous 20th-century American artist, she was enchanted by the spacious landscape and the clarity of the desert light. The brilliant hues of the Southwest—magenta, orange, blue, and chartreuse—soon found their way into her art.

De Kooning's work is on display in museums and galleries around the country and has been featured in numerous special exhibitions.

FURTHER READING
Rubenstein, Charlotte Streifer. *American Women Artists*. New York: Avon, 1982.

Dewson, Mary

SOCIAL WORKER AND REFORMER, SUFFRAGE FIGHTER, DEMOCRATIC PARTY OFFICIAL

Born: February 18, 1874
Quincy, Massachusetts

Died: October 21, 1962
Castine, Maine

Dewson, a leader in the Democratic party during the 1930s, helped make the party and the Presidential administration of Franklin Roosevelt more responsive to women's and workers' needs. As a child, she attended schools in Quincy and Boston, and graduated from Wellesley College in 1897.

She worked first for the Women's Educational and Industrial Union, the largest women's social and reform organization in Boston. From there, she be-

came superintendent of the parole department of the Massachusetts State Industrial School for Girls, a position in which she instituted new ideas in prison reform. She also joined the minimum-wage movement after conducting a statistical study of wages among working women and children in Massachusetts. Her findings helped promote passage of the first minimum wage act in modern industrial America.

Dewson then joined the fight for woman suffrage, because she believed that the ballot was the major tool to achieve other social reforms. During World War I, she worked for the American Red Cross in Europe, then resumed her campaign for minimum wage laws. In 1930, she was a chief proponent of a law in New York State that regulated the work week for women.

She then became active in Democratic party affairs at the state and national level. Working with Eleanor Roosevelt, whose husband had just been elected President, she joined the Women's Division of the Democratic National Committee. In this capacity, she recruited women for key party positions and was responsible for FDR's appointment of Frances Perkins as secretary of labor. In addition, she helped place many other women in New Deal government agencies.

Dewson devoted her energies to ensuring women's equal participation in all levels of Democratic party politics. She continued to lobby for workplace legislation as well, including unemployment insurance and minimum wage laws. In 1937, FDR appointed her a member of the Social Security Board, and she worked on strengthening the delivery of unemployment and old-age assistance. Dewson was part of a vital group of dedicated, talented women who strove to create more humane and representative government programs and policies during the New Deal.

FURTHER READING
Roosevelt, Eleanor and Lorena Hickok. *Ladies of Courage*. New York: Putnam, 1954.

Ware, Susan. *Beyond Suffrage: Women and the New Deal.* Cambridge, Mass.: Harvard University Press, 1981.

———. *Partner and I: Molly Dewson, Feminism and New Deal Politics.* New Haven: Yale University Press, 1987.

Dickinson, Emily

POET

Born: December 10, 1830
Amherst, Massachusetts

Died: May 15, 1886
Amherst, Massachusetts

"I'm nobody! Who are you?" poet Emily Dickinson wrote. "Are you nobody too?" But despite her efforts to remain unknown, Dickinson was indeed somebody—a gifted poet who penned some 1,775 poems during her lifetime.

Born into a prominent Amherst family, she was educated first at Amherst Academy and then at Mount Holyoke Female Seminary in nearby South Hadley. After returning from Mount Holyoke, Dickinson lived the rest of her life in her father's stately house on Main Street in Amherst. But her poet's vision and imagination ranged much farther than the verdant hills surrounding her family home. Although many of her poems are lyrical paeans to the beauties of nature—the May flower, "pink, small, and punctual," the sun arising "a ribbon at a time," and the "phraseless melody" of the wind—Dickinson also penned more brooding meditations in verse about such timeless themes as the fragility of love, the desire for immortality, and the impermanence of life itself.

Though she wrote nearly 1,800 poems, she published only two during her lifetime. As the years passed, she became ever more reclusive and preferred to conduct her friendships through letters rather than in person. But while she withdrew into her solitary world, she enlarged and refined her poetic sensibilities by experimenting with language and rhythm as well as with rhymeless lines.

When she died in 1886, her sister discovered her poems, neatly bound in packets in her dresser drawer, and arranged to have them published. Far from being the work of a nobody, her poetry reveals a fresh, bold artistic vision and a playful love of language.

PUBLICATIONS
Selected Poems and Letters of Emily Dickinson. Edited by Robert N. Linscott (1959)

FURTHER READING

Olsen, Victoria. *Emily Dickinson: Poet.* New York: Chelsea House, 1990.

Whicher, George Frisbie. *This Was a Poet: A Critical Biography of Emily Dickinson.* Ann Arbor: University of Michigan Press, 1938. New edition, 1965.

Wolff, Cynthia Griffin. *Emily Dickinson.* New York: Knopf, 1986.

Dimock, Susan

PHYSICIAN, SURGEON, AND HOSPITAL
ADMINISTRATOR

Born: April 24, 1847
Washington, North Carolina

Died: May 7, 1875
Scilly Islands, England

The daughter of a physician, Susan Dimock evinced an interest in medicine at an early age. She was educated by her mother, who tutored her daughter privately and then opened a school so that Susan could learn in a classroom setting. At 13, she attended a private academy and began to think about a medical career.

She combined teaching with private medical study, and in 1866 entered the New England Hospital for Women and Children as a medical student. She went on to pursue additional clinical work at Massachusetts General Hospital, and then went abroad to complete her medical studies at the University of Zurich. Three years later, in 1868, she graduated with highest honors. After further study in Vienna and Paris, she became one of the best-trained female doctors of the 19th century.

In 1872, Dimock returned to Boston and was appointed resident physician at the New England Hospital for Women and Children. In this position, she reorganized and administered the hospital's training school for nurses, did daily rounds in patient wards, and performed much of the hospital's surgery, with astounding success rates. She also conducted a private practice.

Dimock would have become one of the premier physicians of her time had her life and promising career not been cut short in a ship accident off the coast of England. By her drive and professional accomplishments, she proved that women could excel in a profession from which they had been barred.

PUBLICATION

Memoir of Susan Dimock, Resident Physician of the New England Hospital for Women and Children (1875)

FURTHER READING

Abram, Ruth. *Send Us a Lady Physician: Women Doctors in America, 1835–1920.* New York: Norton, 1986.

Dix, Dorothea Lynde

ADVOCATE FOR MENTALLY ILL,
UNION ARMY NURSING DIRECTOR

*Born: April 4, 1802
Hampden, Maine*

*Died: July 18, 1887
Trenton, New Jersey*

Dorothea Dix left a shining legacy of service on two fronts—as crusader for the mentally ill and director of Union army nursing during the Civil War. After an impoverished childhood, shuttled back and forth between relatives, she secured an education through diligent self-study and opened a school at age 14. She taught for the next 15 years and wrote a science textbook as well as short religious tracts. But teaching did not satisfy her, and she felt a loss of purpose. Her teaching led, however, to her main work in life.

In 1841, she taught a Sunday school class at a Cambridge, Massachusetts, jail. To her horror, she discovered that several insane women had been incarcerated in the same harsh surroundings as criminals. She embarked on an 18-month study of prisons and almshouses in Massachusetts, and exposed the cruel conditions under which the mentally ill were kept. The state legislature grudgingly approved the construction of better treatment facilities, and Dix took her campaign to other states. In New Jersey, she even helped design the state's first mental hospital, and spurred the founding of scores of better mental hospitals in other states. She also toured prisons and hospitals in Europe, and met with Pope Pius IX to report her findings.

When the Civil War began, Dix shifted her attention to a more urgent matter—the recruitment and training of nurses for the Union army. In addition, she helped organize shipments of clothing, medicine, and food to the troops, and established and staffed military infirmaries in and around Washington, D.C. Her high standards and abrasive manner led to clashes with military leaders, but she performed her duties with superlative skill.

After the war, she resumed her campaign for better prisons and mental hospitals until her health gave out. She was a tireless advocate for the mentally ill at a time when they were treated little better than animals.

PUBLICATIONS

Remarks on Prisons and Prison Discipline in the United States (1845)
The Lady and the President: The Letters of Dorothea Dix and Millard Fillmore. Edited by Charles M. Snyder (1975)

FURTHER READING

Schlaifer, Charles. *Heart's Work: Civil War Heroine and Champion of the Mentally Ill.* New York: Paragon House, 1991.

Wilson, Dorothy Clarke. *Stranger and Traveler: The Story of Dorothea Dix, American Reformer.* Boston: Little, Brown, 1975.

Dodge, Grace Hoadley

SOCIAL REFORMER, PHILANTHROPIST

Born: May 21, 1856
New York, New York

Died: December 27, 1914
New York, New York

Grace Hoadley Dodge spurned the frivolous social life of her upper-class peers, and instead carried on her family's sterling tradition of public service. She was educated by private tutors and also attended an exclusive private girls school in Farmington, Connecticut. She made her debut in charity work by joining the advisory board of the New York State Charities Association. She took her work seriously, allowing herself only a two-week vacation each year, and tried to befriend the struggling young women who benefited from her good works.

In 1881, she organized a group of factory women into a social club. Within several years, club members had rented a house for a meeting place, organized a library and classes in sewing and cooking, and hired a woman physician as a resident medical advisor. The idea soon caught on, and similar clubs were organized in other cities. Dodge helped form an association of working girls' societies in New York City and across the nation. She urged other affluent club sponsors not to patronize the working women but to share in fellowship with them.

Dodge also organized the Industrial Education Association to develop manual training programs in New York's public schools. Because of her efforts, she was appointed to the New York City Board of Education in 1886, where she continued to expand manual training in the public school system. She also served as treasurer of the newly organized New York College for the Training of Teachers (later Teachers College), handling the school's financial affairs with fiscal soundness and a genius for fund-raising. Beyond her financial duties, she participated in hiring professors and top administrators.

Dodge worked for other organizations that helped working women. In 1907, she organized the New York Travelers Aid Society to provide housing and employment assistance to young women moving to New York City. She also served on the national board of the YWCA and contributed thousands of dollars to the organization.

Dodge was part of a group of wealthy, reform-minded women who, while unwilling to promote radical social and political change, greatly helped to improve daily life for working-class citizens, especially women.

FURTHER READING

Lagemann, Ellen. *A Generation of Women.* Cambridge: Harvard University Press, 1979.

Dreier, Mary

LABOR REFORMER, SUFFRAGIST

Born: September 26, 1875
Brooklyn, New York

Died: August 15, 1963
Bar Harbor, Maine

Mary Dreier followed her sister Margaret Dreier Robins into the exciting world of social reform. Like Margaret, Mary was privately educated and never attended college. And like Margaret, she shunned the carefree world of the debutante, which was her birthright, to work for social change.

She first worked at Asacog House, a Brooklyn settlement house, and in the early 1900s joined the Women's Trade Union League (WTUL), a coalition of upper- and working-class women dedicated to improving working conditions for factory women.

From 1906 to 1914, Dreier led the New York WTUL. These were the organization's most productive years. In 1909, she was arrested during the "Uprising of the Twenty Thousand," the famous garment worker's strike in New York City. Her reports of police brutality against the strikers aroused public support for the strike. Dreier's participation in the strike converted her into a dedicated advocate for women workers and won for her their enduring trust.

Two years later, after the horrific Triangle Shirtwaist Company fire, which killed 146 workers, mostly women and children, Dreier joined the New York State Factory Investigating Commission and helped draft legislation that revolutionized New York's labor laws by setting better safety standards and guidelines for wages and hours. Alfred Smith, vice chairman of the commission, called Dreier, the only woman on the commission, the "soul" of its work.

From there, Dreier turned her attention to woman suffrage and chaired the New York City Woman Suffrage party. She stayed active in the WTUL until 1950, when it was disbanded. She also served on government and private-sector panels related to women and labor. After World War II, she campaigned for nuclear disarmament. In her eighties, she participated in antinuclear rallies and circulated petitions for her favorite causes.

PUBLICATION
Margaret Dreier Robins: Her Life, Letters and Work (1950)

Duncan, Isadora
DANCER

Born: May 27, 1878
San Francisco, California

Died: September 14, 1927
Nice, France

Born to break the rules, Isadora Duncan enjoyed a bohemian childhood in San Francisco. Her mother introduced her to the creative wonders of poetry, dance, music, and nature.

After studying classical ballet, she realized that she did not like the rigid, intricate movements of this dance form and wanted instead to recapture the flowing, expressive movement that had been the hallmark of ancient dancing. She studied sculpture and the natural world, seeking inspiration for new movements to express the range of human awareness and emotion, from joy to despair.

Although Duncan regarded that most American of poets, Walt Whitman, as her spiritual father, American audiences shunned her daring new style of dance. They were shocked by her revealing costumes and her emphasis on the beauty of the human body in motion. They also condemned her unconventional way of life, including her many love affairs and her out-of-wedlock children.

European audiences were far more responsive to her art, and after 1900 Duncan lived primarily in Europe and Russia. She performed across Europe and established dance schools for gifted young women. European musicians and painters embraced her as one of their own.

Duncan died as dramatically as she had lived. Climbing into an open sports car in Nice, the luxurious resort town on the French Riviera, she waved and called out to friends, "Adieu mes amis. Je vais a la gloire." ("Good-bye my friends. I am going to glory!") As the car pulled away, her long, fringed scarf—her trademark apparel—caught in the spokes of the rear wheel and broke her neck. She died instantly. Duncan's legacy lay not only in the new dance form she had pioneered but in her passion to celebrate the mystery of human existence in her art as well as her life.

PUBLICATION
My Life (autobiography, 1927)

FURTHER READING
Blair, Fredrika. *Isadora: A Portrait of the Artist as a Woman.* New York: McGraw-Hill, 1986.

Kozodoy, Ruth. *Isadora Duncan: Dancer*. New York: Chelsea House, 1988.

Loewenthal, Lillian. *The Search for Isadora: The Legend and Legacy of Isadora Duncan*. Princeton, N.J.: Princeton University Press, 1993.

Duniway, Abigail Jane Scott

WESTERN SUFFRAGE LEADER, JOURNALIST

Born: October 22, 1834
Groveland, Illinois

Died: October 11, 1915
Portland, Oregon

Abigail Scott Duniway's commitment to women's rights was born out of the hardships that both she and her mother suffered as women. She was raised on a farm and spent her childhood years in arduous toil in the fields, with an occasional respite to attend school. She recalled her mother saying, "Poor baby! She'll be a woman some day.... A woman's lot is so hard!"

Against her mother's wishes, her father moved the family by wagon train to Oregon. Both Abigail's mother and young brother died along the way. After teaching school briefly, Abigail married Benjamin Charles Duniway and, like her mother, began the hard life of a farmer's wife. When her husband became disabled, she resumed schoolteaching and opened a millinery shop to support her growing family.

In 1871, after years of listening to her customers' tales of woe about unjust husbands, she joined the women's rights movement by launching a suffrage journal, the *New Northwest*. She also began lecturing, and for the next 25 years she crisscrossed Oregon, Washington, and Idaho speaking about women's rights. Her lectures and lobbying efforts helped steer woman suffrage to victory in Washington Territory and Idaho.

Founder of the Oregon Equal Suffrage Association and a leader in the western suffrage campaign,

Duniway often clashed with her suffrage sisters in the East. They tried to remove her from the presidency of the Oregon suffrage group, but when Oregon's voters finally endorsed woman suffrage in 1914, Duniway was credited with the victory. Brisk in manner and colorful in speech, she was a hardy, unstoppable voice for women's rights in the west.

PUBLICATIONS
From the West to the West (novel, 1905)
Path Breaking (autobiography, 1914)

FURTHER READING
Moynihan, Ruth Barnes. *Rebel for Rights: Abigail Scott Duniway*. New Haven: Yale University Press, 1983.

Durr, Virginia Foster

SOCIAL REFORMER

Born: August 6, 1903
exact location unknown

Virginia Foster Durr grew up in the shadow of the southern Confederacy, with the same aristocratic values and racist ideas that had marked her forebears of the white gentry class. She was forced to question her presumptions of white superiority when she moved north to study at Wellesley College in Massachusetts. There, for the first time, she met American blacks as equals.

In 1926, she married Clifford Durr, a lawyer who became a New Deal government official. In Washington, the Durrs circulated among other reform-minded Southerners, and her growing outrage at the indifference of big business toward its workers during the hard years of the Depression prompted her to get involved in Democratic party politics. During these years, she also became a founding member of the Southern Conference for Human Welfare (SCHW).

Hard times came to the Durrs in the early 1950s after they protested American involvement in the Korean War and the American government's policy of demanding a loyalty oath from workers and government officials. Friends and professional associates shunned them for speaking out.

But they found a welcome niche during the civil rights movement. While her husband defended civil rights workers in Alabama, Durr joined an organization of white sympathizers and published articles supporting the movement. In the late 1960s, she worked for the Alabama National Democratic party, which opposed Governor George Wallace's pro-segregation faction of the Democratic party. Durr had traveled a long and courageous path to fight for social justice and civil rights.

PUBLICATION

Outside the Magic Circle: The Autobiography of Virginia Foster Durr. Hollinger F. Barnard, ed. (1985)

Duston, Hannah

INDIAN CAPTIVE

Born: December 23, 1657
Haverhill, Massachusetts

Died: ca. 1736
Haverhill, Massachusetts

Hannah Duston was captured by Indians—and fought back. The daughter of a shoemaker, she married Thomas Duston, a bricklayer and farmer, on December 3, 1677, and over the course of their 45-year marriage bore 13 children.

On March 15, 1697, while recovering from the delivery of her 12th child, Hannah, her infant son, and Mary Neff, a neighbor who was caring for Hannah, were captured during an Indian raid on Haverhill. Though Thomas Duston, who had first spied the oncoming attackers while working in the field, managed to rescue his older children, he was unable to protect his wife and her infant son and nurse.

The two women and the infant were captured by a band of about 20 Indians and forced to march toward Canada. Along the way, their captors killed the infant. They stopped in a small island off of New Hampshire, where they came upon an Indian settlement and also another captive, Samuel Lennardson, a young Englishman. There Hannah was told by her captors that a brutal punishment awaited her and the other prisoners.

Determined to fight back, on the night of March 30, 1697, she and Lennardson attacked the Indians with hatchets as they slept. Lennardson killed one warrior and Hannah killed nine more. One wounded squaw and a child somehow got away. Duston and her fellow captives turned to flee but, concerned that no one would believe their story, they quickly returned to their victims and scalped the dead Indians for evidence.

After reaching Haverhill safely, they presented the scalps to the General Court in Boston. For her daring escapade, Duston received a cash reward. She returned to Haverhill, where she quietly resumed her life as a colonial goodwife.

FURTHER READING

The Story of Hannah Duston (pamphlet, 1950)

Dyer, Mary

QUAKER MARTYR

Born: date unknown
England

Died: June 1, 1660
Boston, Massachusetts

Mary Dyer gave her life to the cause of religious freedom. Little is known about her early years except that she was born in England and came from a family of means.

On October 27, 1633, she married William Dyer, a milliner and a Puritan. In late 1634 or early 1635, they immigrated to Boston, where they joined the Puritan church. They soon became embroiled in religious conflict by supporting Anne Hutchinson's unprecedented assault on the religious authority of the church. Hutchinson declared that the religious experience of divine grace was inward and private, known at once to the faithful; in contrast, most Puritans believed that religious salvation could be recognized only by the outward signs of material success and good works. Hutchinson's views challenged the church's authority to determine who had been saved. Instead, men—as well as women—had the power to determine their state of grace without seeking the approval of religious leaders.

Despite, or perhaps because of, her heretical beliefs, Mary Dyer supported Hutchinson, and even went so far as to accompany her out of church when Hutchinson was excommunicated, or banished, from the Puritan church in Boston. In turn, Dyer and her husband were excommunicated. They moved to Newport, Rhode Island, where religious freedom prevailed, and bore five sons. William Dyer became a leading citizen in the colony.

In 1652, the Dyers returned to England on political business, and Mary Dyer joined the Society of Friends, the Quaker church. The Quakers believed that each person harbored the divine spirit; like Hutchinson, they emphasized a direct and immediate relationship between the individual and God, unbeholden to the authority of ministers or other religious leaders.

Upon Dyer's return to New England in 1657, she was imprisoned in Boston for espousing Quaker ideas, a religion declared illegal by Boston's Puritan leaders. Although her husband secured her freedom by promising to keep her quiet, she continued to preach her heretical Quaker beliefs. When the Massachusetts General Court passed a law imposing the death penalty on practicing Quakers, Dyer was banished from Boston.

Defiantly, she returned to challenge the law and was sentenced to death in the fall of 1659. A last-minute reprieve freed her, and she reluctantly left Massachusetts. But she returned to Boston the following spring, again to defy the law. On May 31, 1660, she was sentenced to death once more

and was hanged the following day. To the end, she refused to renounce her Quaker beliefs. Moments before she was hanged, she declared, "In obedience to the will of the Lord I came, and in His will I abide faithful to the death."

FURTHER READING
Bacon, Margaret Hope. *Mothers of Feminism.* New York: HarperCollins, 1986.

Earhart, Amelia
AVIATOR

Born: July 24, 1897
Atchison, Kansas

Died: ca. July 2, 1937 (exact date unknown)
Pacific Ocean

Amelia Earhart made aviation history when she became the first woman to fly solo across the Atlantic Ocean. As a child, she spent many happy hours outdoors, playing sports and horseback riding. She entered college but dropped out to work as a Red Cross volunteer during World War I. Hearing the exploits of Canadian pilots who were recovering in the military hospital where she worked aroused her interest in flying.

In Glendale, California, she took her first airplane ride—and was hooked. After taking private lessons, she made her first solo flight in 1921. For the next several years, she supported herself by teaching at Denison House, a settlement house in Boston. But her real passion was flying.

After serving as copilot on a promotional flight from Canada to Wales—for which she merely kept the records—she earned the nicknames of "Lady Lindy," in imitation of aviator Charles Lindbergh, and "First Lady of the Air." Her fame as an aviator was now assured. She flew in air shows, became vice president of an airline, and cofounded the Ninety-nines, an international organization of women pilots.

In 1931, she married the book publisher George Palmer Putnam, and he financed—and shamelessly promoted—his wife's flying exploits. Troubled that her fame was undeserved, Earhart proved her true mettle by flying alone from Canada to Ireland in 1932—the first woman to make the 15-hour trip alone across the Atlantic Ocean. Her exploit earned her several awards, including the Cross of the French Legion of Honor.

She made several other daring solo flights to demonstrate the safety of air travel, then turned in her pilot's wings to work as a career counselor at Purdue University. But she wanted to make "just one more long flight," and on June 1, 1937, she and one crew member took off from Miami, Florida, for a round-the-world trip.

There is evidence to suggest that this was more than just a final daredevil flight: Earhart may have been on a spying mission to photograph Japanese military installations for the United States military. According to faint radio messages received by the Coast Guard on July 2, the plane ran into trouble over the Pacific Ocean. Earhart may have wandered into forbidden Japanese military airspace and been shot down or forced to land. On July 5, according to U.S. State Department records, Earhart radioed that she had been captured by a Japanese shore patrol. That was the last communication from her. Neither the plane nor Earhart and her crew member were heard from again, and their fate remains a tantalizing mystery. Despite her unfortunate end, Earhart, a wiry woman with boundless energy, won the public's approval for airplane flight and for women aviators.

PUBLICATIONS

The Fun of It (1932)
Last Flight (posthumous, 1937)

FURTHER READING

Brink, Randall. *Lost Star: The Search for Amelia Earhart*. New York: Norton, 1994.
Rich, Doris L. *Amelia Earhart: A Biography*. Washington, D. C.: Smithsonian Institution Press, 1989.
Shore, Nancy. *Amelia Earhart*. New York: Chelsea House, 1987.
Ware, Susan. *Still Missing: Amelia Earhart and the Search for Modern Feminism*. New York: W.W. Norton, 1993.

Eastman, Crystal

FEMINIST, SOCIAL REFORMER, LAWYER

Born: June 25, 1881
Marlborough, Massachusetts

Died: July 8, 1928
Erie, Pennsylvania

Crystal Eastman was a social and political rebel with a vision of change that ranged from global peace to new forms of marriage. She inherited her feminist and progressive ideas from her mother, an ordained Congregational minister and advocate of women's rights. Crystal attended local schools in Elmira, New York, and graduated from Vassar College in 1903. She went on to earn a master's degree in sociology from Columbia University and a law degree from New York University.

In 1907, she joined a fact-finding team to investigate the effects of industrialism on urban workers. This was the first such study in the United States, and her findings helped pave the way for new laws to compensate workers when job-related accidents prevented them from working.

But Eastman achieved her greatest influence as a fighter for women's rights and international peace. She campaigned tirelessly for woman suffrage and was a founding member of the Congressional Union (CU), the militant wing of the suffrage movement. A staunch feminist, she opposed protective legislation that regulated working women's hours and wages without providing similar protections for male workers.

She served as chair of the Woman's Peace party, which promoted global peace, and strenuously opposed American entry into World War I. During the war, she helped establish the Civil Liberties Bureau to assist men who, for reasons of conscience refused to fight. After the war, she continued to work for women's rights, demanding besides suffrage, equal employment opportunities, access to birth control, and a single standard of morality for men and women.

Eastman, a member of the bohemian Greenwich Village crowd, was a social rebel as well. Perhaps her most daring and original idea was her proposal for "marriage under two roofs"—separate households for husbands and wives to prevent marriages from going stale. Illness cut short her brilliant career, but in her day Eastman was a passionate and persuasive advocate for new and more fulfilling ways to live.

PUBLICATION
Crystal Eastman on Women and Revolution. Blanche Wiesen Cook, ed. New York: Oxford University Press, 1978.

Edwards, Sarah Pierpont
PURITAN MYSTIC

Born: January 9, 1710
New Haven, Connecticut

Died: October 2, 1758
Philadelphia, Pennsylvania

Sarah Pierpont Edwards, wife of Puritan minister Jonathan Edwards, was an early Puritan mystic who gave eloquent voice in her diary to her exalted religious beliefs. Her life story demonstrates that the Puritan outlook, while solemn and severe in tone, also offered inner peace, gladness, and even high-flown reveries of joy.

Sarah Pierpont was the daughter of a pastor who also founded Yale College, and as such she grew up in a pious and cultured home. By her 13th year, she

apparently had developed a reputation for being spiritual as well as good-natured. Jonathan Edwards, who had not yet met her, commented in his diary in 1723, "They say there is a young lady in [New Haven] who is beloved of that Great Being, who made and rules the world." Four years later, on July 20, 1727, she and Jonathan Edwards were married. Throughout their 30-year marriage, which produced 11 children—7 daughters and 4 sons—Sarah Edwards presided over her husband's parsonage, first in Northampton, Massachusetts, and later in an Indian mission in Stockbridge, Massachusetts, with grace, warmth, and piety. Her home was a haven for scores of visitors each year, some of whom stayed for long periods of time. A skillful household manager, she once provided some 800 meals for soldiers quartered at the Indian mission.

During the Great Awakening, an ecstatic religious revival movement that swept the colonies along the Atlantic seaboard during the 1730s and 1740s, Sarah Edwards embraced an ever-deepening religious faith. Though consumed by despair at times over "my own unworthiness" and "abasement of soul," she found a deep joy, even an ecstasy, in her devotion to God. This sense of communion with the divine remained with her for the rest of her life and brought her intense joy.

She wrote in her diary of an almost physical rising above all earthly concerns and sensations toward the divine, feeling "removed from myself." She seemed to "float or swim, in these bright, sweet beams" of "divine love."

But Sarah Edwards was as hardy in deed as she was fleet of spirit. Through remote woods she would ride alone on horseback to be with a daughter who needed her. She embodied earthly love and devotion to her family as well as fervent piety and grace.

PUBLICATION
Chapter XIV of *The Works of President Edwards,* edited by Sereno E. Dwight (1830), includes Sarah Edwards's diary of her religious experiences.

FURTHER READING

Dodds, Elisabeth D. *Marriage to a Difficult Man: The "Uncommon Union" of Jonathan and Sarah Edwards.* Philadelphia: Westminster Press, 1971.

Farnham, Eliza Wood Burhans

PRISON REFORMER, AUTHOR, LECTURER

Born: November 17, 1815
Rensselaerville, New York

Died: December 15, 1864
New York, New York

Eliza Farnham was a lone but dedicated crusader for better prisons and more humane treatment of criminals. Abandoned to harsh, uncaring foster parents when she was only five, she educated herself by reading intensively and then attended a Quaker boarding school and the Albany Female Academy in New York State.

In 1836, she married Thomas Jefferson Farnham, a young lawyer. Her interest in prison reform began in 1844, when she joined the staff at Sing Sing prison, in New York State, as a matron of the women's division. In this position, she experimented with less repressive ways of maintaining order. She offered instruction in various subjects, rewarded the well behaved with privileges, and repealed a ban on spoken communication among prisoners. Although her methods won the avid support of prominent social reformers, prison authorities were far less enthusiastic, and she was forced to resign in 1848.

She moved to Boston and worked with Samuel Gridley Howe, director of the Perkins Institute for the Blind. She also tried to organize a contingent of unmarried women to move to California and civilize that rough and tumble Gold Rush frontier. Only a few women accompanied her, but, undiscouraged, she moved to northern California, where she taught school and tried to improve conditions at San Quentin Prison. During the Civil War, she volunteered to nurse Union soldiers wounded in the fierce battle of Gettysburg, and died of consumption shortly after.

Besides her prison reform work, Farnham is most well known for her treatise *Woman and Her Era* (1864), in which she proclaimed the superiority of the female sex and the almost godlike power, in her view, of women's reproductive ability. She disavowed the women's rights movement, fearing that women would stoop to men's unworthy position in life by demanding equal rights, and declared instead that women were made for higher purposes.

MAJOR PUBLICATIONS

Life in Prairie Land (a study of frontier development, 1846)
My Early Days (autobiography, 1859; republished in 1864 as *Eliza Woodson*)
Woman and Her Era (1864)

Fauset, Jessie Redmon

WRITER, EDITOR, TEACHER

Born: April 26, 1882
Fredericksville, New Jersey

Died: April 30, 1961
Philadelphia, Pennsylvania

Jessie Redmon Fauset, daughter of a minister, helped give birth to the Harlem Renaissance, the glorious celebration of African-American literature and culture in the 1920s. She grew up in a small town in New Jersey and attended Cornell University, where she was elected to Phi Beta Kappa—perhaps the first African-American woman to receive that honor. In 1919, she earned an M.A. in French from the University of Pennsylvania and continued her studies at the Sorbonne in Paris.

Meanwhile, she had embarked upon a teaching career in Washington, D.C., and began to contribute articles and book reviews to *The Crisis*, the journal of the National Association for the Advancement of Colored People (NAACP). From 1919 to

1926, she was the journal's literary editor, and showcased the talented writers and poets of the Harlem Renaissance. Among them, poet Langston Hughes praised her as one of those who "midwifed the so-called New Negro literature into being." She warmly encouraged authors and held gatherings for Harlem Renaissance writers in her home.

Fauset herself was a talented writer. Her poetry and fiction explored the lives of middle-class blacks who strive for success amidst mounting prejudice. She portrayed characters who aspired to succeed within the larger American culture without neglecting their responsibility to their own people.

Fauset continued to teach both high school and college. Her interest in promoting black culture and literature waned in the 1930s, but she never stopped encouraging black writers.

MAJOR PUBLICATIONS
Plum Bun (1929)
The Chinaberry Tree (1931)
The Chinaberry Tree and Selected Writings. Foreword by Marcy Knopf. Reprint of 1931 edition; Boston: Northeastern University Press, 1994.

Flexner, Eleanor

SCHOLAR

Born: October 4, 1908
New York, New York

Eleanor Flexner's ground-breaking book, *Century of Struggle: The Women's Rights Movement in the United States,* inspired a generation of scholars and readers to uncover the rich, complex history of American women.

Flexner was raised to pursue the life of the mind. Her father, Abraham Flexner, was a highly respected educator, social reformer, and writer, and her mother was a playwright "at a time when such an achievement was still unusual for a woman," according to Flexner. After graduating from Swarthmore College in 1930, Flexner spent a year at Oxford University in England.

Although she has published other scholarly works, *Century of Struggle* remains her best-known book. She published the first edition of this landmark book in 1959, a full decade before academic and popular interest in American women's history had emerged—because, she said, there was no such book on the subject. In the 1960s, her book was an invaluable resource for scholars who were defining this new field of research.

Flexner published a revised edition in 1975, incorporating new questions and research findings. The book remains remarkably up to date for its inclusive treatment of women from different class backgrounds and ethnic and political groups. It covers the social, intellectual, and political progress of American women, and was perhaps the first book to focus on women in the American labor movement. A pioneering work, *Century of Struggle* laid the groundwork for the scholarly study of American women's history.

Flexner lives in Northampton, Massachusetts, where she continues to write and reflect about women's lives.

PUBLICATIONS
American Playwrights, 1918–1938 (1939)
Century of Struggle (1959; revised ed., 1975)
Mary Wollstonecraft: A Biography (1972)

FURTHER READING
DuBois, Ellen. "Eleanor Flexner and the History of American Feminism," *Gender and History* 3 (1991): 81–89.

Flynn, Elizabeth Gurley

LABOR ORGANIZER, RADICAL POLITICAL ACTIVIST

Born: August 7, 1890
Concord, New Hampshire

Died: September 5, 1964
Moscow, U.S.S.R.

For more than half a century, Flynn was a tireless warrior for workers' rights. She was born into a socialist family with Irish roots and witnessed first-hand the ruinous impact of urban poverty on people's lives. She attended public elementary and high school in New York City, where she met anarchist Emma Goldman. After a brief flirtation with anarchism, she found her political home in socialism.

As a teenager, she led street-corner rallies and quickly became a featured speaker for the Socialist party and the Industrial Workers of the World (IWW). During the 1910s, she helped organize the textile workers' strikes in Lawrence, Massachusetts, and Paterson, New Jersey, as well as smaller walkouts. In Lawrence, alone, 10,000 workers walked off the job until management met their demands for better pay and a shorter work week.

When the federal government unleashed a campaign of terror against political radicals after World War I, Flynn helped establish the Workers' Defense Union (WDU) and the American Civil Liberties Union (ACLU) to protect the legal rights and free speech of workers and immigrants. In the late 1920s, she joined the newly organized Communist Party USA (CPUSA) and helped organize labor strikes in a variety of industries. She also joined the women's commission of the party and wrote on feminist issues for the *Daily Worker*, the journal of the CPUSA.

During the late 1940s, an era of rabid anti-communist sentiment in the United States, Flynn bravely remained a staunch supporter of communist ideas—and, as a result, served two years in prison on a false charge of conspiring to overthrow the United States government by violent means.

In 1961, she became the first woman to lead the CPUSA. Despite strong misgivings about some of the party's actions, she remained steadfast in her vision of a socialist America, where equality of opportunity flourished and workers were no longer exploited or persecuted when they demanded a fair wage and better working conditions.

PUBLICATIONS
I Speak My Own Piece (autobiography, 1955; reissued 1973 as *The Rebel Girl*)

Alderson Story (account of her imprisonment, 1955, 1963)

FURTHER READING
Baxandall, Rosalyn Fraad, ed. *Words on Fire: The Life and Writings of Elizabeth Gurley Flynn.* New Brunswick, N.J.: Rutgers University Press, 1987.

Foster, Abigail Kelley
ABOLITIONIST, WOMEN'S RIGHTS
LECTURER

Born: January 15, 1810
Pelham, Massachusetts

Died: January 14, 1887
Worcester, Massachusetts

For 30 years, Abigail Kelley Foster zealously fought two battles: one for the abolition of slavery, the other for women's rights. Raised in the Quaker faith, she early on displayed an independent mind and a searching spirit. She was educated at the Providence (Rhode Island) Friends' School and went on to teach in another Friends' school in Lynn, Massachusetts. There she became a committed abolitionist and joined the Lynn Female Antislavery Society.

As secretary of the society, she circulated petitions, raised funds, and distributed literature. She also joined the Lynn Female Peace Society and was an early supporter of radical abolitionist William Lloyd Garrison. She declared that improving mankind was "the only object worth living for." In 1838, she made her first public address at a major antislavery convention. Her speech was so effective that Sarah and Angelina Grimké and Lucretia Mott, among others, urged her to lecture for abolition full time.

Kelley resigned her teaching position and lectured for the American Antislavery Society. She endured much personal hardship, including the anger and threats of proslavery sympathizers and others who denounced her as a "Jezebel" for speaking in public. Undeterred, she traveled throughout New

England, New York, Pennsylvania, Ohio, and Indiana, carrying Garrison's message of "No Union with Slaveholders." She was an uncompromising abolitionist and condemned any institution—including church and state—that protected slavery.

Kelley promoted women's rights by sponsoring other female speakers and urging women to join the abolitionist and women's rights movements. Among those whom she inspired were future feminist leaders Lucy Stone, Susan B. Anthony, and Paulina Wright Davis.

In 1845, she married Stephen Symonds Foster, who shared her progressive ideas, and they lectured together. During the 1850s, she also addressed temperance and women's rights meetings. But after the Civil War, ill health prevented her from actively participating in social reform. She spoke out when her health permitted and on several occasions refused to pay taxes, arguing that she was taxed without representation. Her passionate support of equal rights for women and blacks remained undiminished.

FURTHER READING

Bacon, Margaret Hope. *I Speak for My Slave Sister: The Life of Abby Kelley Foster*. New York: Crowell, 1974.

Sterling, Dorothy. *Ahead of Her Time: Abby Kelley and the Politics of Anti-slavery*. New York: Norton, 1991.

Fox, Kate and Margaret

SPIRITUALIST MEDIUMS

Born: ca. 1833 (Margaret)
ca. 1839 (Kate)
Canada

Died: March 8, 1893 (Margaret)
July 2, 1892 (Kate)
New York, New York

Daughters of a ne'er-do-well farmer and his wife, Margaret and Kate Fox spent their youth on a small farm in Hydesville, a village in upstate New York. They each received a rudimentary education, and their lives might have followed the unremarkable path to adulthood taken by their peers—had they not, one spring night in 1848, heard mysterious rapping sounds bouncing off their bedroom wall. Neighbors who heard the sounds concluded that spirits had made them, and curious onlookers soon swarmed over the house. Kate and Margaret went to live with relatives, but the mysterious rappings followed them.

Though people had earlier claimed to communicate with the spirit world, the mysterious rappings that followed Kate and Margaret ignited a new religious movement, one in which other young women like themselves held audiences spellbound while they communicated with the spirits of the dead. Spiritualism, as this movement was called, swept through the eastern United States—beginning in western New York, the region where Kate and Margaret lived and the site of an earlier evangelical religious movement that also drew young female converts.

While claiming to make contact with the spirits of the dead, Spiritualists also espoused some of the most progressive ideas of the day regarding women's rights, abolition, and social reform. Shy, naive, and even confused, Kate and Margaret did not fully understand the impact of the movement they had set into motion. Like other Spiritualists, they gave public demonstrations and conducted séances, but their gatherings more often resembled a circus rather than a profound mystical experience.

Although Spiritualism enhanced many women's lives—those who carved out new roles as mediums as well as those who heeded the spirits' "commands" to reform their lives—Kate and Margaret were not so fortunate. Fame and notoriety as mediums brought pressures they could not handle. Both women were briefly married and both succumbed to alcoholism.

In later years, they sank into poverty as first they exposed their spiritualist activities as a hoax, then reversed themselves and once again affirmed their belief in Spiritualism. But they never regained their earlier following, and they spent their last years in poverty and disrepute. Neither sister was able to marshal the strength, wisdom, and serenity that Spiritualism had bestowed on other women mediums and followers.

FURTHER READING
Braude, Ann. *Radical Spirits*. Boston: Beacon Press, 1991.

Franklin, Deborah Read

WIFE OF BENJAMIN FRANKLIN

Born: ca. 1707
Birmingham, England, or
Philadelphia, Pennsylvania

Died: December 19, 1774
Philadelphia, Pennsylvania

Deborah Franklin managed her husband's affairs while he was off trying to prevent a revolution. She was born either in England or Philadelphia, Pennsylvania, where she grew up. She first caught a glimpse of her future husband in October 1723 as he strolled down a Philadelphia street munching a roll after having escaped from an abusive employer in Boston. Their friendship deepened when Franklin boarded in her parents' house.

He courted Deborah, but her mother prevented them from marrying because she thought they were too young. While Franklin was away in England, Deborah met John Rogers, a potter, and they were married on August 5, 1725. The marriage did not work out—it was rumored that he had another wife—and Deborah left him.

When Franklin returned from England in 1730, he and Deborah rekindled their courtship and on September 1, 1730, they entered into a common-law marriage—a marriage not legally recognized by church or state—because Deborah had never legally severed ties with her former husband.

They lived in Philadelphia, and Deborah gave birth to two children and operated the book and stationery store that Franklin owned as part of his printing business. Though Deborah had only a rudimentary education and shared none of Franklin's wide-ranging scientific and intellectual interests, their marriage, from all appearances, was harmonious and intimate.

Deborah managed Franklin's business affairs during his long absences in England from 1757 to 1762 and again from 1764 to 1775, where he tried to stave off war between the British crown and its colonies. They wrote letters back and forth, but Franklin rarely shared political matters with her and she steadfastly refused to join him in England. Thus their lives went along separate paths—while he quickly became a player in world affairs, she quietly took care of his home and business.

In about 1773, her health began to decline and she beseeched Franklin to come home. But Franklin, hoping to avert an ever-looming war between England and its colonies, remained in London. In December 1774, Deborah Franklin suffered a stroke and died. Franklin returned home three months later, to mourn for his wife and prepare for revolution. Two years after she died, he sorrowfully wrote a friend, "I have lately lost my old and faithful Companion; and I every day become more sensible of the greatness of that Loss; which cannot now be repair'd."

FURTHER READING
Franklin, Benjamin. *Autobiography of Benjamin Franklin*. New York: Vintage Books/Library of America, 1990.
Lopez, Claude-Anne and Eugenia W. Herbert. *The Private Franklin: The Man and His Family*. New York: Norton, 1975.

Friedan, Betty

AUTHOR, FEMINIST LEADER

Born: February 4, 1921
Peoria, Illinois

Betty Friedan is a founding mother of the present-day women's movement. Her book *The Feminine Mystique,* published in 1963, questioned the traditional view of domesticity as women's main role in life and urged women to find meaningful work outside of the home. The book quickly became a best-seller and inspired thousands of women, mostly from the middle class, to combine marriage and motherhood with paid work and other activities.

After graduating from Smith College in 1942, Friedan married, raised three children, and embarked upon a career as a freelance magazine journalist. In *The Feminine Mystique,* Friedan wrote about the "problem that has no name"—the attempt to find fulfillment solely from marriage and motherhood—and her career as a feminist was launched.

In 1966, Friedan helped to establish the National Organization for Women (NOW), a feminist group that fought for women's social, economic, and legal equality within American society. She served as president from 1966 to 1970. Under her leadership, NOW expanded into a national organization with local chapters, but it did not address the needs of all American women. Instead, it catered mostly to educated white professional women who had different concerns from those of women from other ethnic and class backgrounds. The first organization to emerge from the feminist activism of the 1960s, NOW sparked the formation of other groups, which fought for ideas and positions that NOW would not endorse.

Friedan has served on numerous other commissions and councils relating to women and has taught journalism and women's studies at colleges around the country. She also serves on several editorial boards and has written for a variety of popular and scholarly publications.

Over the years, she has modified her initial thinking; by the early 1980s, she urged women—and men—to make family life a feminist priority and to share household responsibilities. She is also interested in helping men and women turn the process of aging into a fruitful, enjoyable part of life.

MAJOR PUBLICATIONS
The Feminine Mystique (1963)
It Changed My Life: Writings on the Women's Movement (1976)
The Second Stage (1981)
The Fountain of Age (1993)

FURTHER READING
Blau, Justine. *Betty Friedan: Feminist.* New York: Chelsea House, 1990.

Fuller, Margaret

AUTHOR, CRITIC, JOURNALIST, FEMINIST

Born: May 23, 1810
Cambridgeport, Massachusetts

Died: July 19, 1850
at sea off of Long Island, New York

Margaret Fuller was the female Voltaire of her era—a brilliant, voracious seeker of new ideas whose intellectual home was the world. At the age of six, she could already read Latin. She was educated primarily by her father, who was disappointed that she was not a boy. To compensate for this deficiency, he decided to give her an education befitting a son, and she was soon reading the Greek and Roman classics as well as Shakespeare, Cervantes, and Molière. At 14, she attended school in Groton, Connecticut, and solidified her mastery of French, Italian, and Greek.

By the late 1820s, she had gained entrée into Cambridge's elite intellectual circles—though she was still in her teens. When her father died, she taught school to support her mother and siblings. But teaching did not challenge her enough. Bemoaning the indifference to women's intellectual development, she offered a series of "Conversations" in Elizabeth Peabody's bookstore in Boston. In these two-hour sessions, open only to women, she briefly introduced the topic of the day and then led a discussion.

She was also active in the New England Transcendentalist movement, a group of thinkers and writers who challenged traditional religious thought and sought inspiration and wisdom from the natural world. Besides Fuller, other proponents of Transcendentalism included Ralph Waldo Emerson, Henry David Thoreau, Bronson Alcott, and Elizabeth Peabody—all highly original and iconoclastic thinkers.

Fuller was the first editor and a chief contributor to their journal, the *Dial*. She also published other writings, and in 1844 she moved to New York City to write for the *New York Tribune*. There she expanded her focus from airy philosophical ideas to a concrete concern for urban poverty, prison reform, and other social ills.

Restless once again for new challenges, she became the *Tribune*'s foreign correspondent in 1846 and traveled throughout Europe. In Italy, she met her future husband, Angelo Ossoli, and immersed herself in the country's political turmoil. Eventually, she and her husband and their young son were forced to flee, and they sailed for America. She died tragically in a shipwreck off Long Island.

For Margaret Fuller, life was an adventure to be savored. Before the emergence of an organized women's rights movement, she urged women to strike down all barriers that kept them from becoming full human beings. "Very early," she once wrote, "I knew that the only object in life was to grow." That she did, in spirit and intellect during her brief, luminous life.

MAJOR PUBLICATIONS

Woman in the Nineteenth Century (1845)
Memoirs of Margaret Fuller Ossoli (posthumous, 1852)
At Home and Abroad (posthumous collection of essays, 1856)
Life Without and Life Within (posthumous collection of essays, 1859)

FURTHER READING

Balducci, Carolyn. *Margaret Fuller: A Life of Passion and Defiance*. New York: Bantam, 1991.
Capper, Charles. *Margaret Fuller: An American Romantic Life—The Private Years*. New York: Oxford University Press, 1992.

Gage, Matilda Joslyn
WOMEN'S RIGHTS ADVOCATE

Born: March 25, 1826
Cicero, New York

Died: March 18, 1898
Chicago, Illinois

Matilda Joslyn Gage was right-hand captain to Elizabeth Cady Stanton and Susan B. Anthony in the struggle to achieve women's rights. She acquired her progressive ideas from her father, an abolitionist and women's rights advocate who taught her Greek, mathematics, and physiology—a highly rigorous and unusual curriculum for a young woman of her time. She completed her education at the Clinton Liberal Institute in Clinton, New York.

In 1845, at age 18, she married Henry H. Gage, a merchant, and over the next several years bore five children. In 1852, she made her first speech at a women's rights convention, "trembling in every limb," she later said. She advocated equal educational opportunities and political and legal rights.

Gage was a founding member of Stanton and Anthony's National Woman Suffrage Association (NWSA) and wrote for its newspaper, the *Revolution*. She was also vice president and secretary of the New York State Woman Suffrage Association, and in 1875 served as head of the National Woman Suffrage Association. Gage was both a skillful organizer and writer. She penned several pamphlets, including *Woman As Inventor* (1870), edited a monthly newspaper for NWSA, and coauthored with Stanton and Anthony the first three volumes of the monumental *History of Woman Suffrage.*

In later years, she blamed women's social inequality on organized religion and formed her own organization, the Woman's National Liberal Union, to challenge conservative church teachings regarding women. In 1893, she published *Woman, Church, and State,* which spelled out her views.

Gage remained a dedicated women's rights activist until her death. Her gravestone is inscribed with her lifelong motto: "There is a word sweeter than Mother, Home, or Heaven; that word is liberty."

MAJOR PUBLICATION
Woman, Church, and State (1893)

Gaynor, Janet

ACTRESS

Born: October 6, 1906
Philadelphia, Pennsylvania

Died: September 14, 1984
Palm Springs, California

Janet Gaynor, the innocent-eyed actress who won the first Academy Award for best actress, was one of the most popular Hollywood stars of the 1930s and 1940s. She portrayed sweet, naive young women in a spate of musicals and comedies for Fox Films.

She was born Laura Gainor and began working as an extra in Hollywood while still in her teens. At 18, she signed her first contract, a five-year commitment to Fox Films. In 1928, she won the first Academy Award for best actress in three films: *Sunrise* (1927), *Seventh Heaven* (1927), and *Sweet Angel* (1928). By 1934, she was making the princely sal-

ary of more than $250,000 a year. Later she boasted that she "never had an acting lesson in my life."

In 1937, she starred in the dramatic motion picture *A Star Is Born*—a departure from the light, frothy roles she had been playing. This role would be the high point of her film career. Two years later, she gave up acting to start a family. As she explained at the time: "Making movies was really all I knew of life. I just wanted to have time to know other things. Most of all I wanted to fall in love. I wanted to get married. I wanted a child."

Gaynor had already married and divorced once. But in 1939 she married Gilbert Adrian, a Hollywood fashion designer, with whom she had a child and shared a loving marriage. She also took up painting and exhibited her work in galleries in Palm Springs, New York, and Chicago.

Gaynor, who occasionally acted on stage in later years, was one of the first actresses to abandon the more restrained realm of silent pictures and work in the glamorous, new industry of talking movies.

FURTHER READING
Billips, Connie J. *Janet Gaynor: A Bio-Bibliography.* Westport, Conn.: Greenwood Press, 1992.

Gilman, Charlotte Anna Perkins Stetson

FEMINIST, AUTHOR, LECTURER

Born: July 3, 1860
Hartford, Connecticut

Died: August 17, 1935
Pasadena, California

Perhaps the most brilliant and original thinker among early 20th-century feminists, Charlotte Perkins Gilman proposed bold new ways to free women from household drudgery and expand the scope of their lives.

Her own childhood became a tableau of poverty and dislocation after her father deserted the family. Despite having to work, the young Charlotte Perkins managed to attain some schooling, including a brief period of study at the Rhode Island School of Design. She supported herself as a commercial artist, art teacher, and governess.

In 1884, she married Charles Walter Stetson, and a year later gave birth to a daughter. Shortly after the child was born, she fell into a deep depression and could no longer carry out routine household tasks. Her husband and her doctor, a well-respected physician, both suggested round-the-clock bed rest. But she soon realized during a recuperative trip to California that the root problem was her feelings of entrapment in her marriage, and she divorced her husband.

She now devoted herself to writing and lecturing. In 1892, she published "The Yellow Wall-Paper," a short story based on her nervous breakdown. The story was to become a classic feminist tale. Attracted to the ideas of utopian socialist Edward Bellamy, she lectured about women, labor, and new forms of social relations, and formulated many of the ideas she later wrote about.

Her lecture tours took her across the country, and she seldom stayed in one place for long. She also journeyed to London to attend a Socialist conference, though she never joined the Socialist party. But she was greatly influenced by several English Socialists, including the playwright George Bernard Shaw, and incorporated their ideas into her own thinking.

In 1898, she published her most famous book, *Women and Economics,* in which she argued that women, through their domestic roles, had become wholly dependent upon men and must sever that dependence through paid work. To free women from full-time domesticity, she proposed the construction of "feminist apartment houses" with centralized nurseries and kitchens run by a trained staff. There, mothers could leave their children and also purchase their families' meals to allow themselves more time

for work and other activities. She promulgated these ideas in the *Woman's Journal,* the main newspaper of the women's rights movement, and in two books, *Concerning Children* (1900) and *The Home* (1903).

After marrying again, she continued to lecture and write, and in 1909 she launched her own journal, the *Forerunner,* to convey her feminist ideas. Her final major work was *Herland,* a feminist fantasy novel published in 1915, which portrayed an ideal society inhabited only by women.

Fiercely independent to the end, Gilman took her own life when she feared that illness would render her a burden on her family. She was brilliant, audacious, and visionary in her thinking.

MAJOR PUBLICATIONS
"The Yellow Wall-Paper" (1892)
Women and Economics (1898)
Man-Made World (1911)
Herland (1915)
The Living of Charlotte Perkins Gilman (autobiography, published posthumously, 1935)

FURTHER READING
Lane, Ann J. *To Herland and Beyond: The Life and Work of Charlotte Perkins Gilman.* New York: Pantheon, 1990.

Goldman, Emma

POLITICAL ACTIVIST AND AGITATOR, WRITER, LECTURER

Born: June 27, 1869
Kovno, Lithuania

Died: May 14, 1940
Toronto, Ontario, Canada

Troublemaker, rabble rouser, hero, and visionary—Emma Goldman was all of these, as well as one of the most colorful and committed political rebels to sweep through American history.

She was the daughter of Orthodox Jewish parents and endured a childhood scarred by poverty, religious persecution, and brutal government treatment of Lithuania's lower classes. These harsh conditions, along with her own early exposure to radical political ideas, converted Goldman into a political rebel.

In 1885, Goldman immigrated to the United States and, after a brief, unhappy marriage and divorce, made her home in New York City. There, as she later claimed, her true life began. By day she worked in a garment factory, and in the evenings she attended political meetings and made speeches. Goldman had become an anarchist, and in New York City she met many leading exponents of anarchism, including Alexander Berkman, soon to be her lover and lifelong friend.

Goldman defined anarchism as "the spirit of revolt, in whatever form, against everything that hinders human growth." She opposed central governments, organized religion, private property, and traditional morality as obstacles to achieving social equality and happiness. Instead, Goldman envisioned a society composed of small, cooperative communities unfettered by repressive laws or government institutions.

Goldman fought for her political ideals until the end of her life, crisscrossing the nation to promote her views. From 1906 to 1917, she published *Mother Earth*, a monthly journal of anarchist ideas and other unconventional views. She also urged women to use birth control to regulate the number of children they wanted—a practice that was against the law—and called marriage "legalized prostitution." She supported free love, a philosophy that advocated love and equality between men and women without the legalistic weight of marriage.

Goldman was imprisoned repeatedly for her unpopular ideas until 1919, when the U.S. government deported her, Berkman, and other immigrant radicals back to Russia for allegedly plotting revolution against the United States. Goldman spent the rest of her life in exile, barred from returning to the United States. In later years, she supported the Spanish Republicans in their struggle against Fascist forces in Spain. She died during a visit to Toronto, Canada.

Impatient with efforts to merely reform existing social and political institutions, Goldman wanted to uproot those institutions and build a new society organized around class and gender equality. Fearless, passionate, and uncompromising, she dared to dream of a world governed by harmony, equality, and human fulfillment.

MAJOR PUBLICATIONS
Living My Life (autobiography, 1931)
Emma Speaks: An Emma Goldman Reader (1983)

FURTHER READING
Falk, Candace. *Love, Anarchy, and Emma Goldman.* New York: Henry Holt, 1984.
Waldstreicher, David. *Emma Goldman.* New York: Chelsea House, 1990.
Wexler, Alice. *Emma Goldman: An Intimate Life.* New York: Pantheon, 1984.
———. *Emma Goldman in Exile: From the Russian Revolution to the Spanish Civil War.* Boston: Beacon Press, 1989.

Good, Sarah

ACCUSED WITCH

Born: ca. 1653
Wenham, Massachusetts

Died: July 19, 1692
Salem, Massachusetts

Sarah Good's story is a tale of pathos and misery. Though she was born into an affluent family, she lived most of her life penniless and homeless, and her impoverished status perhaps contributed to the suspicions and ill will shown toward her by her Salem neighbors—and their accusations of witchcraft. Good, along with Tituba and Sarah Osborne, were the first three women accused of witchcraft during the Salem witch-hunt.

Cheated out of her share of a family inheritance by a greedy stepfather, Sarah married Daniel Poole, a poor indentured servant who died shortly after their marriage, leaving her with a huge debt. Her second marriage, to William Good, a weaver and laborer, did not improve her financial prospects. Debts continued to mount and Sarah, William, and their three children were left destitute and homeless. Sarah never attended church in Salem Village, where she begged on the streets, because she did not have the proper clothing. The mutterings she aimed at villagers who refused to give her food or lodgings were interpreted as curses. She was an oddity and outcast in this righteous Puritan community.

On February 29, 1692, therefore, it was natural that Sarah Good should be named as a witch, along with Tituba and Sarah Osborne, when three young Salem girls started to display odd behavior. In their ravings, they accused Tituba of practicing witchcraft, and she in turn named Good and Osborne as fellow witches.

Though Sarah Good refused to confess, she accused Sarah Osborne. To make matters worse, Good's own husband voiced concern that she was either a witch or "an enemy to all good." Sarah was imprisoned first in Ipswich, and then in Boston, where she was kept in chains. Not content with seizing her alone, her accusers also imprisoned her four-year-old daughter and infant son, who died in prison.

After undergoing two humiliating physical examinations for marks of witchcraft, Sarah Good was condemned to death by the presiding court and hanged at Salem on July 19, 1692. When Salem's minister offered her one last opportunity to repent at the gallows, she spat out, "You are a liar. I am no more a Witch than you are a Wizard, and if you take away my Life, God will give you blood to drink."

FURTHER READING

Boyer, Paul and Stephen Nissenbaum. *Salem Possessed: The Social Origins of Witchcraft.* Cambridge: Harvard University Press, 1974.

Demos, John. *Entertaining Satan: Witchcraft and the Culture of Early New England.* New York: Oxford University Press, 1982.

Robinson, Enders A. *The Devil Discovered: Salem Witchcraft, 1692.* New York: Hippocrene Books, 1991, pp. 260–63.

Grable, Betty

ACTRESS

Born: December 18, 1916
St. Louis, Missouri

Died: July 2, 1973
Santa Monica, California

During World War II, Betty Grable was America's sweetheart and one of its premier sex symbols. Innocent but sensual on screen, she symbolized the girl back home and the American way of life the soldiers were fighting to protect. Her picture adorned the tents and foxholes of thousands of American troops stationed in Europe and the Pacific. Women were also drawn to the wholesome, girl-next-door image she projected on screen.

Born Ruth Elizabeth Grable, she was prodded into singing and dancing by her ambitious mother. The young Betty Grable appeared in her first movie when she was barely in her teens. Throughout the 1930s, she played small roles in several movies. In 1939, she appeared in the Broadway show *Du Barry Was a Lady* with Ethel Merman, and her acting career took off. Grable—and especially her shapely legs, which the studio eagerly promoted in publicity shots—became a box-office hit, and she starred in a number of lavish movie musicals throughout the 1940s.

Although these movies were phenomenally successful, by the 1950s a fickle public stopped fawning over her. She continued to make movies, appeared on stage and in night club acts, and also appeared on television occasionally before succumbing to lung cancer in 1973.

MAJOR FILMS

The Gay Divorcee (with Fred Astaire, 1934)
Tin Pan Alley (1940)
Footlight Serenade (1942)
How to Marry a Millionaire (with Lauren Bacall and Marilyn Monroe, 1953)

FURTHER READING
Pastos, Spera. *Pin-Up: The Tragedy of Betty Grable.* New York: Putnam, 1986.

Gratz, Rebecca

CHARITY WORKER, SUNDAY SCHOOL FOUNDER

Born: March 4, 1781
Philadelphia, Pennsylvania

Died: August 27, 1869
Philadelphia, Pennsylvania

Rebecca Gratz was the seventh child in a well-established Jewish family in Philadelphia. Her father had immigrated from upper Silesia in central Europe in the 1750s, and had made his fortune in fur trading, land speculation, and shipping. During the Revolutionary War, he supported the patriot cause. The wealth and prestige of her family gave Gratz entrée into Philadelphia's most elite circles.

But Gratz was not content to be an upper-class lady of leisure. At 20, she began a lifelong career of charity work by helping to organize the nonsectarian Female Association for the Relief of Women and Children in Reduced Circumstances, one of the city's first female relief societies. She also helped establish several other charitable organizations, including the nonsectarian Philadelphia Orphan Asylum (1815), the Female Hebrew Benevolent Society (1819), the Jewish Foster Home and Orphan Asylum (1855), the Fuel Society, and the Sewing Society.

Eager to furnish Philadelphia's Jewish children with a proper religious education, she also organized and taught a Jewish Sunday school. Although the school did not last, Gratz was determined to promote Jewish religious education, and in 1838 she organized the Hebrew Sunday School Society of Philadelphia, a free Sunday school for Jewish boys and girls. It became the model for other Jewish Sunday schools around the United States and was perhaps her most important accomplishment.

Gratz, who was widely admired for her civic and religious volunteer work, was a pioneer social reformer. Through her charitable and religious good works, she helped make Philadelphia a better city.

PUBLICATION
David Philipson, ed. *Letters of Rebecca Gratz.* New York: Arno Press, 1975.

FURTHER READING
Wagenknecht, Edward. *Daughters of the Covenant: Portraits of Six Jewish Women.* Amherst: University of Massachusetts Press, 1983.

Grendon, Sarah

POLITICAL REBEL

Born: date and place unknown

Died: date and place unknown

In an era when colonial women were not expected—indeed, even discouraged from—expressing political opinions, Sarah Grendon, a colonial woman living in Charles City, Virginia, took it upon herself to assist a rebellion against the royal governor. Unhappy with the lukewarm protection provided by royal colonial governor William Berkeley against Indian attacks throughout the summer and fall of 1675, local vigilante groups of men united under two leaders—Nathaniel Bacon and Giles Bland--to oppose the governor. By the spring of 1676, a full-scale insurrection against Berkeley, which came to be known as Bacon's Rebellion, was in force.

Sarah Grendon, whose husband, Thomas, was away from Virginia and therefore not involved in the insurrection, was one of several women who offered food and other assistance to the insurrectionists. Grendon even gave gunpowder to Bacon's forces—but later tried to minimize her actions by claiming that she thought the gunpowder would be used only against Indians. Nevertheless, after the rebellion was quelled, the governor regarded Grendon as a "great encourager and assister in the late horrid Rebellion" and refused to include her in the pardon that he granted to citizens of Charles City in February 1677.

To free his wife from the serious charge of treason, Thomas Grendon requested that the royal commissioners try her themselves. On May 10, 1677, they convened a court in Charles City County and dismissed charges against her. That same day, the governor and attorney general also conducted a hearing on her role in the rebellion and decided not to try her for treason because she acted no more treasonously than others had.

Little is known about Grendon other than her mutinous role during this skirmish between the British governor and his colonial subjects. She had been married and widowed twice before marrying Thomas Grendon, and had no children. When Grendon died in 1685, he left her a sizable estate, suggesting that he bore her no ill feeling for her role in the rebellion or for the embarrassment to him at having such a feisty and independent-minded wife.

FURTHER READING

"Women in Bacon's Rebellion" by Susan Westbury, in Virginia Bernhard et al., eds. *Southern Women: Histories and Identities.* Columbia: University of Missouri Press, 1992.

Grimké, Angelina Emily and Sarah Moore

ABOLITIONISTS, WOMEN'S RIGHTS ADVOCATES

Born: November 26, 1792 (Sarah)
February 20, 1805 (Angelina)
Charleston, South Carolina

Died: December 23, 1873 (Sarah)
October 26, 1879 (Angelina)
Hyde Park, Massachusetts

Daughters of a Charleston, South Carolina, slave owner, Sarah and Angelina Grimké became ardent abolitionists and early women's rights activists. Their remarkable dedication to both causes inspired Lucretia Mott and Lucy Stone, among others, to do battle for both African-American and women's rights.

Both sisters were educated by private tutors, though—to Sarah's chagrin—they were not taught Greek, Latin, philosophy, and law because these were not considered suitable "feminine" subjects. Although they had grown up in a household where slaves served their every need, both sisters came to regard slavery as a moral evil. Sarah was the first sister to act on her beliefs. In 1821, after much soul searching, she joined the Quaker faith, which opposed slavery, and moved to Philadelphia. Angelina also became a Quaker and followed Sarah to Philadelphia. She joined the Philadelphia Female Antislavery Society and pledged her support to radical abolitionist William Lloyd Garrison.

In 1836, Angelina published *An Appeal to the Christian Women of the South,* a pamphlet urging southern women to oppose slavery, and joined the American Antislavery Society as a lecturer. Sarah also joined the society and wrote a pamphlet addressed to southern preachers, *Epistle to the Clergy of the Southern States,* in which she challenged a widely held view that slavery was justified because it was practiced in biblical times.

Soon the sisters were lecturing before audiences of men and women—then a highly unusual practice—and their audacity drew the wrath of several Massachusetts clergymen. In pamphlets published separately, both Sarah and Angelina eloquently defended their right as women to speak in public and their belief in equal rights for women—a full decade before the organized women's rights movement began. Sarah's pamphlet, *Letters on the Equality of the Sexes and the Condition of Women* (1838), remains a classic early manifesto for women's rights.

In 1838, Angelina married Theodore Weld, an abolitionist, and she and her husband and sister continued their antislavery work. By 1840, they had mostly withdrawn from the abolition movement, and later opened a school in New Jersey for both black and white students. Sarah also worked as a journalist. Although their involvement in the abolition movement was brief, they inspired scores of other women, and men, to oppose slavery and also work for women's rights.

PUBLICATIONS

Grimké, Angelina. *An Appeal to the Christian Women of the South* (pamphlet, 1836)

Grimké, Angelina. *Appeal to the Women of the Nominally Free States* (pamphlet, 1837)

Grimké, Sarah. *Epistle to the Clergy of the Southern States* (pamphlet, 1836)

Grimké, Sarah. *Letters on the Equality of the Sexes, and the Condition of Woman* (pamphlet, 1838)

FURTHER READING

Lerner, Gerda. *The Grimké Sisters from South Carolina: Rebels Against Slavery*. Boston: Houghton Mifflin, 1967.

Grimké, Charlotte L. Forten

EDUCATOR, AUTHOR

Born: August 17, 1837
Philadelphia, Pennsylvania

Died: July 23, 1914
Washington, D.C.

Charlotte Forten Grimké came from a prominent African-American family long active in the abolition movement. Her father hired a tutor for her rather than send her to Philadelphia's segregated schools. Early on, she developed a love of learning and a fondness for cultural pursuits, such as music and art, and supplemented her formal education with a rigorous program of self-study. She completed her schooling at the State Normal School in Salem, Massachusetts, and became a teacher. She was the first African American to instruct white students in Salem, and her teaching won accolades from parents, colleagues, and students. She also joined the Massachusetts Female Antislavery Society.

During the Civil War, Forten journeyed south to the Sea Islands, off of Georgia, to teach ex-slaves set free by Union forces. Eager to help her race, she approached the formidable task of educating scores of illiterate children and adults with high hopes. She greatly admired her students' determination to learn and was fascinated by their customs and cultural traditions. But overwork, poor climate, and rugged living conditions, as well as her own exacting standards, took a toll on her health, and she returned to Philadelphia two years later. She resumed teaching and wrote for several publications.

After the war, she married Frances James Grimké, a former slave and pastor in Washington, D.C., and worked for the U.S. Treasury Department. She also wrote for several publications. Though Grimké, in her own life, had known little of the hardship suffered by other African Americans, she was fiercely dedicated to helping her people.

PUBLICATIONS

Stevenson, Brenda, ed. *The Journals of Charlotte Forten Grimké*. New York: Oxford University Press, 1988.

FURTHER READING

Sterling, Dorothy. *We Are Your Sisters: Black Women in the Nineteenth Century*. New York: Norton, 1984.

Guyart, Marie

FRENCH MISSIONARY

Born: ca. 1599
France

Died: ca. 1672
Quebec, Canada

Known after her death as Marie of the Incarnation, Marie Guyart was one of the first female missionaries in New France (now Quebec, Canada). Born to middle-class parents, she married Claude Martin, a silk worker, in 1617, and bore one son.

When her husband died three years later, she secured work as a housekeeper in her sister's family.

In 1632, she left her son in her sister's care and entered the Ursuline Convent in Tours, France. There she claimed to receive numerous divine revelations and also envisioned her future vocation to be missionary work. Seven years later, in 1639, she and three other Ursuline sisters responded to a Jesuit call to form a convent in Quebec. They quickly established a school for the daughters of settlers and Native Americans. Despite sickness, poverty, and hostility from native peoples, the school flourished and even expanded.

In addition to her teaching duties, Guyart compiled and published a French-Algonquian dictionary, composed catechisms, and wrote more than 13,000 letters about life in New France. Despite growing danger from Iroquois Indian attacks in 1648, Marie Guyart and her Ursuline sisters ignored warnings to return to the safety of Europe and instead chose to stay in Quebec. Two collections of her works appeared after her death: *Retraites* (1682) and a compilation of her letters (1681).

Hale, Sarah Josepha Buell

MAGAZINE EDITOR

Born: October 24, 1788
Newport, New Hampshire

Died: April 30, 1879
Philadelphia, Pennsylvania

Sarah Hale edited the 19th century's most popular women's magazine and, in the process, redefined women's social role for thousands of Americans. She was mostly educated at home by her mother, who introduced her to the works of Milton, Shakespeare, and Bunyan. As a young woman she conducted a local dame school and, in 1813, married David Hale, a lawyer. Happy years of domes-

ticity and childrearing followed until 1822, when her husband died.

Forced to support herself and her children, Hale opened a millinery shop and began to write. Her published pieces caught the attention of a minister, who asked her to edit his new *Ladies' Magazine* (later the *American Ladies' Magazine*). For the next nine years, she single-handedly edited this monthly magazine and defined for a generation of readers her view of "woman's sphere"—praising meekness, piety, virtue, and maternal love as women's true attributes. Man, she insisted, was fit for the coarser world of business and politics, while woman was destined to uplift the race from the sheltering walls of her home. Hale even rejected volunteer work for women—though she championed greater educational opportunities because she believed that educated women made better teachers of the nation's children. Indeed, she supported all efforts to improve educational instruction.

In 1836, Hale became editor of the new *Godey's Lady's Book*. She continued to espouse a domestic role for women, but she also rejected the prevailing idea that women should lead an inactive life indoors and urged female readers to get exercise and fresh air, eat sensibly, and wear comfortable clothing. She continued to champion women teachers, and in the 1850s, as the nation's industrial growth forced more women into the labor market, she urged all women to develop a marketable skill, such as teaching, missionary work, and even medicine. She deemed women physicians better suited to treat women patients.

Hale turned *Godey's Lady's Book* into one of the most successful magazines of its time. For all her talk of woman's tender, meek nature, she was a savvy businesswoman who knew how to make her magazine sell. She also edited or published numerous household manuals and children's books. An indefatigable worker, she retired at 89 and died a year later.

MAJOR PUBLICATIONS
Poems for Our Children (1830; included the classic verse "Mary Had a Little Lamb")
Woman's Record (1853)

FURTHER READING
Rogers, Sherbrooke. *Sarah Josepha Hale: A New England Pioneer, 1788–1879.* Grantham, N.H.: Tompson & Rutter, 1985.

Hamer, Fannie Lou

CIVIL RIGHTS ACTIVIST

Born: October 6, 1917
Montgomery County, Mississippi

Died: March 15, 1977
Sunflower County, Mississippi

Fannie Lou Hamer rose up from poverty to work for social justice for African Americans and all poor people. She was the twentieth child of share-cropper parents and at age 6 began the tedious, back-breaking work of picking cotton. No matter how hard her family worked, they remained mired in poverty. Altogether, she had about six years of formal schooling pieced together during periods when her labor was not needed in the fields.

In 1942, she married Perry "Pap" Hamer, a tractor driver. At the plantation where she picked cotton, she gradually worked her way up to timekeeper, a less arduous but still low-paying job.

In 1962, Hamer joined the staff of the Southern Christian Leadership Conference (SCLC), the civil rights organization established by the Reverend Martin Luther King, Jr., and volunteered to challenge voting laws that discriminated against blacks. Not surprisingly, she lost her job and had to flee town. After participating in a civil rights workshop in Charleston, South Carolina, she joined a busload of other blacks trying to integrate segregated bus terminals. They were arrested and jailed in Winona, Mississippi, where she suffered a beating that left her permanently injured.

More committed than ever to ending segregation, Hamer joined other civil rights organizations. In 1964, she was chosen vice president of the newly organized Mississippi Freedom Democratic party, which strove to challenge the all-white state Democratic party. On national television, she told of the cruel treatment that she and other civil rights workers had suffered in the struggle to achieve racial justice. Her riveting account helped convert many people to the cause of civil rights.

In later years, Hamer dedicated herself to other causes besides civil rights. She was an early opponent of the Vietnam War, decrying the bloodshed and money spent abroad while Americans were "starving to death" at home. She also helped establish factories, cooperatives, and day-care facilities in her community to help impoverished workers, and urged black women to lead their communities. "To support whatever is right, and to bring in justice where we've had so much injustice" was how she defined the black woman's role.

In honor of her civil rights and antipoverty work, Hamer received honorary doctoral degrees from colleges and universities across the country. She devoted her life not only to combating racial and economic injustice but to helping blacks and poor people make better lives for themselves.

FURTHER READING
Crawford, Vicki L., Jacqueline Anne Rouse, and Barbara Woods. *Women in the Civil Rights Movement.* Brooklyn: Carlson, 1990.
Lerner, Gerda, ed. *Black Women in White America.* New York: Pantheon, 1972.
Mills, Kay. *This Little Light of Mine: The Life of Fannie Lou Hamer.* New York: Dutton, 1993.

Hamilton, Alice

PHYSICIAN, SOCIAL REFORMER

Born: February 27, 1869
New York, New York

Died: September 22, 1970
Hadlyme, Connecticut

More than 50 years before the present-day environmental movement, Alice Hamilton aroused public awareness of the dangers of workplace pollutants. She grew up in a loving, affluent, and intellectually stimulating home, and from her mother she learned that "personal liberty was the most precious thing in life." Educated at home in literature and the classics, she completed her schooling at an exclusive girls' school in Farmington, Connecticut, and aspired to become a physician. She enrolled in the Fort Wayne College of Medicine in Fort Wayne, Indiana, and then transferred to the University of Michigan, where she received her M.D. degree in 1893.

She pursued rigorous postgraduate training in bacteriology and pathology at the Woman's Medical School of Northwestern University in Chicago. She also joined Jane Addams's pioneering circle of female social reformers at Hull House, where she taught, established a well-baby clinic, and worked for various social causes. But Hamilton was still unsure of her true work—until she discovered a shocking public indifference to health hazards in the workplace.

She spearheaded numerous state and federal investigations of industrial pollutants that caused disease. By 1916, she was the leading expert on lead poisoning and only one of a few specialists in industrial diseases. Three years later, she became an assistant professor of industrial medicine at Harvard University—the first woman to join Harvard's faculty. She used her scientific expertise to speak out for poor and immigrant workers, who were the chief victims of workplace diseases. In 1925, she published *Industrial Poisons in the United States,* the first textbook on the subject.

Hamilton supported numerous other causes that improved people's lives as well, including international peace, laws regulating child labor, legalized birth control, and state-sponsored health insurance. From 1944 to 1949, she was president of the National Consumers' League, and she lived long enough to protest U.S. military involvement in the Vietnam War. Her friendly, soft-spoken manner concealed a fierce determination to create safer working and living conditions for all Americans.

PUBLICATIONS
Exploring the Dangerous Trades (autobiography, 1943)
"A Woman of Ninety Looks at Her World," *Atlantic Monthly* (September 1961)

FURTHER READING
Sicherman, Barbara. *Alice Hamilton: A Life in Letters.* Cambridge, Mass.: Harvard University Press, 1984.

Harland, Marion

See Terhune, Mary Virginia Hawes

Harper, Frances Ellen Watkins
LECTURER, AUTHOR, REFORMER

Born: September 24, 1825
Baltimore, Maryland

Died: February 22, 1911
Philadelphia, Pennsylvania

Frances Ellen Watkins Harper worked for two mighty movements for social justice—woman suffrage and abolition. Born to free parents in Maryland, she was orphaned at an early age and was reared by her uncle, a minister who taught her the value of discipline and the love of freedom. She attended his school for free blacks until 1839, when she became a domestic in the household of a Baltimore bookseller. After finishing her chores each day, she would settle down with a book.

In 1851, she published her first book of poetry and prose, *Forest Leaves.* Meanwhile, she taught sewing at Union Seminary, an African Methodist Episcopal church near Columbus, Ohio, and later in Little York, Pennsylvania.

Around 1853, Watkins met prominent black abolitionists and was inspired to join the antislavery movement. In August 1854 she gave her first antislavery lecture, entitled "Education and the Elevation of the Colored Race," and joined the Maine Antislavery Society as a lecturer. She lectured throughout New England, Pennsylvania, New Jersey, New York, Ohio, and other states. Often called the "Bronze Muse," because she wrote poetry as well, she spoke in a clear, musical voice and impressed audiences with her solemn dignity and sincerity.

Watkins used the pen as well as the lecture platform to convey her ideas. In 1854, she published *Poems on Miscellaneous Subjects,* and also wrote poetry and articles for major abolitionist periodicals. Fast becoming the nation's most popular black poet, she depicted in her poems the horrors of slavery, especially for enslaved women.

Her short story, "The Two Offers," which appeared in *Anglo-African Magazine* in 1859, is said to be the first short story published by an African American. In the story, Harper adroitly reflected upon love, marriage, and women's social role by portraying two women—Janette and Laura—who have made very different choices in their lives. Later, Harper wrote, "The true aim of female education should be, not a development of one or two, but all the faculties of the human soul."

On November 22, 1860, Watkins married Fenton Harper, and they settled on a farm near Columbus, Ohio. The marriage produced one daughter. After her husband died in 1864, Harper continued to lecture, focusing on the needs and concerns of blacks in the postwar period. She exhorted blacks to seek schooling and practice temperance, but she also condemned white racial bigotry. While maintaining a grueling lecture schedule, Harper continued to publish poetry and also a novel, *Iola Leroy.* Published in 1892, the novel recounts the plight of a young quadroon—a person of mixed black and white ancestry—sold into slavery and her rescue. The book was highly popular in its day.

In later years, Harper focused her energies on improving living and working conditions for blacks. From 1883 to 1890, she directed the department of work for blacks for the Woman's Christian Temperance Union (WCTU), a national temperance organization. She also organized African-American Sunday schools in Philadelphia, and worked with local black ministers to prevent delinquency among black youth.

In addition, she supported woman suffrage and participated in the 1875 and 1887 conventions of the American Woman Suffrage Association (AWSA). But she did not flinch from chastising her white sisters in the movement for ignoring the needs of African-American women. Because of racism among white suffragists, she and other African-American women leaders strove to organize black women to help themselves. In 1896, she helped establish the National Association of Colored Women, a federation of black women's clubs, and served as vice president.

MAJOR PUBLICATIONS
Forest Leaves (1851)
Poems on Miscellaneous Subjects (1854)
Moses: A Story of the Nile (1869)
Sketches of Southern Life (1872)
Iola Leroy (1892)
Poems (1900)
Idylls of the Bible (1901)

FURTHER READING
Sterling, Dorothy. *We Are Your Sisters: Black Women in the Nineteenth Century.* New York: Norton, 1984.

Hawthorne, Sophia Amelia Peabody

ARTIST AND WRITER

Born: September 21, 1809
Salem, Massachusetts

Died: March 3, 1871
London, England

The youngest of three talented sisters, Sophia Peabody Hawthorne was muse and chief editor for her famous husband, the novelist Nathaniel Hawthorne. She was an invalid until her early teens and received no formal schooling, except for a brief period of study in her sister Elizabeth Palmer Peabody's classroom. But she read widely and was possessed of an artistic spirit, which she applied to both painting and writing. Her illustrations appeared as the frontispiece to numerous books, including those of her husband.

She and Hawthorne met in the late 1830s and were married in 1842. She bore three children over the next decade, and the family shared a happy but penurious life together. In 1850, Nathaniel Hawthorne published *The Scarlet Letter,* the novel that made him famous. Other novels followed. He read each work in progress to Sophia, eager for her response.

From 1853 to 1860, the family lived in England and Italy. Hawthorne died in 1864, leaving his family financially hard-pressed. To bring in money, Sophia edited and published his notebooks, unfortunately altering some of the distinctiveness of his writing at his editor's suggestion. In 1868, she moved with her children to Germany and then to London, where she died.

In letters to family and friends, Sophia Hawthorne revealed a sparkling prose style and a lively spirit. Had she turned her literary gift to more ambitious purposes, she might have become an accomplished novelist.

FURTHER READING

Herbert, T. Walter. *Dearest Beloved: The Hawthornes and the Making of the Middle-class Family.* Berkeley: University of California Press, 1993.
Tharp, Louise Hall. *The Peabody Sisters of Salem.* 1950. Reprint. Boston: Little Brown, 1988.

Hayden, Sophia Gregoria

ARCHITECT

Born: October 17, 1868
Santiago, Chile

Died: February 3, 1953
Winthrop, Massachusetts

Sophia Hayden enjoyed a prominent but short-lived reputation as the architect of the Woman's Building of the 1893 World's Columbian Exposition in Chicago, Illinois. This building showcased the impressive array of women's work and activities from around the world, including handicrafts, fine arts, textiles, ceramics, inventions, and books.

After attending public schools in Boston, Hayden enrolled at the Massachusetts Institute of Technology in 1886. She was the first female student to study architecture in a new program based on the teachings of the famed École des Beaux Arts in Paris. She mastered both the structural and esthetic principles of architecture, and graduated with honors in 1890. She then taught mechanical drawing at a Boston high school.

In 1891, Hayden submitted drawings for the competition to design a Woman's Building for the upcoming World Exposition. Her design, a structure incorporating the Italian Renaissance style, was chosen by the Board of Lady Managers, and she received an honorarium of $1,000 plus expenses for her work—far below the honoraria paid to male architects who designed the other exposition buildings. Hayden faced down pressures by the Board of Lady Managers to alter her design, and her spacious, graceful building won several important architectural awards.

The Woman's Building was Hayden's major work. She drew up plans for a memorial building for American women's clubs, but the structure was never built. She moved to Winthrop, Massachusetts, and was active in local civic groups, but she left no record of other architectural work.

FURTHER READING

Paine, Judith. "Sophia Hayden and the Woman's Building Competition," in Susana Torre, ed. *Women in American Architecture: An Historic and Contemporary Perspective.* New York: Whitney Library of Design, 1977.
Weimann, Jeanne Madeline. *The Fair Women.* Chicago: Academy Chicago, 1981.

Hellman, Lillian

PLAYWRIGHT, AUTHOR

Born: June 20, 1905
New Orleans, Louisiana

Died: June 30, 1984
New York, New York

Lillian Hellman was a commanding and combative presence in 20th–century American letters and politics. Her plays probed the darker side of human nature and bristled with sharply drawn characters.

Though Hellman was born in the South, she lived most of her life in New York City. She dropped out of New York University to work for a publisher and as a theatrical agent. It was her lover, Dashiell Hammett, a novelist and screenwriter, who urged her to write her first play, *The Children's Hour* (1936), a drama about two Scottish boarding-school teachers accused of having a lesbian relationship. The play enjoyed a long and successful Broadway run because of its explosive theme and Hellman's taut treatment of the plot and characters. Her 1941 drama, *Watch on the Rhine,* a portrayal of the growing menace of fascism, also found a responsive audience.

Hellman wrote other plays as well as three volumes of memoirs. Her writing, honest in spirit if not always in fact, crackles with rich, complex characters and insights.

Throughout her life, Hellman championed political causes such as civil rights and international peace. Like other artists, she was harassed for her leftist politics during the 1950s, an era of virulent anti-Communism in the United States. When called before the House Un-American Activities Committee in 1952 to implicate other writers and artists, Hellman delivered these unforgettable lines: "I cannot and will not cut my conscience to fit this year's fashions." As a result, she and Hammett were blacklisted—spurned professionally—

and she had no work or income for several years. But Hellman, tough to the core, endured these hard years and continued to write. In the 1960s, she taught at Harvard, Yale, and the City University of New York. She was a brilliant, provocative woman and writer.

MAJOR PUBLICATIONS
The Children's Hour (play, 1934)
The Little Foxes (play, 1936)
Watch on the Rhine (play, 1941)
Candide (play, 1957)
An Unfinished Woman (memoir, 1969)
Scoundrel Time (memoir, 1972)
Pentimento: A Book of Portraits (memoir, 1976)

FURTHER READING
Bryer, Jackson. *Conversations with Lillian Hellman.* Jackson: University of Mississippi Press, 1986.
Towns, Sandra. *Lillian Hellman: Playwright.* New York: Chelsea House, 1989.
Wright, William. *Lillian Hellman: The Image, the Woman.* New York: Simon & Schuster, 1986.

Hepburn, Katharine

ACTRESS

Born: November 8, 1909
Hartford, Connecticut

Katharine Hepburn is an American original—a dazzling actress and a dauntless woman who has stood up to the most powerful people in Hollywood. Throughout a long and distinguished career on stage and screen, she has created unforgettable characters that mirror her own bold and brassy style.

Hepburn was born into an affluent and politically progressive family. Her father was a doctor who pioneered the practice of social hygiene, and her mother was a feminist and suffragist whose friends included Margaret Sanger and Emma Goldman. The young Katharine Hepburn was educated by private tutors before attending the exclusive Hartford School for Girls. She graduated from Bryn Mawr College in 1928 and embarked upon an acting career.

Her first roles were small parts in summer stock and on Broadway. She made her breakthrough in

1932 with a winning performance on Broadway in *The Warrior's Husband,* which led to a film contract with RKO Pictures. Over the next six decades, she starred in scores of Hollywood films opposite such distinguished actors as John Barrymore, Cary Grant, Laurence Olivier, Henry Fonda, and Spencer Tracy, the man with whom she shared a deeply loving relationship for 25 years, though he was married. Hepburn had also been briefly married, but decided that "marriage is not a natural institution—otherwise why sign a contract for it?"

Hepburn played assertive women who retained some traditional female attributes—one reviewer called her an "iron butterfly." In her movies with Tracy, she usually played a career woman, such as a columnist, lawyer, or professional athlete. She also played Jo in a film adaptation of *Little Women* by Louisa May Alcott, as well as darker, more complex roles in film adaptations of plays by Tennessee Williams and Eugene O'Neill.

Hepburn has won four Academy Awards and has been nominated twice as many times. With her patrician features and brisk stride, flashing smile, and staccato voice, she has graced the stage and screen with unforgettable presence.

PUBLICATIONS
The Making of the African Queen (1987)
Me: Stories of My Life (1991)

FURTHER READING
Edwards, Anne. *A Remarkable Woman: A Biography of Katharine Hepburn.* New York: Morrow, 1985.
Latham, Caroline. *Katharine Hepburn: Actress.* New York: Chelsea House, 1988.

Hobby, Oveta Culp

ORGANIZER AND DIRECTOR OF THE
WOMEN'S ARMY CORPS (WACS) DURING
WORLD WAR II

Born: January 19, 1905
Killeen, Texas

Oveta Culp Hobby has spent most of her life steeped in political affairs and public service.

As a child, she often sat in her father's law office, reading the *Congressional Record* or listening to discussions of legal questions.

She dropped out of Mary Hardin-Baylor College after one year to accompany her father to sessions of the Texas House of State Representatives, where she heard debates about the woman suffrage amendment to the U.S. Constitution and about the League of Nations. Subsequently she received her law degree from the University of Texas. By age 20, she was an assistant city attorney in Houston and also served as parliamentarian of the Texas state legislature, a position she held from 1926 to 1931. In addition, she wrote a textbook on parliamentary procedure and helped revise the banking laws of Texas.

In 1931, she married William Hobby, owner and publisher of the *Houston Post* and a former governor. Their marriage produced two children. While raising her family, Hobby quickly found a niche for herself at the newspaper, and by 1938 she was executive editor.

The beginning of World War II found Hobby active in war preparation. Six months before Japanese planes attacked American warships at Pearl Harbor, she was appointed head of the Women's Interest Division of the army's Public Relations Bureau, and in 1942 became head of the newly formed Women's Auxiliary Army Corps (WAAC), the first organization of women to be part of the regular American military. Despite protests that she was too young—she was 37 at the time—and that she would show bias against black recruits because she was a Southerner, she organized and directed a military unit of more than 100,000 women to perform noncombat military service around the world. She ensured that a fair proportion of African-American women were promoted to officer status.

In 1943, the WAAC was changed to the Women's Army Corps (WAC) and made an official branch of the military service. At the end of the war, Hobby became the first woman to receive the

U.S. Army's Distinguished Service Medal.

After the war, Hobby resumed her work at the *Post* and took on new responsibilities as station director for a television and radio station in Houston. She also served on several corporate boards and campaigned for Dwight Eisenhower in the 1952 presidential election. When he took office, he appointed her secretary of the newly formed Department of Health, Education, and Welfare (HEW)—the second woman in American history to hold a cabinet-level position in a Presidential administration.

Hobby presided over a tumultuous era in the nation's social welfare. In 1954, the Supreme Court struck down segregation in the nation's schools, and polio epidemics were a frightening nationwide scourge. Controversy over the use of a new polio vaccine marred her tenure. She resigned from office in 1955 and returned to work in the private sector.

In 1983, Hobby was the only woman included on a list of the "twenty most powerful Texans" compiled by *Texas Business* magazine. Though she sold her ownership in the *Houston Post*, she continues to work in television broadcasting. She supports educational and cultural causes, and has received numerous honorary degrees and awards.

FURTHER READING
Doris Weatherford. *American Women's History.* New York: Prentice Hall, 1994, pp. 167–68.

Hope, Lugenia Burns

ACTIVIST, CLUBWOMAN

Born: February 19, 1871
Natchez, Mississippi

Died: August 14, 1947
Nashville, Tennessee

Lugenia Burns Hope devoted her life to the betterment of her fellow African Americans. Neighborhood day-care centers, antilynching laws, and other causes became her life's work. She received her first exposure to social reform as a teenage volunteer in Jane Addams's Hull House. Between 1890 to 1893, she attended the Chicago Art Institute, the Chicago School of Design, and the Chicago Business College. In 1897, she married John Hope, an educator, and they had two sons.

When her husband became the first black president of Morehouse College in Atlanta, Georgia, in 1906, she carved out her own niche as an instructor of physical education and arts and crafts for female students. In Atlanta, she helped open day-care centers for working-class children and was a founder of the Neighborhood Union, Atlanta's first female social welfare agency. For 25 years, she directed the agency, which provided medical, educational, recreational, and civic services for Atlanta's black community.

During World War I, she worked with the YWCA to provide better recreational and social services to black soldiers; because of her work, she was promoted to a national position within the YWCA. She also worked with Jessie Daniel Ames, a leader of the all-white Association of Southern Women for the Prevention of Lynching (ASWPL), to stop the lynching of southern blacks. And in Atlanta, she worked tirelessly to create better schools and medical and recreational services for the city's black citizens.

During the 1930s, she served as an assistant to Mary McLeod Bethune, director of the Negro Affairs Division of the National Youth Administration, and was first vice president of the Atlanta chapter of the National Association for the Advancement of Colored People (NAACP). An active clubwoman, Hope was affiliated with numerous black women's organizations, including the National Association of Colored Women's Clubs and the National Council of Negro Women.

FURTHER READING
Rouse, Jacqueline A. *Lugenia Burns Hope: Black Southern Reformer.* Athens: University of Georgia Press, 1989.

Hosmer, Harriet Goodhue

SCULPTOR

Born: October 9, 1830
Watertown, Massachusetts

Died: February 21, 1908
Watertown, Massachusetts

In an era when few women had the resources or the training to become professional artists, Harriet Hosmer achieved recognition as the first well-known female sculptor in America. After an active childhood spent mostly out of doors, she was sent by her father to a finishing school in Lenox, Massachusetts, to cultivate more traditional feminine traits. There she met the actress Fannie Kemble, who inspired her to become a sculptor.

Hosmer set up a studio at home and took private lessons in art technique. Her father, a physician, gave her some instruction in anatomy—a subject not commonly taught to women of her day—but she felt she needed more instruction. When no medical school in the East would admit her to anatomy classes because she was a woman, she moved to St. Louis, where she received additional private instruction.

In 1852, she felt ready to study in Rome, a mecca of great painting and sculpture. There she studied the work of Michelangelo and other masters. Her father helped her obtain private instruction with a well-known English sculptor, and within two years she was selling her work.

Hosmer's reputation quickly spread and she soon had commissions for work from English and American patrons. She created statues and busts as well as ornamental gates and fountains. Hosmer lived a charmed life; her work fulfilled her and she enjoyed the friendship of other artists and writers. The combination of personal drive, parental support, and an encouraging mentor enabled her to succeed where other aspiring female artists could not.

Around 1900, she returned to the United States. She spent her final years inventing and refining a perpetual motion machine powered by magnets.

PUBLICATION
Harriet Hosmer, Letters and Memories (1912)

FURTHER READING
Sherwood, Dolly. *Harriet Hosmer, American Sculptor, 1830–1908.* Columbia: University of Missouri Press, 1991.

Howe, Julia Ward

WOMEN'S CLUB AND SUFFRAGE LEADER

Born: May 27, 1819
New York, New York

Died: October 17, 1910
Newport, Rhode Island

Julia Ward Howe not only was author of the "Battle Hymn of the Republic," she was a dedicated club woman and a keen observer of American society. Born to affluence, she later decried the grasping materialism of the post–Civil War years. She was educated by private tutors and attended exclusive female academies. Early on, she showed a fondness for intellectual pursuits and published essays in scholarly journals.

In 1841, she married Samuel Gridley Howe, a Bostonian and director of the Perkins Institute for the Blind. Her marriage, however, was not happy; she never felt accepted by her husband or by the rest of Boston society. She retreated inward, studying foreign languages, religion, and philosophy, and also wrote poetry and drama.

During the Civil War, Howe volunteered for the women's auxiliary of the New England Sanitary Commission, a soldiers' relief organization. As she watched Union soldiers march off to battle in 1861, the words of a poem formed in her mind. Her verses were later set to the haunting strains of "John Brown's Body," and by 1864 Northerners had embraced the "Battle Hymn of the Republic" as their own, for it seemed to embody the ideals for which they were fighting.

In the years immediately following the war, Howe wrote essays and tried to launch a literary magazine, but the journal quickly went under. As the postwar women's rights movement regained momentum, she found her true work. In 1868, she joined Lucy Stone and others in founding the New England Woman Suffrage Association, and a year later she became a leader of the American Woman Suffrage Association (AWSA), one of the two competing factions in the national suffrage movement.

Suffrage work imbued her life with purpose and direction. She spoke at conventions and legislative hearings and helped direct state, regional, and national suffrage campaigns. She was also a guiding spirit behind the growing women's club movement; she helped to organize women's clubs across the country and presided over the New England Women's Club from 1871 until her death. In 1890, she helped establish the General Federation of Women's Clubs, a national network of local clubs, and later served as president of the Massachusetts Federation of Women's Clubs.

Beyond her club work, Howe lectured throughout the country on the need to reaffirm core American values during an age rife with greed and corruption. In 1908, she was the first woman elected to the American Academy of Arts and Letters—a resounding honor and belated acknowledgment of her contribution to her country's cultural life.

MAJOR PUBLICATIONS
Reminiscences (autobiography, 1900)
At Sunset (1910)
The Walk with God (1919)

FURTHER READING
Clifford, Deborah Pickman. *Mine Eyes Have Seen the Glory: A Biography of Julia Ward Howe.* Boston: Little, Brown, 1979.

Howland, Emily
EDUCATOR, SOCIAL REFORMER

Born: November 20, 1827
Cayuga County, New York

Died: June 29, 1929
Cayuga County, New York

In her later years, Emily Howland characterized herself as "a little girl who played too little and who thought too much." As an adult, however, she looked outward, as the nation plunged grimly toward war, to find purpose in her life. Born on a farm, she was raised in the Quaker tradition and drew much inspiration from her religious upbringing. She attended a dame school in a nearby town and spent two years at the Poplar Ridge Seminary in upstate New York.

Her mother's illness forced her to return home and assume household responsibilities—a task she was decidedly not suited for. "I am as a bell that cannot ring," she bemoaned to a friend. But she found an outlet by joining the abolition movement. In 1857, she journeyed to Washington, D.C., to fill in for Myrtilla Miner, the ailing headmistress of a school for African-American girls, and found her calling through teaching. During the Civil War, she taught and served as a nurse at several camps for former slaves in and around Washington. After the war, she helped to resettle ex-slaves on a piece of land that her father had bought in Virginia, and there she opened a school.

After her mother died, Howland became mistress of the family farm in New York State, a position she occupied with grace and generosity. She endowed a nearby Quaker school, provided interest-free loans to female college students, contributed money to more than 30 schools—mostly black—and staunchly supported the women's rights movement. She was a regular delegate and occasional speaker at conventions of the National American Woman Suffrage Association (NAWSA).

In later years, Emily Howland proudly looked back on her life. The words she chose for her epitaph were apt: "I strove to realize myself and to serve."

FURTHER READING
Breault, Judith Colucci. *The World of Emily Howland: Odyssey of a Humanitarian.* Millbrae, Calif.: Les Femmes Pub., 1976.

Howland, Marie Stevens Case

UTOPIAN REFORMER

Born: 1836 (exact date unknown)
Lebanon, New Hampshire

Died: 1921 (exact date unknown)
Fairhope, Alabama

Marie Howland bravely challenged traditional notions of home and family to give women greater freedom in their lives. She envisioned cooperative working and living arrangements in which women were no longer chained to household drudgery. Declaring that the "loss of respectability as defined by hypocrites and prudes" was women's first step toward liberation, she sought mightily to put these words into action.

She knew what it was like to earn her own living. After her father died, she went to work in the textile mills of Lowell, Massachusetts, where from dawn to dark she operated four looms at a time. After years of this exhausting labor, she moved to New York City and taught in a tenement district. She attended a teacher-training school at night, and by 1857 she had become a primary school principal.

That same year, she married Lyman W. Case, a lawyer whom she had met at The Club, a group of like-minded New Yorkers interested in new ideas. The Club drew feminists, anarchists, and others who espoused radical ideas. Howland and her husband joined a cooperative living arrangement called the Unitary Household.

When this communal household broke up during the Civil War, she traveled to France to study other forms of cooperative living. There she married Edward Howland, another resident of the Unitary Household who had gone to France. After returning to the United States in the late 1860s, Howland drafted detailed plans for a community composed of apartments situated around cooperative kitchens, laundry facilities, libraries, and recreational facilities. Each community also included a nursery for children. Howland wanted to liberate women from full-time domesticity in order to seek paid work and other endeavors. She also urged women to enjoy a variety of sexual relationships outside of marriage.

Her plan never came to fruition, and Howland, who had moved to a community of like-minded reformers in Mexico, gave up and returned to the United States. She settled in Alabama, where she quietly lived and worked as a librarian in yet another reform community. Her visionary ideas inspired other thinkers to devise new ways of integrating work and family life for women.

PUBLICATION
Papa's Own Girl (novel, 1874)

FURTHER READING
Hayden, Dolores. *The Grand Domestic Revolution.* Cambridge, Mass.: MIT Press, 1981.

Hunt, Harriot Kezia

PHYSICIAN, REFORMER

Born: November 9, 1805
Boston, Massachusetts

Died: January 2, 1875
Boston, Massachusetts

Harriot Hunt, who was twice barred from entering Harvard Medical School because she was a woman, studied medicine on her own and pioneered the field of preventive health care. She was educated in local dame schools, and her parents encouraged her to read widely and frame her own opinions. Like other educated young women, she opened her own school, but her professional life changed dramatically when her sister, Sarah, became seriously ill. Traditional treatments, such as blistering, leeches, prussic acid, and ointments proved fruitless, and Sarah's condition worsened—until she underwent nontraditional forms of treatment and made a stunning recovery.

Both Harriot and Sarah studied these new treatments, and in 1835 they opened their own practice. With their mother's steadfast encouragement, they gradually built up a successful practice, prescribing a commonsensical regimen of good nursing, a healthy diet, bathing, rest, exercise, and sanitation. In addition, Harriot examined possible connections between physical illness and emotional distress.

She also advocated health education and gave public lectures on physiology and hygiene in Boston's working-class neighborhoods. Early on, she joined the women's rights movement, and urged women to work for the abolition of slavery.

In 1847 and again in 1850, Hunt applied to Harvard's medical school but was rejected both times. Finally, in 1853, the Female Medical College of Philadelphia granted Hunt an honorary medical degree. For the rest of her life, Hunt vigorously worked for the advancement of women and progressive social change.

PUBLICATION
Glances and Glimpses (1856)

FURTHER READING
Abram, Ruth. *Send Us a Lady Physician: Women Doctors in America, 1835–1920.* New York: Norton, 1986.

Hunton, Addie W.
SUFFRAGIST, EDUCATOR, CLUBWOMAN,
WOMEN'S RIGHTS ACTIVIST

Born: July 11, 1875
Norfolk, Virginia

Died: June 21, 1943
Brooklyn, New York

Addie W. Hunton stood at the forefront of the twin struggles for women's rights and civil rights. She attended public schools in Norfolk, Virginia, and Boston, where she lived with relatives after her mother died, and attended Spencerian College of Commerce in Philadelphia. She graduated in 1889—the first black woman to graduate from that college—and taught school in Portsmouth, Virginia. A year later, she became principal of the State Normal and Agricultural College in Alabama.

In 1893, she married William Hunton, an official in the YMCA, and through him became active in the YWCA. She also served on the committee that created the National Association of Colored Women (NACW) in 1896, a national network of black women's clubs. As a national organizer for the NACW and, later, president of the New York State chapter, she promoted the strength and dignity of black womanhood and helped expand the club's activities and membership.

During World War I, Hunton joined a select group of African-American women to work among 200,000 black soldiers in France. She taught literacy courses, conducted a weekly discussion group on cultural and political topics, and helped establish libraries and a variety of educational, cultural, and religious activities.

After the war, she joined the Women's International League for Peace and Freedom, and served as president of the Circle for Peace and Foreign Relations. She supported women's suffrage and conducted voter-education programs throughout the South for the National Association for the Advancement of Colored People (NAACP) and NACW. After American women gained the right to vote, she and other black women urged leading white feminists to denounce discrimination against black women voters in the South, but their pleas went unheard. Hunton was a vice president and field secretary for the NAACP, and also belonged to numerous women's clubs.

PUBLICATIONS
"Negro Womanhood Defended," *Voice of the Negro* (July 1904): 280–82
Two Colored Women with the American Expeditionary Forces (written with Kathryn M. Johnson)

FURTHER READING
Davis, Elizabeth Lindsay. *Lifting As They Climb.* Washington, D.C.: National Association of Colored Women's Clubs, 1933.

Hurston, Zora Neale

WRITER, ANTHROPOLOGIST

Born: ca. January 7, 1901
Eatonville, Florida

Died: January 28, 1960
Ft. Pierce, Florida

Zora Neale Hurston, troubadour of rural black folk life, grew up in a home and community that inspired her creative yearnings. Her mother urged her to "jump at de sun," and her father, a Baptist preacher and mayor of their tiny all-black town, gave her the confidence to believe in herself. From the townspeople of Eatonville, she learned to appreciate the beauty and dignity of her rural roots.

After her mother died, Hurston said, her life became "a series of wanderings." At 14, she left home and signed on as a wardrobe girl with a traveling Gilbert and Sullivan theater troupe. Her education continued sporadically, first at Morgan Academy in Baltimore and then at Howard University in Washington. She also started to write, and her work caught the attention of leading writers of the Harlem Renaissance, a movement promoting black artistic expression.

In 1925, she moved to New York City and worked as secretary and chauffeur to novelist Fanny Hurst, who introduced her to other important literary figures. She also attended Barnard College, where she studied with the anthropologist Franz Boas. The first African-American student at Barnard, she graduated in 1928 with an A.B. in anthropology. She went on several expeditions to Florida, Alabama, Louisiana, and the Bahamas to record folktales, songs, prayers, sermons, and other cultural practices of rural blacks. In 1935, she published her findings in *Mules and Men.*

While continuing her anthropological fieldwork, Hurston used her gift of language and her interest in folklore to write fiction. Her finest novel, *Their Eyes Were Watching God* (1937), explored a woman's search for self-fulfillment. The main character, like Hurston herself, refused to settle for less than the chance to achieve her dreams.

During the 1930s, Hurston also worked briefly as a drama coach and editor for the Federal Writers' Project. But over the following two decades, her work was neglected and she fell into poverty. She worked as a domestic while she wrote and published a few magazine articles, and died alone and impoverished in a county welfare home. A new generation of readers in the 1970s rediscovered her writing, and Hurston is now celebrated for her vibrant evocation of rural black life.

MAJOR PUBLICATIONS
Jonah's Gourd Vine (1934)
Their Eyes Were Watching God (1937)
Dust Tracks on a Road (autobiography, 1942)

FURTHER READING
Howard, Lillie P. *Zora Neale Hurston.* Boston: Twayne, 1980.
Lyons, Mary E. *Sorrow's Kitchen: The Life and Folklore of Zora Neale Hurston.* New York: Scribners, 1990.
Walker, Alice. "In Search of Zora Neale Hurston," *Ms.* (March 1975).

Hutchinson, Anne

RELIGIOUS REBEL

Born: ca. 1591
Alford, Lincolnshire, England

Died: ca. August 1643
Pelham Bay Park, New York

Anne Hutchinson courageously spearheaded the first organized challenge to Puritan religious authority in the Massachusetts Bay Colony. Born in England, she was baptized into the Anglican church. But from her father, an Anglican clergyman who challenged certain church practices, she acquired an intimate knowledge of religious ideas as well as an independent mind.

In 1605, her family moved to London, where she remained until her marriage to William Hutchinson, a prosperous merchant, on August 9, 1612. Over the course of a long and loving marriage, they had 13 children and he supported her independent thinking on religious matters.

While still living in England, Anne Hutchinson embraced the controversial views of John Cotton, an Anglican minister who dismissed the importance of performing good works as a way to ensure religious salvation. Instead, he claimed that the presence of salvation was an inward experience—though he still insisted that followers try to act morally. Hutchinson carried his beliefs even further by maintaining that the gift of grace was entirely independent of human efforts to be moral and good—and was also beyond the authority of any religious leader to judge. Her heretical views challenged the accepted authority of church leaders.

In 1634, Hutchinson and her family followed Cotton to the New World. The Hutchinsons settled in Boston, the center of the Massachusetts Bay Colony, and William Hutchinson prospered as a cloth merchant while his wife continued to expound her unorthodox views. She preached first to women and then to larger meetings of men and women, held in her home twice a week. Some of Boston's most prominent citizens, including the colony's governor, endorsed her views.

By 1637, Anne Hutchinson commanded a strong following throughout the colony—one that challenged the authority of the established religious leadership. One Salem minister told her, "You have stept out of your place, you have rather been a Husband than a Wife and a preacher than a Hearer."

That same year, her opponents—followers of the established Puritan leadership—elected John Winthrop governor and managed to unseat some of her supporters in the colony's General Court. A few months later, the court put her on trial for "traducing the ministers and their ministry." With Cotton's assistance, she nearly cleared herself of all charges—until she claimed that she had received a direct communication from God—"an immediate voice"—that He would destroy her opponents. For this heretical claim of divine communion, the court banished her from the colony.

Hutchinson remained in the colony under detention until the spring thaw permitted safe travel. Boldly, she continued to challenge church teachings, and in March 1638 she was publicly tried for heresy. Though she hesitantly recanted, she was formally excommunicated from the Congregational church of the Boston Puritans.

A few days later, she and her children left Massachusetts for an island off of Rhode Island, where her husband and other followers had already settled. In 1642, after her husband died, Hutchinson and her six youngest children moved to the Dutch colony of New Netherland (now New York City). A year later, she and all but her youngest daughters were killed by Indians.

Though Anne Hutchinson displayed remarkable courage in challenging the Puritan establishment, she did not do so under the guise of religious freedom. She did not champion the right of others to hold beliefs different from her own; instead, she believed that her way was the right way. Nevertheless, by staunchly upholding her own religious beliefs, she struck the first blow for religious freedom in what later became the new American nation.

FURTHER READING
Ilgenfritz, Elizabeth. *Anne Hutchinson.* New York: Chelsea House, 1991.

Jackson, Helen Hunt

AUTHOR, CRUSADER FOR NATIVE AMERICAN RIGHTS

Born: October 15, 1830
Amherst, Massachusetts

Died: August 12, 1885
San Francisco, California

Though she was a native New Englander, Jackson's spiritual home was the Southwest, where she developed a deep respect for Native American cultural traditions. While living in Colorado, she was awakened to the injustices perpetrated against Native Americans and rose up to defend them.

After attending private female academies in and around Boston, she married Edward Bissell Hunt, an army engineer, and bore two sons. Years of travel followed because of her husband's career. Tragedy followed as well, for within 20 years she had lost her husband and both sons to fatal illness and accident. She wrote poetry to assuage her grief and was soon published in *The Nation* and other journals. She began to write essays as well, and her work appeared in the leading magazines of the day.

In 1875, she married William Sharpless Jackson, a banker in Colorado, and settled down to the work that defined the rest of her life. After years of indifference to reform causes, she was aroused to fight for better government treatment of American Indians. She appealed to the secretary of the interior and spent several months at the New York Public Library doing research. In 1881, she published *A Century of Dishonor,* a scathing indictment of governmental policy toward Indian tribes. At her own expense, she sent copies of her book, bound in blood-red covers, to numerous government officials, including every member of Congress.

In 1882, Jackson was commissioned by the U.S. Interior Department to investigate the needs of Native Americans living on the West Coast. She reported her findings the following year, but government officials ignored them. She decided to expose the ill treatment of Indians through fiction. In 1884, she published *Ramona,* a historical novel about a Native American woman in California. "I did not write *Ramona,*" she later declared. "It was written through me. My life-blood went into it—all I had thought, felt and suffered for five years on the Indian question." Though simplistic and sentimental, the novel focused public attention on the plight of Native Americans.

One year after the novel was published, Jackson died of cancer at age 54. Her final request was to be buried in Colorado, her spiritual and creative homeland.

MAJOR PUBLICATIONS
Verses (1870)
Bits of Travel (1872)
A Century of Dishonor (1881)
Ramona (1884)

FURTHER READING
Mathes, Valerie Sherer. *Helen Hunt Jackson and Her Indian Reform Legacy.* Austin: University of Texas Press, 1990.

Jacobi, Mary Corinna Putnam

PHYSICIAN

Born: August 31, 1842
London, England

Died: June 10, 1906
New York, New York

Mary Putnam Jacobi, a dedicated physician, fought for women's entry into the medical profession. Educated mainly by her mother, she briefly attended a private school in Yonkers, New York, and a public school in Manhattan. Early on, she aspired to a career in science, though she had shown a talent for writing and had even published an essay in the *Atlantic Monthly* when she was 17. She graduated from the New York College of Pharmacy in 1863 and received her medical degree in 1864 from the Female (later Woman's) Medical College of Pennsylvania.

After working at the New England Hospital for Women and Children in Boston, and also volunteering at Union army camps and hospitals during the Civil War, she sailed to France for advanced medical training. She was the first woman to enroll at the École de Medécine, and graduated with high honors in 1871. In her spare time, she also published articles in several general-interest magazines.

After returning to New York, she quickly became America's most well-known female physician. She published scores of medical articles, taught at the Woman's Medical College of the New York Infirmary for Women and Children, founded by Elizabeth Blackwell, and was consulting physician at several other hospitals, including Mount Sinai.

In 1873, she married Dr. Abraham Jacobi, a fellow physician who shared her passion for science. They had three children.

In later years, Jacobi campaigned for woman suffrage and for working women's advancement. She was a cofounder of the Working Women's Society in New York City, an organization that fought for better wages and job opportunities for working women. She was an exacting teacher with her female medical students and firmly believed in women's right to equal educational and employment opportunities.

PUBLICATION

Life and Letters of Mary Putnam Jacobi (1925)

FURTHER READING

Abram, Ruth. *Send Us a Lady Physician: Women Doctors in America, 1835–1920.* New York: Norton, 1986.

Jacobs, Harriet Ann

WRITER, CIVIL WAR NURSE

Born: 1813 (exact date unknown)
Edenton, North Carolina

Died: March 7, 1897
Cambridge, Massachusetts

Harriet Jacobs, an escaped slave, wrote *Incidents in the Life of a Slave Girl* (1861), a remarkable autobiography that chronicled her dreadful years of bondage. Writing under the pseudonym Linda Brent, Jacobs portrayed the unique oppression of female slaves—their sexual exploitation by white masters, the ordeal of coping with jealous mistresses, and the fear of being sold away from their own children. Though scholars at first dismissed Jacobs's book as fiction, it has since been proved factual, and from it come the details of her life.

Jacobs was born into slavery and was given to new owners when her mother died. Her new mistress, Margaret Horniblow, treated her well and taught her how to read, spell, and sew. When she died in 1825, the young slave, now 12, once again went to new owners—where her troubles began.

Over a 10-year period, her new master, Dr. James Norcom, made repeated sexual advances toward her. She managed to fend him off, and he retaliated by forbidding her to marry. To regain some control over her life, she became intimately involved with a young white lawyer, with whom she bore two children. Her master's harassment did not stop, however, and when he threatened to sell her away from her children, she escaped.

At first, she hid with sympathetic whites, then spent seven years in her grandmother's attic—"in a tiny crawlspace above a storeroom," according to her account. There she passed the time, reading, writing, and sewing.

Finally, she made her way to New York State,

where she worked as a nursemaid and joined the antislavery movement. She also worked on her autobiography and published it in installments in the *New York Tribune,* starting in 1855. After no book publisher would take it, a Boston printer published the book in 1861. In her preface, she said that she hoped to "arouse the women of the North to a realizing sense of the condition of two millions of women at the South, still in bondage, suffering what I suffered, and most of them far worse." Her book has proved to be a vital firsthand glimpse of the dreadful system of slavery.

During the Civil War, Jacobs worked as a nurse and teacher among freed slaves, and lived the remainder of her life in Washington, D.C.

PUBLICATION
Jean Fagan Yellin, ed. *Incidents in the Life of a Slave Girl, Written By Herself* (1987)

FURTHER READING
Yellin, Jean Fagan. *Women & Sisters.* New Haven: Yale University Press, 1989.

Jemison, Mary
INDIAN CAPTIVE

Born: 1743 (exact date unknown)
en route to United States from Ireland

Died: September 19, 1833
Buffalo Creek Reservation
(near Buffalo, New York)

Known as the "White Woman of the Genessee," Mary Jemison was captured by Indians and spent much of her remarkable life as a member of a Native American tribe. Born on ship during her family's voyage from Ireland to America, she enjoyed a quiet childhood on her family's farm near what is now Gettysburg, Pennsylvania. In 1758, during the French and Indian War, a raiding party of French soldiers and Shawnee Indians attacked her family's farmstead. The two eldest sons escaped, but Mary

and her parents and other siblings were captured. She, alone, was spared by her captors—and was witness to her family's death at the hands of their attackers.

A Seneca family adopted her and took her to their home on the Ohio River. Thus began her life as a Native American. For the rest of her life she straddled two cultures—Native American and the white Western culture of her youth. In 1760, she married a Delaware Indian. When he died, she married a Seneca warrior. In these two marriages, she bore eight children.

Over the years, she acquired land and livestock and enjoyed a modest affluence. Like Native American women, she planted, cultivated, and harvested her crops; tended her cattle; ground cornmeal and prepared foodstuffs; and raised her children. In 1817, she became a naturalized U.S. citizen but continued to practice many Native American customs. She felt at home with both Native Americans and Anglos. Although she converted to Christianity, she spent the remainder of her life on an Indian reservation.

Jewett, Sarah Orne
WRITER

Born: September 3, 1849
South Berwick, Maine

Died: June 24, 1909
South Berwick, Maine

Sarah Orne Jewett, a well-respected author and a native New Englander, chronicled the land and people of her beloved state of Maine. In her writings, she celebrated the quiet strength and dignity of rural people, striving to capture on paper the texture of deeply rooted lives. Her stories evoked the land and illuminated as well the gentle character of the people who lived there.

Despite bouts of ill health during her childhood, she attended a private school for girls, and graduated in 1865 from the Berwick Academy. But her real education came from accompanying her father, a country physician, on his rounds. She absorbed the landscape as well as his stories about the region and its inhabitants, and her own stories became a loving extension of the tales they had shared during their carriage rides to visit his patients.

As a young woman, she lived in Boston and traveled repeatedly throughout Europe, but in her imagination and writing she continually returned to her homeland of coastal Maine. In 1877, she published her first book, *Deephaven,* a collection of sketches that had earlier appeared in *Atlantic Monthly.* Other collections of stories followed, culminating in her most famous novel, *The Country of the Pointed Firs* (1896). Like her other stories, it was set in coastal Maine and portrayed the rough-hewn inhabitants of a small coastal town.

Jewett followed a style of writing known as "local color"—the attempt to re-create the texture, telling details, even the dialect of a particular region. In later years, she described what she had hoped to achieve in her writing: "I determined to teach the world that country people were not the awkward, ignorant set those persons seemed to think. I wanted the world to know their grand, simple lives."

But Jewett's own outlook and interests extended far beyond Maine to encompass philosophical and literary traditions in Europe. In later years, she gave Willa Cather, a fellow artist, this sound advice: "One day you will write about your own country. In the meantime, get all you can. One must know the world so well before one can know the parish."

Jewett died from a stroke and was buried in her beloved hometown, where she had spent so many nourishing years.

MAJOR PUBLICATIONS
Deephaven (1877)
A Country Doctor (1884)
A Marsh Island (1885)
A White Heron, and Other Stories (1886)
The Country of the Pointed Firs (1896)
The Tory Lover (1901)

FURTHER READING
Blanchard, Paula. *Sarah Orne Jewett: Her World and Her Work.* Reading, Mass.: Addison-Wesley, 1994.
Silverthorne, Elizabeth. *A Writer's Life.* Woodstock, N.Y.: Overlook Press, 1993.

Jones, Mary Harris
LABOR ACTIVIST

Born: May 1, 1830
Cork, Ireland

Died: November 30, 1930
Silver Spring, Maryland

Known as "Mother Jones" because of her lifelong crusade against child labor, Mary Harris Jones emigrated to North America as a child and attended public and normal schools in Toronto, Canada. She first taught in a convent in Monroe, Michigan, but soon moved to Chicago to start a dressmaking business. She married in 1861 but lost her husband and four young children six years later in an epidemic of yellow fever.

Resuming her dressmaking business, she gradually became more aware of economic inequity by sewing clothes for wealthy families. She began attending meetings of the Knights of Labor and was soon drawn into the struggle to improve working conditions.

By 1880, she had fully committed herself to the labor movement. With no home and few possessions, she took to the road, journeying from one industrial area to another, wherever she could organize a strike or educate workers in their rights. As an organizer for the United Mine Workers union, she traveled thousands of miles to organize strikes in West Virginia, Colorado, Arizona, and elsewhere. She also marched with striking machinists for the Southern Pacific Railroad.

Mother Jones's most dramatic march came in 1903, when she led a group of striking children from the textile mills of Kensington, Pennsylvania, to Oyster Bay, New York, the summer home of U.S. President Theodore Roosevelt, to protest child labor. She was imprisoned at least three times, testified before numerous congressional committees, and helped organize the Social Democratic party in 1898 and the radical Industrial Workers of the World (IWW) in 1905. She also worked in textile mills and factories to get a firsthand view of the danger and drudgery of the work.

Uncompromising and thoroughly devoted to workers and their children, she was still organizing strikes into her 90s. Her popularity and trust among workers was such that, according to one observer, "she could keep the strikers loyal month after month on empty stomachs and behind prison bars."

PUBLICATION
The Autobiography of Mother Jones (1925)

FURTHER READING
Atkinson, Linda. *Mother Jones: The Most Dangerous Woman in America.* New York: Crown, 1978.

Kearney, Belle

MISSISSIPPI TEMPERANCE REFORMER, SUFFRAGIST, STATE LEGISLATOR

Born: March 6, 1863
Madison County, Mississippi

Died: February 27, 1939
Jackson, Mississippi

Belle Kearney was one of scores of southern women who found greater opportunities for personal and professional advancement after the devastation of Civil War. Her family, once prosperous planters, sank into poverty after the war, and she was forced to drop out of school because her father could no longer afford the tuition. Instead, she opened a school in her bedroom. Despite her father's opposition, she went on to teach in a public school.

At 26, she joined the Woman's Christian Tem-

perance Union (WCTU) and promptly worked her way up the ranks of national leadership. She was elected president of the Mississippi WCTU in 1895 and was soon traveling across the country to lecture on temperance. From 1904 to 1905, she also lectured throughout Europe. Perhaps because of her own experiences, she regarded the WCTU as the liberator of southern women.

She also joined the woman suffrage movement, serving as president of the Mississippi Woman Suffrage Association from 1906 to 1908. Her support for female enfranchisement, however, was not a commitment to justice for all; she viewed suffrage as a tool, in her words, to "retain the supremacy of the white race over the African."

During World War I, Kearney lectured on behalf of American involvement in the war. In 1922, after winning a state senatorial race in Mississippi, she became the first woman to serve in a southern state legislature. Until she retired, she worked actively for the Democratic party.

PUBLICATIONS
A Slaveholder's Daughter (autobiography, 1900)
Conqueror or Conquered? (1921)

Kelley, Florence

SOCIAL REFORMER, SECRETARY OF THE NATIONAL CONSUMERS' LEAGUE

Born: September 12, 1859
Philadelphia, Pennsylvania

Died: February 17, 1932
Philadelphia, Pennsylvania

Florence Kelley was part of a remarkable circle of women who, during the Progressive era, accomplished an impressive array of social and economic reforms. Raised in an enlightened antislavery family, she was educated at home and in private academies and Quaker schools. With her father's encouragement, she enrolled at Cornell University in 1876. Health problems curtailed her studies for a time, and she did not graduate until 1882. She pursued graduate work at the University of Zurich, the only European university to admit women, where she joined the Socialist movement in Europe.

After marrying a Russian medical student, who was also a Socialist, she returned to the United States and plunged into working for the Socialist Labor party. When her marriage failed, she moved to Chicago with her three children and became a resident counselor at Jane Addams's Hull House. Now her true work began.

Kelley soon focused her energies on combating child labor, and in 1892 she investigated employment conditions among child workers in the garment industry. Her findings led to passage of a state law prohibiting child labor and regulating women's working hours. She continued to investigate factories and even earned a law degree in 1894 from Northwestern University Law School to help prosecute offenders of the law.

Her interest in child labor and factory inspection thrust her into the top ranks of the National Consumers' League, a nationwide organization that used consumer pressure to force factories and department stores to improve working conditions. As general secretary of the organization from 1899 to the end of her life, she traveled throughout the country, lecturing and organizing 60 local groups in 20 states. But her main goal was the abolition of child labor and the creation of protective legislation for women workers, and to this end she helped draft passage of several state minimum-wage laws.

Kelley was also a founding member of the National Association for the Advancement of Colored People, and worked for international peace during World War I. In 1912, she joined the Socialist party and worked for woman suffrage as a vice president of the National American Woman Suffrage Association (NAWSA). She was also a member of the executive committee of the National Woman's party (NWP) throughout the 1910s. Although she did not achieve her final goal—a Constitutional amendment

prohibiting child labor—for more than 30 years she had played a vital role in lessening factory exploitation for thousands of workers.

PUBLICATIONS
Kathryn K. Sklar, ed. *Notes of Sixty Years: The Autobiography of Florence Kelley* (1985)
Our Toiling Children (pamphlet, 1889)
Some Ethical Gains Through Legislation (1905)

FURTHER READING
Goldmark, Josephine C. *Impatient Crusader: Florence Kelley's Life Story.* 1953. Reprint. Westport, Conn.: Greenwood Press, 1976.

King, Mary

ACTIVIST AND GOVERNMENT OFFICIAL

Born: ca. 1942
New York, New York

Mary King and Casey Hayden, two white women working for civil rights during the 1960s, challenged male domination in the civil rights movement—and helped spark the resurgence of the women's movement. King, the daughter of a Methodist minister and a nurse, grew up, as she said, with "a strong sense of public service and working to make my life count for something."

While attending Ohio Wesleyan University, she joined the Student Nonviolent Coordinating Committee (SNCC), the student-led branch of the civil rights movement. Like fellow SNCC workers, she endured many hardships, including spending Christmas 1963 in an Atlanta jail for protesting a black friend's right to eat at a segregated coffee shop. She served as communications coordinator for SNCC in Georgia and Mississippi, and in 1964 she helped organize the Mississippi Freedom Democratic party to put civil rights on the agenda of the 1964 Democratic Presidential convention.

In that year as well, she and Casey Hayden, having tired of the condescending, second-class treatment endured by all women workers in SNCC, published a position paper on women's roles in the movement; in clear, reasoned, and persuasive language, they denounced men's arrogance toward women within SNCC and the lack of leadership roles available to women. "[The] assumption of male superiority [among SNCC men is] as widespread and deep-rooted and as crippling to women as the assumptions of white supremacy are to the Negro." Regardless of the hard work that women performed for SNCC, they had little voice or power within the organization. "This is no more a man's world than it is a white world," the paper concluded, and it was time for men in SNCC to realize that.

In 1965 she and Hayden refined their position in another paper, "Sex and Caste: A Kind of Memo." They made a direct link between women and blacks, claiming that both were "caught up in a common law caste system." They went on to urge women to organize on their own behalf: "Perhaps we can start to talk to each other more openly than in the past and create a community of support for each other so we can deal with ourselves and others with integrity and therefore keep working." What they suggested was the forerunner of a consciousness-raising group—a collective way to explore the issues and concerns they shared as women in order to act together to achieve sexual equality. The civil rights movement had imbued King and Hayden with a vision of freedom, equality, and community, which they used to challenge men's domination within the movement as well as within American society. This early demand for gender equality, inspired by frontline work for racial equality, was one of the gears that set in motion a powerful women's movement—a movement that continues to this day.

After leaving the civil rights movement, King went on to become one of President Jimmy Carter's chief advisers on women's issues and health care. She also operated her own management consulting firm, providing research and technical assistance for setting up health-care and community-action services. In later years she served as executive director of the U.S.-Iraq Business Forum, a consortium of over 40 American corporations with business interests in Iraq. In this position, she worked to expand the market for American goods and services to less-developed nations.

Her first marriage, to another civil rights activist, ended in divorce in the mid-1960s, and she later married Peter Bourne, a psychiatrist and mental health administrator.

PUBLICATION
Freedom Song: A Personal Story of the 1960s Civil Rights Movement (1987)

FURTHER READING
Evans, Sarah. *Personal Politics: The Roots of Women's Liberation in the Civil Rights Movement and the New Left.* New York: Knopf, 1979.

Knight, Sarah Kemble

COLONIAL DIARIST

Born: April 19, 1666
Boston, Massachusetts

Died: September 25, 1727
New London, Connecticut

At a time when few women could read or write, Sarah Kemble Knight wrote an engaging diary that later became a classic account of travel and manners in New England. Knight, the daughter of a Boston merchant and landowner, had managed to acquire the rudiments of an education. Sometime before her father's death in 1689, she married Richard Knight, a bricklayer and carver. On May 8, 1689, she gave birth to a daughter, Elizabeth.

In October 1704, Sarah Knight embarked on a journey from Boston to New Haven, Connecticut. She kept a journal of her travels, humorously describing the travails of journeying on bumpy roads and overflowing rivers. She also described the various lodgings and fellow travelers she met along the way. Her jottings revealed a keen eye and ear for local color and dialect. She returned home the following March.

In 1706, she was apparently widowed, for after that her husband's name disappears from the records. She supported herself and her daughter by running a boardinghouse and shop.

When her daughter married and moved to New London, Connecticut, Sarah Knight followed her. There she opened a shop, bought land, and established an inn. Besides possessing a keen wit, she was clearly entrepreneurial. She died in 1727, and her diary remained in private hands until it was published in 1825. It is an early and revealing glimpse into life and customs in 18th-century New England.

PUBLICATION
The Journal of Madam Knight (1825)

La Follette, Suzanne

WRITER AND EDITOR

Born: ca. 1894
Washington State

Died: April 23, 1983
Stanford, California

Feminist writer Suzanne La Follette came from a long line of progressive politicians. Her cousin, Senator Robert M. La Follette of Wisconsin, initiated numerous reforms to make state government more accountable to its constituents, protect citizens from corrupt business practices, and protect working people's welfare and rights. But Suzanne La Follette's political views were harder to pinpoint—and were also more conservative than those of her famous cousin. As she declared in 1964, "I haven't moved. The world has moved to the left of me."

She was born on a large wheat ranch in Washington State and lived for many years in New York City, where she wrote and edited such magazines as the *Nation,* the *American Mercury,* and the *Freeman,* a weekly journal of opinion that she helped establish in 1930. She founded the *Freeman,* she said, because "newspapers have no policy of enlighten-

ment anymore and do not inform the public what is actually going on." She also wrote several books, including *Concerning Women* (1926), in which she advocated equal rights for women.

Early on, she participated in anti-Soviet causes and served as secretary to a national commission that investigated the Soviet trial of Communist leader Leon Trotsky; the commission concluded that he had been framed by the Soviet government. In 1964, she ran unsuccessfully on the Conservative party ticket for a seat in the U.S. House of Representatives from the 19th District of New York City.

PUBLICATIONS
Concerning Women (1926)
Art in America (1929)

Lamallice, Madame

INDIAN INTERPRETER

Born: date and location unknown

Died: date and location unknown

Madame Lamallice was a Chipewyan Indian who married the brigade guide at Fort Wedderborn, the command post of the Hudson Bay fur-trading company on Lake Athabasca, Canada. She managed to carve out a position of power for herself as the post's only interpreter with nearby tribes. She also exerted considerable influence with these tribes—to the extent that her demands for extra rations and favored treatment were met by the company's leaders to prevent her from leaving.

She was apparently quite shrewd and resourceful. In the spring of 1821, when food was scarce and the fort's other residents were forced to fend for themselves, Lamallice had managed to stock up an abundance of fish for her family. She also peddled food and other goods on the side for profit—an act that did not sit well with the company's officers. When they threatened to stop her activities, she in turn threatened to turn the Indians against the company. Though her influence soon waned, she exemplified the visible role that some Native American women played in facilitating relations between their people and white settlers.

FURTHER READING
Sylvia Van Kirk. *Many Tender Ties: Women in Fur-Trade Society, 1670–1870*. Norman: University of Oklahoma Press, 1980.

Lange, Dorothea
PHOTOGRAPHER

Born: May 26, 1895
Hoboken, New Jersey

Died: October 11, 1965
San Francisco, California

Dorothea Lange is best known for her stark, poignant photographs of Americans ravaged by the Great Depression. As a child, she preferred to wander the streets of New York City observing the details and drama of urban life rather than attend school. In 1913, she graduated from a public high school and, though she already knew she wanted to be a photographer, she attended a teacher-training school in New York. But she also enrolled in a photography class at Columbia University and apprenticed herself to two photographers.

In 1919, after moving to San Francisco, Lange opened her own photography studio. For the next 10 years, she took portraits of San Francisco's wealthy merchant class—until the overwhelming suffering wrought by the Depression stirred her to use her camera to document the plight of newly impoverished Americans.

During the 1930s, she worked for state and federal agencies to record in visual image the plight of migrant workers in California, the Midwest, and the South. She collaborated with Paul S. Taylor, a social economist, on reports about living conditions among migrant workers. Their shocking findings galvanized the Roosevelt administration to build better sanitary facilities for migrant workers.

In 1941, Lange shifted her lens to another dispossessed group—Japanese Americans, who were forced by the federal government to resettle in internment camps. Although she was hired by the government to record the process, Lange's sympathies clearly lay with the Japanese Americans. During World War II, she worked for the Office of War Information, and many of her photographs appeared in military magazines. In later years, she took photographs of current events for *Life* magazine and other publications.

PUBLISHED COLLECTIONS OF HER PHOTOGRAPHS:
An American Exodus: A Record of Human Erosion (1939)
Dorothea Lange (1966)
Dorothea Lange Looks at the American Country Woman (1967)
Celebrating a Collection: The Work of Dorothea Lange (1978)

FURTHER READING
Meltzer, Milton. *Dorothea Lange: A Photographer's Life*. New York: Farrar, Straus and Giroux, 1978.

Lathrop, Julia Clifford
SOCIAL WORKER AND REFORMER

Born: June 29, 1858
Rockford, Illinois

Died: April 15, 1932
Rockford, Illinois

Julia Lathrop dedicated her life to improving institutional care for the mentally ill and for juvenile delinquents. She came from a family that championed social reform. Both of her parents avidly supported women's rights, and her father advocated civil service reform and better treatment for the insane.

After high school, she attended Rockford Seminary for one year and graduated from Vassar College in 1880. For the next 10 years, she worked as a secretary in her father's law office and read law on her own.

In 1890, she joined Jane Addams's talented circle of women at Hull House. From there, she rose rapidly in the field of public welfare, serving first as a volunteer investigator of relief applicants in the neighborhood surrounding Hull House. In her investigations, she exposed the notorious conditions of county infirmaries and insane asylums.

In 1893, she was appointed to the Illinois Board of Charities and investigated each of the 102 county farms and almshouses in the state. In her findings, she urged separate facilities each for delinquent children and the mentally ill, and protested the inadequate training of attendants and other employees of these institutions.

To rectify this problem, in 1903 she helped organize the social work curriculum for the Chicago School of Civics and Philanthropy, and she created the first training program in occupational therapy for attendants of the insane. Along with Jane Addams and others, she also helped obtain legislation to establish the first juvenile court and detention home in the United States.

Her work on behalf of child welfare and juvenile delinquents earned her the first directorship of the Children's Bureau, a newly created federal agency. Under her leadership, the bureau investigated infant mortality, nutrition, juvenile delinquency, out-of-wedlock births, mental illness, and child labor. Lathrop's tireless crusade for more government spending on behalf of infant and maternal health care helped secure passage of the Shepard-Towner Act in 1921, the first legislation to provide federal money to states for this purpose.

After retiring from the Children's Bureau in 1921, Lathrop lectured on social work issues, served as president of the Illinois League of Women Voters, investigated conditions on Ellis Island as part of a Presidential commission, and worked on international child welfare concerns for the League of Nations. Until her death, she lobbied to secure a re-

duced sentence for a 17-year-old boy committed to death row.

FURTHER READING
Addams, Jane. *My Friend, Julia Lathrop* . New York: Macmillan, 1935. Reprint. Arno Press, 1974.

Lee, Ann

RELIGIOUS LEADER

Born: February 29, 1736
Manchester, England

Died: September 8, 1784
Niskeyuna, New York

Ann Lee was the founder of the United Society of Believers in Christ's Second Coming, a utopian religious group known as the Shakers. The Shakers' belief in the sanctity of hard work, disciplined living, and frugality; their vision of social equality; and their regard for individual conscience continue to resonate deeply among Americans seeking a more spiritual way of life.

The young Ann Lee had no formal schooling and spent her early teens working in a Manchester textile mill. She matured into a deeply introspective, religious young woman, and joined a new religious sect—an offshoot of Quakerism—known for its unusual form of worship. Singing, dancing, shouting, shaking, and speaking in tongues—these were the hallmarks of their exuberant spiritual expressiveness—and they became known as the Shakers. Beyond believing that the second coming of Christ was imminent, they had no defined creed.

After enduring a loveless marriage and the traumatic deaths of all four of her children in infancy, Ann Lee retreated into a harsh regimen of no sleep and meager amounts of food; she was doing penance for what she believed to be her "violation of God's laws." Spiritually reborn, she rose to a leadership position in the Shakers, and offered this new

Shaker precept: a belief that the "cohabitation of the sexes" was sinful, indeed the root of all evil.

In 1772 and 1773, Lee and her followers were arrested for violating the Sabbath. In prison, she had a vision that she had been called to complete Christ's work, and when she was released the Shakers decided that their new eden lay in the New World.

In 1774, Ann Lee and seven disciples sailed for America and landed in New York. Two years later, after raising the necessary funds, they established a Shaker colony in Niskeyuna (later Watervliet), near Albany, New York. As word spread of the millennium brought by "the woman clothed with the sun," followers flocked to Niskeyuna, and the Shaker community grew rapidly. When Lee, known as "Mother" to her followers, died in 1784, 11 Shaker communities were in various stages of planning.

Lee's teachings were simple—confession and celibacy led to salvation—and very progressive. Like the Quakers, she opposed slavery, weapons, and oaths, and she envisioned a society in which all members enjoyed equal rights regardless of sex, race, or social class.

FURTHER READING

Campion, Nardi Reeder. *Ann the Word: The Life of Mother Ann Lee, the Founder of the Shakers.* Boston: Little, Brown, 1976.

———. *Mother Ann Lee: Morning Star of the Shakers.* Hanover, N.H.: University Press of New England, 1990.

Leopold, Alice

SECRETARY OF STATE OF CONNECTICUT

Born: ca. 1909
Scranton, Pennsylvania

Alice Leopold's career exemplified women's voluntarism during World War II—a voluntarism that led to new paths to power. She graduated from Goucher College in 1927 and married Joseph Leopold four years later. While caring for two young children, she established her own toy manufacturing business in 1946.

During World War II, she took charge of two war bond drives and a fund-raising campaign for the Red Cross. She also served as president of the League of Women Voters. These highly visible volunteer positions opened new professional opportunities for her: In 1949, she was elected to the Connecticut Assembly and wrote the state's equal pay and minimum wage bills, which both passed. In 1950, she was elected the state's secretary of state, and three years later President Dwight Eisenhower appointed her director of the Women's Bureau and also assistant to the secretary of labor. She was charged with the task of planning and executing a program to benefit women workers. Though she initially supported an Equal Rights Amendment for women, she reversed her position.

While she favored sex-based legislation protecting women's wages and working hours, Leopold believed that women must determine for themselves their goals in life. She once said: "A woman has to know what she wants to do, why she wants to do it, and how to proceed. If she believes in herself sufficiently, she will not be easily discouraged."

Levertov, Denise

POET, AUTHOR

Born: October 24, 1923
Essex, England

Denise Levertov is a major 20th-century poet. Born in England, she was educated mostly at home by her mother and private tutors. She served as a nurse during World War II and, in 1947, married writer Mitchell Goodman. They emigrated to the United States a year later, and she became a naturalized citizen in 1955.

Levertov began writing poetry as a teenager and published her first book of verse in her early 20s. She has taught at several American universities and has served as poetry editor for *The Nation*. She was an early critic of the Vietnam War and continues to combine writing with social activism, especially in favor of nuclear disarmament.

Levertov's poetry ranges from the intensely personal to the consciously political—from the details of domestic life to the global concerns of war and environmental destruction. Her poetic voice also ranges from gentle humor to irony and outrage. She has received numerous awards for her poetry.

MAJOR PUBLICATIONS
Jacob's Ladder (1961)
Footprints (1972)
The Poet in the World (1973)
The Freeing of the Dust (1975)
Collected Earlier Poems, 1940–1960 (1979)
Light Up the Cave (1981)
A Door in the Hive (1989)

FURTHER READING
Marten, Harry. *Understanding Denise Levertov.* Columbia: University of South Carolina Press, 1988.

Lewis, Edmonia

SCULPTOR

Born: July 4, 1845
Greenbush, New York

Died: after 1909 (exact date unknown)
Rome, Italy

Born to a Chippewa Indian mother and an African-American father, Edmonia Lewis, a sculptor, found artistic inspiration from her unique birthright. She was educated at Oberlin College and settled in Boston. A statue of Benjamin Franklin in front of Boston's city hall may have inspired her to become a sculptor. Her first work was a medallion of the fiery abolitionist John Brown. Indeed, many

of her works celebrate the emancipation of American slaves. Her sculpture *Hagar in the Wilderness,* completed in 1868, was a dramatic portrayal of a biblical slave. Lewis chose to render Hagar, she claimed, because of a "strong sympathy for all women who have struggled and suffered."

Lewis soon gained professional acclaim, and by the early 1870s she was doing commissioned work for patrons in England and Italy. Diminutive and vivacious, she sported a crimson working cap and aroused interest and admiration among all who knew her.

At the Centennial Exposition of 1876 in Philadelphia, Pennsylvania, Lewis exhibited six sculptures, including a large marble rendering entitled *The Death of Cleopatra.* As new trends in sculpture emerged, her popularity declined. She is best remembered for her desire to capture in stone the sufferings of her people and the joy of freedom.

Lockwood, Belva

LAWYER, WOMEN'S RIGHTS ADVOCATE

Born: October 24, 1830
Royalton, Niagara County, New York

Died: May 19, 1917
Washington, D.C.

Belva Lockwood fought for women's right to practice law. Born on a farm, she attended country schools and at age 15 became a teacher. After her first marriage ended with her husband's death, she resumed teaching and also returned to school. She attended a local academy and then enrolled at Genesee College in Lima, New York (later Syracuse University). She graduated in 1857 and became preceptress of a school in New York before opening her own coeducational school in Washington, D.C.

In 1868, she married Ezekiel Lockwood, a dentist. She had studied law on her own for several years and now wished to go to law school—but was repeatedly turned down because she was a woman. Finally, in 1871, she was admitted to National University Law School in Washington, D.C. Two years later, she was admitted to the Washington bar. After lobbying for a bill to permit women lawyers to argue before the Supreme Court, in 1879 she became the first female lawyer to do so. In turn, she sponsored the first African-American lawyer to appear before the high court.

Lockwood, a staunch feminist, worked actively for women's rights. In 1867, she helped organize the Universal Franchise Association, a Washington, D.C., suffrage organization. Equal pay for equal work, better protection of married women's property rights, and woman suffrage were among the goals she fought for. She supported Victoria Woodhull's campaign for U.S. President in 1872, then ran for President herself as a candidate of the National Equal Rights party in 1884 and 1888. Her platform included equal rights for all, temperance, standardized marriage and divorce laws, and universal peace. Although she lost both times, she received a substantial vote.

In later years, she devoted her energies to world peace. She attended international peace conferences as a delegate of the Universal Peace Union and even served on the nominating committee for the Nobel Peace Prize. Meanwhile, she also conducted a successful law practice. In 1906, she won a major settlement for the Eastern Cherokee Indians against the U.S. government. Determined and energetic, Lockwood challenged professional barriers against women lawyers and personally helped many aspiring female attorneys.

PUBLICATIONS
"My Efforts to Become a Lawyer," *Lippincott's* (February 1888)
"How I Ran for the Presidency," *National Magazine* (March 1903)

FURTHER READING
Fox, Mary Virginia. *Lady for the Defense: A Biography of Belva Lockwood.* New York: Harcourt Brace Jovanovich, 1975.

Loos, Anita
AUTHOR, SCREENWRITER

Born: April 26, 1893
Sissons, California

Died: August 18, 1981
New York, New York

Witty and tart-tongued Anita Loos symbolized the insouciant flapper of the 1920s. A highly successful screenwriter, she bobbed her hair, raised her hemline, and claimed for all women the right to live as they pleased. A former child actress with a traveling theater company, she was mostly self-educated, with scattered periods of formal schooling. Revealing a gift for light humor, she became, at 13, a correspondent for the *New York Morning Telegraph,* a theatrical newspaper. From there, she turned to writing movie scenarios. By 1915, she had sold more than 100 scripts to D. W. Griffith, a leading film producer.

In 1915, she married Frank Palmer, Jr.—only to desert him after one night to set out for Hollywood. Her light comic style gradually caught on, and she worked with such famous movie stars as Douglas Fairbanks, Lillian Gish, and Mary Pickford. In the 1920s, she moved to New York, where she befriended critic H. L. Mencken and other celebrated literary figures. Satirizing his interest in beautiful but mindless blonde women, she wrote a fictional piece for *Harper's Bazaar,* which she expanded and published in 1925 as the best-selling *Gentlemen Prefer Blondes.* The novel became a hit Broadway musical and, later, the inspiration for two movies. Among Loos's fans were British Prime Minister Winston Churchill, the Italian dictator Benito Mussolini, and the acclaimed author James Joyce.

For more than three decades, Loos reigned as one of Hollywood's most successful screenwriters. She wrote the screenplay for the movie *Gigi,* a charming tale about the romance between a sophisticated older man and a naive young woman, and continued to write for Broadway. Loos was part of the generation of actors and writers who turned Hollywood into a mecca for the rich and famous. As a member of this new elite, she helped create the modern culture of celebrity and typified the woman who expressed newfound social freedom not in working for political change but in pursuing personal fulfillment.

MAJOR PUBLICATIONS
Cast of Thousands (1977)
Gentlemen Prefer Blondes (1925)
A Girl Like I (autobiography, 1972)
Kiss Hollywood Good-By (autobiography, 1974)
Ray Pierre Corsini, ed. *Fate Keeps on Happening* (an anthology of her writings, 1984)

FURTHER READING
Carey, Gary. *Anita Loos: A Biography*. New York: Knopf, 1988.

Lyon, Mary
EDUCATOR

Born: February 28, 1797
Buckland, Massachusetts

Died: March 5, 1849
South Hadley, Massachusetts

Mary Lyon was a true pioneer. Driven by a desire to improve women's education, she established Mount Holyoke Seminary—now the oldest four-year women's college in the United States. Lyon was born in the gentle hill country of western Massachusetts and enjoyed a childhood securely nestled in the rustic surroundings and loving attention of family and kin. She attended local schools and began teaching in 1814. She also took additional courses, alternating her teaching with full-time study.

In 1824, she opened a girls' school in her hometown of Buckland. The school thrived in part because of Lyon's innovative teaching methods. Instead of relying on rote memorization—the main

method of teaching at that time—she urged students to read current periodicals and express their ideas in discussion groups.

During the summer of 1833, Lyon traveled throughout New York, Pennsylvania, and Michigan. She visited schools and colleges, and a plan gradually took shape in her mind to open a "residential seminary to be founded and sustained by the Christian public." She raised the first thousand dollars from women in and around Ipswich, Massachusetts, and in 1837 Mount Holyoke Female Seminary opened its newly varnished doors to 80 female students, age 17 and older.

Lyon was principal of the seminary and also a teacher there. She believed that women were uniquely suited to be teachers in the home and at school, and she groomed her students for teaching careers. The school followed a rigorous curriculum—covering academic as well as more traditional female subjects such as elocution and needlework—and students also attended lectures by visiting professors. Among Mount Holyoke's distinguished alumnae was the poet Emily Dickinson. Lyon herself spent the remainder of her life at Mount Holyoke.

PUBLICATION
A Missionary Offering (1843)

FURTHER READING
Green, Elizabeth Alden. *Mary Lyon and the Beginnings of Mount Holyoke*. Hanover, N.H.: University Press of New England, 1979.

Mahoney, Mary Eliza
NURSE

Born: April 16, 1845
Roxbury, Massachusetts

Died: January 4, 1926
Boston, Massachusetts

Mary Eliza Mahoney was the first African-American nurse to graduate from an accredited nursing program. Little information exists about her early years, but she was apparently employed as a domestic at the New England Hospital for Women and Children in Boston before enrolling in its nursing school.

In 1878, Mahoney was among 40 applicants for 18 openings in the nursing school. Sixteen months later, only four students, including Mahoney, graduated from the program. Besides lectures and demonstrations, the training included 12 months of rotation among the hospital's medical, surgical, and maternity wards and 4 months of private-duty nursing in a private home.

Mahoney's sterling academic record helped to break down prejudices against other African-American female nursing students. Over the next 20 years, four other black nurses graduated from the nursing program at the New England Hospital for Women and Children.

Mahoney went on to pursue a career as a private-duty nurse. She was widely respected for her calm manner and quiet efficiency. Actively involved in African-American medical groups in Boston, she joined the National Association of Colored Graduate Nurses and was said to be one of the first women to vote in Boston after American women were enfranchised.

FURTHER READING

Miller, Helen S. *Mary Eliza Mahoney, 1845–1926: America's First Black Professional Nurse: A Historical Perspective.* Atlanta, Ga.: Wright Publishing Company, 1986.

Mann, Mary Tyler Peabody

EDUCATOR

Born: November 16, 1806
Cambridge, Massachusetts

Died: February 11, 1887
Boston, Massachusetts

Mary Peabody Mann was the middle sister in a family of talented women. Her older sister, Elizabeth Peabody, was a well-known educational reformer, and Sophia Peabody Hawthorne, her younger sister, was an accomplished artist. All three sisters grew up in a family that valued learning—an "atmosphere of education," as Mary later recalled.

Though she had little formal schooling, Mary was sufficiently learned to teach school in Maine and then in Brookline, Massachusetts, where she helped Elizabeth conduct a dame school.

Mary left teaching for a time to work as a governess in Cuba, then returned to the United States and resumed teaching. In 1843, she married Horace Mann, a lawyer and educator whom she had met many years before. When her husband, after having been elected to Congress, challenged the Compromise of 1850, which protected slavery in some new states entering the Union, Mary staunchly supported him.

In 1853, Mary and Horace Mann and their three children moved to Yellow Springs, Ohio, where Mann had accepted the presidency of Antioch College, a new coeducational school. Mary served as an unofficial dean of women.

After her husband's death, she returned to Massachusetts and conducted an infant school in Concord. In 1860, her sister Elizabeth established the first formal kindergarten in the United States, and Mary assisted her at the school, which was located in Boston. Both sisters held highly progressive ideas about educating young children; they believed that children were innately good and wise and must be awakened to their inborn talents with gentle urging rather than harsh discipline.

In later years, Mary and Elizabeth sponsored the work of Sarah Winnemucca, a Native American activist fighting for her people's rights. Mary also wrote a novel about her experiences in Cuba.

PUBLICATIONS

Christianity in the Kitchen: A Physiological Cookbook (1857)
Juanita: A Romance of Real Life in Cuba Fifty Years Ago (1887)

FURTHER READING

Tharp, Louise. *The Peabody Sisters of Salem*. 1950. Reprint. Boston: Little, Brown, 1988.

Mansfield, Arabella Babb

PROFESSOR, LAWYER

Born: May 23, 1846
Sperry Station, Iowa

Died: August 2, 1911
Aurora, Illinois

Although Arabella Babb Mansfield was the first woman to be admitted to the American bar, she never practiced law. Instead, she became a college professor. As a child, she attended local public schools and in 1863 enrolled at the Methodist-affiliated Iowa Wesleyan University in Mount Pleasant, Iowa. She graduated in 1866 and taught first at Simpson College in Indianola, Iowa, then at Wesleyan.

In 1868, she married John Melvin Mansfield, a fellow professor, and together they studied law. A year later they both applied for admission to the Iowa bar. Fortunately, the presiding judge, Francis Springer, and his two associates supported the women's rights movement; construing the words "men" and "male" in the state's laws to include women as well, Springer immediately admitted Arabella Mansfield to the bar.

But she chose not to practice law and continued teaching history and English at Wesleyan University. She received a master's degree in 1870 and an LL.B. degree in 1872. A year later, she studied at the Sorbonne in Paris, then moved to Greencastle, Indiana, where she and her husband both accepted faculty appointments at Indiana Asbury University (later Purdue). There she taught history, esthetics, and music and also served as dean of the schools of art and music. She also gave Sunday afternoon lectures in art, literature, history, and religion.

Although Mansfield clearly supported a woman's right to equal educational and employment opportunities, her involvement in the organized women's rights movement was limited. From 1870 to 1872, she helped organize the Iowa Woman Suffrage Society and served as its recording secretary.

Matthews, Victoria Earle

SOCIAL REFORMER, CLUBWOMAN, AUTHOR

May 27, 1861
Fort Valley, Georgia

Died: March 10, 1907
New York, New York

Victoria Earle Matthews was a prime mover in the African-American clubwomen's movement of the late 19th century. Born into slavery, she was raised in her former master's household after the Civil War. In 1873, she and her mother and sister moved to New York City. She attended public school, but soon had to drop out and work as a domestic. She read on her own and seized every opportunity she could for intellectual and cultural improvement.

After marrying William Matthews, a coachman, in 1879, she began writing articles for the *New York Times* and other local newspapers and magazines. Most of her articles dealt with nostalgic childhood memories.

But her chief interest was clubwork, not a literary career. In 1896, she helped to organize the National Association of Colored Women, a powerhouse network of black women's clubs. Matthews worked for the association and lectured on race pride and African-American women's community roles. She urged blacks to preserve their history by collecting and compiling the writings of famous black men and women.

Concerned about a rising rate of prostitution among young black women, she shifted her interests once again to investigate the causes and solutions to this troubling problem. In 1897, she founded the White Rose Industrial Organization in New York

City and helped establish a working girls' home for young black women new to the city. There they learned employment skills—mostly in domestic servantry—and received shelter and counseling. The home also ran a social center for neighborhood black women and offered classes for children. White Rose agents patrolled piers in New York City and elsewhere to ensure that no one took advantage of young black women travelers—especially traffickers in prostitution.

Matthews, once described by a reporter as "a missionary, a teacher, a preacher, a Sister of Mercy, all in one," died before she could give the full measure of her abilities and commitment to her race. But she left a sterling record of service and accomplishment in striving to improve the quality of African-American life.

PUBLICATION
Aunt Lindy (1893)

McCarthy, Mary
AUTHOR

Born: June 21, 1912
Seattle, Washington

Died: October 25, 1989
New York, New York

For nearly half a century, Mary McCarthy graced American letters with her witty, erudite, and often sardonic voice. Like Margaret Fuller, a 19th-century intellectual, McCarthy was wholly engaged by ideas, and her intellectual interests embraced literature, history, politics, and social reform.

Her emergence as an accomplished author did not come easily. After a childhood spent in the care of abusive relatives whom, she later recalled, had "a positive gift for turning everything sour and ugly," she went to live with her grandparents. They sent her to exclusive private schools and later to Vassar College.

McCarthy graduated Phi Beta Kappa from Vassar in 1933 and worked as a book reviewer for the *New Republic* and *The Nation.* She also worked for a New York publishing house. From 1937 to 1948, she wrote for *Partisan Review,* a lively journal of arts and politics that embodied the zeal and optimism of left-wing political activism during the 1930s. Through her work, she joined a prominent circle of radical intellectuals who made New York City the nerve center of the nation's political and intellectual life. Her novel *The Group* (1963) captured the exhilaration, hopes, ideals, and ultimately the disillusionment of a life immersed in ideas and ideologies.

In the 1940s, McCarthy taught at Bard and Sarah Lawrence colleges. Married four times, she did not begin writing until her second husband, the critic Edmund Wilson, urged her to try her hand at fiction. A week after they were married, she wrote her first short story, launching a long and distinguished writing career. McCarthy has been called a "first lady of letters" with a "subversive soul."

MAJOR PUBLICATIONS
The Company She Keeps (1942)
The Groves of Academe (1952)
A Charmed Life (1955)
Memories of a Catholic Girlhood (autobiography; 1957)
On the Contrary: Articles of Belief, 1946–1961 (1961)
The Group (1963)
How I Grew (1987)

FURTHER READING
Brightman, Carol. *Writing Dangerously: Mary McCarthy and Her World.* New York: Clarkson Potter, 1992.
Gelderman, Carol W. *Mary McCarthy: A Life.* New York: St. Martin's, 1988.

McCauley, Mary Ludwig Hays
REVOLUTIONARY WAR SOLDIER AND PATRIOT

Born: ca. October 13, 1754
near Trenton, New Jersey

Died: January 22, 1832
Carlisle, Pennsylvania

If eyewitness accounts are trustworthy, Mary McCauley was the first woman soldier in American history. The daughter of a German immigrant, she worked as a domestic before marrying John Caspar Hays, a barber.

When the American Revolution began, John Hays enlisted as a gunner in a Pennsylvania unit. At first, Mary remained behind; then, like other wives, she followed her husband to his camp, eager to be closer to him. There, she worked as a laundress, cook, and nurse.

During a battle on June 28, 1778, she earned the nickname "Molly Pitcher" by carrying water in a pail or pitcher from a nearby spring to the thirsty soldiers. When her husband was wounded in battle, the story goes, she took his place and loaded his cannon for the rest of the battle. Her quick actions helped her unit defeat their British foes.

When the Revolution ended, Mary and her husband returned home. After his death, she married John McCauley, also a former soldier. She lived quietly and worked as a charwoman. In 1822, the Pennsylvania state legislature awarded her an annual pension of $40 for her "services" during the American Revolution. Acquaintances characterized her as rough-hewn—she supposedly "swore like a trooper" and chewed tobacco—but generous in spirit and courage.

Mead, Margaret
ANTHROPOLOGIST

Born: December 16, 1901
Philadelphia, Pennsylvania

Died: November 15, 1978
New York, New York

Margaret Mead was a world-famous anthropologist who pioneered the study of cultural change. In her fieldwork and writing, she studied the ways in which members of a particular culture are socialized and the shaping of gender roles within a culture. She was especially interested in the process of cultural change and continuity, and hoped to apply her insights from studying primitive cultures to the concerns of modern-day technological societies.

Although her father was a scholar who taught her the value of facts, it was Mead's paternal grandmother who most influenced her early life by educating her at home. After graduating from high school, Mead enrolled at Depauw University but transferred to Barnard College, where she studied with the renowned anthropologist Franz Boas. She received her A.B. in 1923 and embarked upon graduate work at Columbia University. While working on her Ph.D., Mead began her fieldwork in Samoa. Five years later, she published her first and most popular book, *Coming of Age in Samoa,* a study of adolescence in Samoan society.

In 1929, Mead received her Ph.D. and became curator of ethnology at the American Museum of Natural History in New York City, a position she held for the rest of her life. She also taught at several universities and did fieldwork in the Admiralty Islands, New Guinea, Bali, and elsewhere. She received numerous honorary degrees and awards and served as president of the American Anthropological Association in 1960.

Beyond her research, Mead made two important contributions to the study of anthropology: She helped to attract popular interest to this sometimes arcane subject by writing for the general public, and she integrated the study of culture and personality into anthropology. In the process, she demonstrated that patterns of personality and behavior, such as gender roles, are not biologically determined but instead are shaped by a specific cultural setting. She was a brilliant scholar and an insatiably curious student of the world.

MAJOR PUBLICATIONS

Coming of Age in Samoa (1928)
Sex and Temperament in Three Primitive Societies
(1935)
*Culture and Commitment: A Study of the Generation
Gap* (1970)
Blackberry Winter (autobiography, 1972)
World Enough: Rethinking the Future (1975)

FURTHER READING

Bateson, Mary Catherine. *With a Daughter's Eye.*
New York: Morrow, 1984.
Ludel, Jacqueline. *Margaret Mead.* New York:
Franklin Watts, 1983.
Ziesk, Edra. *Margaret Mead: Anthropologist.* New
York: Chelsea House, 1990.

Meyer, Agnes Elizabeth Ernst

JOURNALIST, WRITER, PHILANTHROPIST

Born: January 2, 1887
New York, New York

Died: September 1, 1970
Mt. Kisco, New York

Agnes Ernst Meyer grew up in an immigrant
German home that instilled a love of Western
culture. She attended public schools in Pelham Heights, New York, where her family
moved when she was a child. Over her father's
objections she enrolled in Barnard College, supporting herself through scholarships and part-
time jobs.

After graduation, she became one of the first
women reporters at the *New York Sun*. A year later,
she left the newspaper to study at the Sorbonne in
Paris. But she found cafe and literary life more interesting than academia, and spent her time with
illustrious artists such as the photographer Edward
Steichen, the writer Gertrude Stein, and the sculptor Auguste Rodin.

She returned to the United States, and in 1910
married Eugene Meyer, a financier and multimil-
lionaire. His wealth afforded her a life of travel,
dabbling in the arts, and leisurely study. When

he purchased the *Washington Post* in 1933, she
resumed her career as a reporter and wrote a number of articles for the *Post*, including a series criticizing President Franklin Roosevelt's New Deal
policies.

World War II turned Meyer's politics and interests around. As she toured the homefront in England and the United States, she discovered a profound need for social reform. She wrote articles de-
tailing the failure of American communities to provide for the educational and housing needs of their
growing populations; after the war, she exposed the
unfair treatment of veterans and migrant workers
and wrote about discrimination and overcrowded
schools. Educational reform remained a special concern of hers.

Although she urged American women to choose
a life of domesticity, she did not follow her own
advice. Instead, she played a vital role in expanding
social programs to meet community needs. She lobbied for greater governmental support for education, and urged the establishment of what came to
be the Department of Health, Education, and Welfare in the federal government. She also supported
expanded social security, better health services, and
integration and more economic opportunities for
American blacks.

In addition, she organized and funded a variety of philanthropic projects, mostly aimed at improving public education, and served on government commissions studying health, education, the
status of women, and employment. President
Lyndon B. Johnson credited her with exerting
great influence on his educational policies. Meyer
received 14 honorary degrees and numerous
awards for her work on behalf of education and
social welfare.

PUBLICATIONS

Journey Through Chaos (collection of her articles
written during World War II, 1944)
Out of These Roots (autobiography, 1953)
Education for a New Morality (a collection of
lectures, 1957)

Millay, Edna St. Vincent

POET

Born: February 22, 1892
Rockland, Maine

Died: October 19, 1950
Austerlitz, New York

The bard of the Jazz Age, Edna St. Vincent Millay expressed in her poetry the hopes, dreams, and vitality of a new generation. Her poetry captured the aspirations of the New Woman of the 1920s who yearned for a full life. "My candle burns at both ends," Millay wrote. "It will not last the night / But ah, my foes, and oh, my friends / It gives a lovely light."

After an unsettled childhood, scarred by poverty and divorce, she graduated from high school in Maine and went to Vassar College, determined to become a poet. Her mother had first encouraged her artistic ambitions by teaching her to write poetry. Upon graduation, Millay moved to New York's Greenwich Village, the heart of bohemian life in the city. She joined the Provincetown Players, an avant-garde theater troupe, and wrote poetry as well as magazine articles.

In 1921, she became a foreign correspondent for *Vanity Fair,* a trendy journal of art and gossip. For the next two years, her candle did indeed burn at both ends as she traveled throughout France, Italy, and Austria writing poetry and essays. She returned to the United States to become one of the country's most popular poets. Readers found in her poetry a glimpse of the footloose, bohemian life they wanted for themselves. In 1923, her *Ballad of the Harp-Weaver,* a collection of her poetry, received the Pulitzer Prize.

That same year, Millay married Eugen Jan Boissevain, a businessman who urged her to dedicate herself to her vocation. They divided their time between upstate New York and a brownstone in Greenwich Village. It seemed that Millay had the best of both worlds—the high-spirited excitement of Greenwich Village and the quiet beauty of rural life.

As the nation plummeted into depression and then war, Millay shifted her poetic themes to suit the times. But she was unable to make compelling poetry out of social concerns, and her work went mostly unnoticed. Her poetry had spoken to an earlier era, one more youthful, adventurous, and innocent. She was not able to stir a readership toughened by hard times. During World War II, she worked for the Red Cross and the Writers' War Board, and enjoyed an active public life. But her final years were isolated and lonely, as her poetry became eclipsed by a new generation of poets.

PUBLICATION
Edna St. Vincent Millay: Selected Poems, The Centenary Edition (1991)

FURTHER READING
Cheney, Anne. *Millay in Greenwich Village.* Mobile: University of Alabama Press, 1975.
Daffron, Carolyn. *Edna St. Vincent Millay: Poet.* New York, Chelsea House: 1990.
Sheean, Vincent. *The Indigo Bunting: A Memoir of Edna St. Vincent Millay.* New York: Schocken, 1973.

Mitchell, Maria

ASTRONOMER

Born: August 1, 1818
Nantucket, Massachusetts

Died: June 28, 1889
Lynn, Massachusetts

Perhaps America's most renowned woman scientist in the 19th century, Maria Mitchell learned astronomy while helping her father chart the position of stars for Nantucket's whaling industry. She attended local dame schools, as well as the school her father opened, and established her own school for young women in Nantucket.

But astronomy was her first love, and in 1847 she discovered a new comet, which was later named after her. Her discovery earned her Denmark's gold medal and the distinction of being the first woman elected to the American Academy of Arts and Sciences in Boston. Two years later, in 1850, she was elected to the American Association for the Advancement of Science.

In 1865, Maria Mitchell was appointed head of the astronomy department at newly opened Vassar College—though she herself had never attended college. She proved to be one of the most untraditional teachers there, refusing to grade her students or require attendance. "I mourn over any loss of individuality," she explained.

At Vassar, she continued doing research and also served as a mentor for women students, especially those who wanted to pursue a scientific career. In 1873, she helped found the Association for the Advancement of Women, and urged an end to all barriers against women's advancement in the sciences. In 1869, she was elected to the American Philosophical Society in recognition of her keen mind and broad accomplishments.

Monroe, Marilyn

ACTRESS

Born: June 1, 1926
Los Angeles, California

Died: August 5, 1962
Los Angeles, California

Born Norma Jean Baker, Marilyn Monroe overcame a childhood spent in foster homes and orphanages to become the nation's premier sex symbol. But her life, while exciting and glamorous on the surface, was filled with the pressures and personal conflicts brought on by fame.

She dropped out of high school in Los Angeles to marry an aircraft factory worker. During World War II, while he was away at sea on a merchant freighter, she went to work in a factory in Van Nuys, California, assembling military aircraft. There she was chosen as a model for an article on women workers—and her film career was launched.

A modeling agency signed her up, and soon she was posing for magazine covers and calendars. With her shapely, full-chested figure, high cheekbones, porcelain-clear skin, and curly, blond hair, she was at once sexy and innocent looking.

In 1946, she took a screen test for Twentieth-Century Fox and signed a film contract. She also changed her name to Marilyn Monroe. Her first roles were bit parts, but she gradually achieved more visible roles. She soon developed a persona as a "blonde bombshell"—a sexy, gorgeous woman who was more beauty than brains.

By the mid-1950s, Marilyn Monroe was Hollywood's reigning sex queen and movie star—though she portrayed a limited range of characters. She tried to inject greater emotional depth into her roles, and she showed a real talent for comedy. But she was unable to break out of the gilded cage into which Hollywood had locked her. This pressure to maintain an image of allure, along with three failed marriages and several affairs, no doubt contributed to her growing emotional instability. During 1961, she was briefly hospitalized after a mental breakdown. She returned to work, but her behavior continued to be erratic. In August 1962, she died from an overdose of sleeping pills in her home in Los Angeles.

MAJOR FILMS:
The Asphalt Jungle (1950)
All About Eve (1950)
The Seven-Year Itch (1954)
Bus Stop (1956)
Some Like It Hot (1959)

FURTHER READING
Spoto, Donald. *Marilyn Monroe: The Biography.* New York: HarperCollins, 1993.
Steinem, Gloria. *Marilyn.* New York: Henry Holt, 1986.

Moody, Helen Wills

TENNIS PLAYER

Born: October 6, 1905
Centerville, California

One of the first women to gain international acclaim as a tennis champion, Helen Wills Moody began playing tennis as a child. Her father, a physician, taught her the game, and at age 17 she won the American singles title.

From 1926 to 1938, she played in major tournaments at Wimbledon, England; Forest Hills, New York; and Paris—and captured 31 titles. She achieved a world record for both men's and women's tennis by winning eight singles tournaments at Wimbledon.

In 1929, she married Fred Moody, and for the next nine years she combined marriage and professional tennis. After defeating Helen Jacobs, a long-standing competitor at Wimbledon in 1938, she retired from professional tennis and took up painting. In 1958, Moody was inducted into the International Tennis Hall of Fame.

Moreno, Luisa

LABOR ORGANIZER

Born: (dates unknown)
Guatemala

Luisa Moreno was a leader in the United Cannery, Agricultural, Packing and Allied Workers of America, a union within the Congress of Industrial Organizations (CIO). She was also a principal organizer in the Congreso de Pueblos que Habla Espanola (National Congress of Spanish-Speaking People).

A former correspondent for a Guatemalan newspaper, Moreno immigrated to the United States in 1928 and went to work in a garment factory in Spanish Harlem. The harsh working conditions there appalled her and, after joining a left-wing Latino organization, she decided to become a labor organizer. She organized Puerto Rican women garment workers in Spanish Harlem, and in 1935 she became a professional organizer for the American Federation of Labor (AFL).

Moreno left the AFL when it took a strong anti-Communist stand, and joined the CIO. She helped organize unions in cigar factories in New York City, Philadelphia, and Pennsylvania, then focused her efforts on helping Mexican pecan shellers in Texas. She organized the first Congress of Spanish-Speaking People to bring together all Spanish-speaking workers in the United States. During the anti-Communist hysteria that swept the United States after World War II, the U.S. government deported her on grounds that she was an agitator.

FURTHER READING
Ruiz, Vicki. *Cannery Women, Cannery Lives.* Albuquerque: University of New Mexico Press, 1987.

Morris, Margaret

QUAKER NURSE

Born: 1737
exact date and birthplace unknown

Died: 1816
exact date and place of death unknown

Although she sympathized with the cause of the American Revolution, Margaret Morris, a widow who lived in Burlington, New Jersey, bravely hid a British soldier in her cellar. Her quick actions saved the soldier's life when American troops came looking for him.

But Morris clearly supported the cause of the American Revolution. She referred to Washington's army as "hers" and provided food and shelter to

American soldiers. After Washington's forces defeated the British at the Battle of Trenton on December 26, 1776, she fed and housed the victorious, but hungry and weary, soldiers in a nearby empty house.

Later that spring, she nursed several soldiers and their wives, who were living temporarily at the governor's mansion. Morris was one of scores of patriotic American women who extended services to American troops out of concern for the young, bedraggled men—"pritty innocent looking lads," as she wrote in her diary—as well as their mothers who had relinquished them to battle.

Mott, Lucretia Coffin

QUAKER MINISTER, ABOLITIONIST, WOMEN'S
RIGHTS ADVOCATE

Born: January 3, 1793
Nantucket, Massachusetts

Died: November 11, 1880
near Philadelphia, Pennsylvania

For more than half a century, Lucretia Mott was a voice of liberation—for enslaved African Americans, for women seeking equality, and for religious and political freedom. Born into a Quaker seafaring community, in which women were accustomed to speaking their minds and fending for themselves while their husbands were away on whaling or trading expeditions, Lucretia Mott came of age among many strong and independent women. She attended both public and Quaker schools and, at 15, became an assistant teacher.

In 1811, she married James Mott. They had six children and were truly partners in marriage. James Mott proved to be his wife's greatest booster as she became more politically active. He assisted her and heartily endorsed the causes that she championed.

In 1821, Lucretia Mott became a Quaker minister and quickly embroiled herself in the clash between Quakers who espoused more traditional and authoritarian ideas and those who advocated more equality between the sexes within the church. Mott and her husband cast their support with the latter group, and Mott continued to evolve in her religious thinking. She had a remarkable capacity to embrace new, more enlightened ideas.

As her thinking became more independent, her opposition to slavery strengthened. After meeting William Lloyd Garrison, the radical abolitionist who called for the immediate emancipation of all slaves, in 1833 she helped form the Philadelphia Female Antislavery Society. She also joined the American Antislavery Society when it finally accepted female members. Her continued support for Garrison's radical views, as well as her willingness to work with non-Quakers, aroused the disapproval of more conservative Quakers. But Mott, who by now was accustomed to facing down vicious antiabolitionist mobs, was thoroughly unmoved by their opposition.

From championing abolition and social and political equality for American blacks, Mott took but a short step to help launch the organized women's rights movement. In 1848, she and Elizabeth Cady Stanton, along with three other women, organized the Seneca Falls convention, the birthplace of the American women's rights movement. Mott delivered the opening and closing speeches and played a leading role in getting the "Declaration of Sentiments," a list of demands for women's social and political equality, passed.

From then on, she fought for women's rights as well as abolition. After the Civil War, she campaigned for both female and African-American suffrage and worked to provide assistance and schooling for former slaves. She also raised money for the establishment of Swarthmore, a Quaker college.

In 1866, she was elected president of the American Equal Rights Association, the first organization dedicated to achieving American women's rights, and presided over a critical and stormy period in the American women's rights movement. Until her death, she crusaded for the causes dearest to her heart—the elevation of African Americans into full American citizenship and the end of sexual inequality. Beneath her gentle demeanor lay a fiercely independent and broadly humane spirit. Deeply respected by all who knew her, she was an accomplished reformer and a towering human being.

FURTHER READING
Bacon, Margaret. *Valiant Friend: The Life of Lucretia Mott.* New York: Walker, 1980.

Murray, Judith Sargent

AUTHOR, FEMINIST

Born: May 1, 1751
Gloucester, Massachusetts

Died: July 6, 1820
Natchez, Mississippi

Long before the organized women's rights movement began, Judith Sargent Murray decried women's unequal social and political status. During and after the Revolutionary War, she publicly urged women to claim their equal rights. Murray was the daughter of a wealthy shipowner and merchant. Early on, she displayed a love of learning and a quick intelligence, and attended her brother's tutorial lessons. Later he helped her continue her studies.

The opportunity to receive an education not readily available to other young women inspired her to advocate equal educational opportunities for both men and women. After her first marriage in 1769, she aspired to write poetry, but found the essay form more to her liking.

As the American colonies lurched toward war with England, all the talk of liberty and equality inspired Murray to question women's unequal social and political status. In 1779, she wrote an essay endorsing better educational opportunities for women. Six years later, she published another essay, entitled "Desultory Thoughts upon the Utility of Encourag-

ing a Degree of Self-Complacency, Especially in Female Bosoms." In this piece, she cautioned women not to rush into marriage merely to avoid the social stigma of spinsterhood. Instead, she wanted women to get an education that would prepare them for earning their own livelihood. She urged women to marry only when they had met a suitable mate and, after marriage, to assist their husbands in their work. That way, women would be able to support themselves and their children if their husbands became incapacitated or died.

Murray's first marriage ended with her husband's death in 1786, and she remarried two years later. Although she bore two children, one of whom died in infancy, she devoted more of her time to her writing and soon published a monthly column in the *Massachusetts Magazine* called "The Gleaner." Under the byline "Mr. Vigillus," she held forth on a variety of topics—religious, political, educational, and social. Highly popular, she also wrote about women's status, urging that "'the Rights of Women' begin to be understood." Among those rights she singled out greater educational and employment opportunities. "Yes, ye lordly, ye haughty sex," she addressed men, "our souls are by nature equal to yours . . . we are not fallen lower than yourselves."

PUBLICATION
The Gleaners (reissued 1992 by Union College Press, Schenectady, N.Y.)

Murray, Pauli

LAWYER, AUTHOR, EDUCATOR, RELIGIOUS
LEADER, CIVIL RIGHTS ACTIVIST, FEMINIST

Born: November 20, 1910
Baltimore, Maryland

Died: July 1, 1985
Pittsburgh, Pennsylvania

Pauli Murray was a 20th-century Renaissance woman—a person of astonishingly diverse interests and accomplishments. Her genealogy spanned the American mosaic—black, white, and Cherokee Indian; slave, free black, and white planter class.

She graduated from a public high school in Durham, North Carolina, where she went to live when her parents died. After working a year to save up tuition, she entered Hunter College in New York City and graduated in 1933 with a major in English and a minor in history. She was one of only 4 black students in a class of 247 women.

During the 1930s, she worked for the Works Progress Administration (WPA) as a reading teacher in the New York City public school system. But writing was always her first love. At age 15 she had published her first novel, *The Angel of the Desert,* in serial form in a black-owned newspaper. She continued to write while she taught and soon came to know the writers and poets of the Harlem Renaissance.

In the fall of 1941, hoping to become a civil rights lawyer, she enrolled at Howard University Law School. As a law student, she organized and led demonstrations to desegregate restaurants in Washington, D.C. She also joined the Congress of Racial Equality (CORE) and worked with the National Association for the Advancement of Colored People (NAACP). In 1944, she won a Rosenwald Fellowship for graduate law study at Harvard University— but the law school rejected her because she was a woman.

After receiving her law degree, she practiced law in California and New York. She rose rapidly to the top of her profession, and in 1951 she published a landmark study of civil rights law, *States' Laws on Race and Color,* which U.S. Supreme Court Justice Thurgood Marshall called "the Bible" for civil rights lawyers.

In 1966, Murray found a new focus for her commitment to social justice—the reborn women's movement. She spoke to Betty Friedan of her desire to form a national civil rights organization for women, and in the fall of 1966 she became one of 32 founding mothers of the National Organization for Women (NOW).

She served in a variety of high-level professional and administrative positions, and then shifted her interests once again—to spiritual concerns. At the age of 63, she decided to become a minister and enrolled at the General Theological Seminary. She was the only black woman and the oldest student. Three years later, she received a master's of divinity degree and in 1977 was ordained an Episcopal priest—the first black woman to achieve that status. While continuing to write, she served parishes in North Carolina, Washington, D.C., Virginia, and Maryland. Murray was possessed of a prodigious intellect and a restless, searching spirit. Throughout her life, she sought new ways to work for social equality and a better life for all.

MAJOR PUBLICATIONS
Proud Shoes: The Story of an American Family (1956, reissued 1978)
Song in a Weary Throat: An American Pilgrimage (1987)

Nash, Diane

CIVIL RIGHTS ACTIVIST, EDUCATOR

Born: 1938 (exact date unknown)
Chicago, Illinois

Diane Nash, risked her life for integration and equality during the civil rights battles of the 1960s. Born in Chicago, Nash had never experienced segregation until she went South. She was profoundly affected by the discrimination she witnessed as a student at Fisk University in Nashville, Tennessee. There she joined other African-American students from Fisk and nearby colleges to protest Nashville's segregated stores and restaurants. Without using force or fighting back, they boycotted stores and sat at segregated lunch counters, where they were harassed and even physically harmed.

Nash soon became an unofficial leader of the first group of students to employ this new nonviolent technique. She endured racial slurs and threats, and quickly learned the true meaning of courage: "I found beautiful things in people," she said later, "who would care enough about other people to put their bodies between another person and danger."

Nash, now a convert to nonviolent protest, soon became a leading strategist and coordinator of the growing civil rights movement. She went to jail repeatedly, even when she was pregnant, and dropped out of college to work as a salaried field worker for the Student Nonviolent Coordinating Committee (SNCC). She helped orchestrate the Freedom Rides, in which blacks and whites rode buses together through the Deep South to integrate interstate public bus transportation, and she helped organize voter registration drives among southern blacks— who had been denied their constitutional right to vote.

In 1962, Nash went to work for the Southern Christian Leadership Conference (SCLC), an organization established by the Reverend Martin Luther King, Jr. During this time, she married James Bevel, another civil rights activist, and they worked together for the SCLC.

During the late 1960s, Nash joined the organized student protest against the Vietnam War. In later years, she taught school in Chicago and lectured around the country on women's rights and the civil rights movement.

PUBLICATION

"Inside the Sit-ins and Freedom Rides: Testimony of a Southern Student," in Mathew H. Ahmann, ed. *The New Negro*. Biblo & Tannen, 1969.

FURTHER READING

Branch, Taylor. *Parting the Waters: America in the King Years, 1954–63.* New York: Simon & Schuster, 1988.

Giddings, Paula. *When and Where I Enter: The Impact of Black Women on Race and Sex in America.* New York: Bantam, 1984.

Hampton, Henry and Steve Fayer. *Voices of Freedom: An Oral History of the Civil Rights Movement from the 1950s Through the 1980s.* New York: Bantam , 1990.

Powledge, Fred. *Free at Last? The Civil Rights Movement and the People Who Made It.* Boston: Little, Brown, 1991.

Nestor, Agnes
TRADE UNION LEADER

Born: June 24, 1880
Grand Rapids, Michigan

Died: December 28, 1948
Chicago, Illinois

Trade unionist Agnes Nestor resolved to work for labor reform because of the hardships that she and her parents had endured as factory workers. At an early age, she went to work in a glove factory, putting in an average of 60 hours a week. After enduring years of harsh, exploitive treatment on the job, she led her fellow glovemakers out on strike. Ten days later, their list of demands was met. These included raises for lower-paid workers, a union shop, and an end to the practice of charging workers for use of the machines.

Nestor became president of her own local and a delegate and officer of the International Glove Makers Union. She helped form a glovemaker's cooperative and also served as director of research and education for the union.

But she made her greatest contribution to trade unionism through her work for the Women's Trade Union League (WTUL). As president of the Chicago branch and a member of the national league's executive board, she helped organize strikes and union drives among garment workers, waitresses, nurses, and teachers. She also lobbied for protective legislation for women and children, and was primarily responsible for the passage of an eight-hour workday bill in 1937.

She also worked for a guaranteed minimum wage for women, the abolition of child labor, the establishment of a Women's Bureau in the Department of Labor, health-care programs for pregnant women and infants, and woman suffrage. In addition, she served on numerous state and federal commissions pertaining to labor and employment. In all of these activities, Nestor played a vital role in improving wages, working conditions, and the quality of life for thousands of workers.

PUBLICATION
Woman's Labor Leader (autobiography, 1954)

Norton, Eleanor Holmes

LAWYER, GOVERNMENT OFFICIAL, POLITICIAN, EDUCATOR

Born: April 8, 1938
Washington, D.C.

Eleanor Holmes Norton has spent her life fighting to protect the rights of others. Raised by parents who worked as public servants and who believed in the value of a good education, she attended public schools before enrolling at Antioch College in Yellow Springs, Ohio. After graduating, she earned a master's degree in American Studies in 1963 and a law degree in 1964.

One year later, she married Edward Norton, a fellow lawyer. Her career path was set when she joined the American Civil Liberties Union (ACLU) as assistant legal director. During her tenure, she defended Vietnam war protestors, civil rights activists, feminists—and Governor George Wallace, a staunch segregationist who had tried to prevent black students from attending the University of Alabama. Norton believed that Wallace's freedom of speech had been violated. "If people like George Wallace are denied free expression," she explained, "then the same thing can happen to black people." Besides practicing law, she also taught black history at the college level.

In 1970, Norton was appointed chair of the New York City Commission on Human Rights. She was the first woman to occupy this powerful position. She covered a range of discrimination cases—from obtaining better maternity benefits for working women in New York City to urging businesses to hire Vietnam veterans and older workers.

From 1977 to 1983, she carried her battle against discrimination to the national level by chairing the Equal Employment Opportunity Commission (EEOC), a civil rights agency that reports directly to the President of the United States.

After stepping down from this position, she joined the faculty of Georgetown University Law School. Since 1990, she has served as the nonvoting congressional delegate from the District of Columbia in the U.S. House of Representatives. She is the recipient of almost 50 honorary degrees from colleges across America and works with numerous professional, political, and community-service organizations.

O'Keeffe, Georgia

ARTIST

Born: November 15, 1887
Sun Prairie, Wisconsin

Died: March 6, 1986
Santa Fe, New Mexico

Artist Georgia O'Keeffe captured the mystery and beauty of the American Southwest in her painting. Her work had a stark, unromantic—indeed, even an unsparing—quality, but it spoke with a poetry all its own. Huge poppies and purple hollyhocks; the dry, brittle canyons and towering mountains surrounding her home in Abiquiu, New Mexico; the bleached bones of animals long perished in the hot desert sun—these were the subjects that seized her imagination and filled her canvases.

O'Keeffe was born in a prairie town far from the arid New Mexican landscape, but she grew up with a love of wide, open spaces and cloudless blue skies. "The brightness of the light," she later recalled, was one of her earliest memories. She was raised in an austere middle-class farm family and attended public schools. She received her first art instruction from a teacher who boarded with her family, then completed her high school education at a public school in Milwaukee and a private girls' school in Virginia. There she first aspired to be an artist, and she enrolled at the Art Institute of Chicago and the Art Students League of New York City, where she studied with famed artist William Merritt Chase.

From 1912 to 1914, O'Keeffe taught art at a high school in Amarillo, Texas. Her artistic vision expanded in the spacious landscape of Amarillo; she exulted in the feeling of endless sky and rolling, grassy flatlands. Over the next several years, she taught in Virginia and Texas and refined her style, painting the wondrous sunsets and brilliant star-spangled nights of the Texas Panhandle.

In 1919, she moved to New York City. There she worked exclusively on her art and struck up a relationship with Alfred Stieglitz, a photographer and gallery owner who had been exhibiting her paintings. They married in 1924, and O'Keeffe, now a well-known artist, continued to experiment with style and color, painting both the New York skyline and the gentle, rolling landscapes of upstate New York, where she and Stieglitz spent their summers.

In 1929, O'Keeffe traveled to New Mexico, a state she had visited once before, and was instantly enraptured by the clarity and light of the desert landscape. For the next two decades she divided her time between the East Coast and the Southwest. After Stieglitz died in 1949, she moved to New Mexico permanently.

Certain that she had at last come home, she painted the New Mexican landscape with an inner calm not apparent in her earlier work. She gave her life wholly over to her art and, except for brief periods of travel, made the arid New Mexican landscape the center of her life and her art. She also experimented with ceramic sculpture and pottery.

Over the years, O'Keeffe exhibited her work at major museums around the country and won numerous awards and honors. She was perhaps the most famous woman artist of the 20th century.

PUBLICATION
Georgia O'Keeffe (1976)

FURTHER READING
Berry, Michael. *Georgia O'Keeffe.* New York: Chelsea House, 1988.
Eisler, Benita. *O'Keeffe and Stieglitz: An American Romance.* New York: Doubleday, 1991.
Lisle, Laurie. *Portrait of an Artist: A Biography of Georgia O'Keeffe.* Albuquerque: University of New Mexico Press, 1986.

O'Reilly, Leonora

LABOR LEADER AND REFORMER

Born: February 16, 1870
New York, New York

Died: April 3, 1927
Brooklyn, New York

In the early years of the 20th century, Leonora O'Reilly helped lead the struggle to achieve better working conditions for all workers. Born into an impoverished family in New York City's Lower East Side, the heart of immigrant working-class life in the city, she attended public school for a few years before dropping out to work in a collar factory. Early on, her mother exposed her to trade union activism by taking her to labor meetings.

In 1886, O'Reilly joined the Knights of Labor, a nationwide union of industrial workers. She also organized the Working Women's Society to expose the harsh conditions under which sales and factory women worked. This organization, in turn, inspired several middle- and upper-class women to form the Consumers' League, a national organization dedicated to improving these working conditions. O'Reilly soon befriended leading thinkers and reformers, including Lillian Wald, and joined social reform groups—though she continued to work 10 hours a day in a shirtwaist factory.

In 1898, she enrolled at the Pratt Institute in Brooklyn to strengthen her meager formal education. She graduated two years later and for the next several years taught at the Manhattan Trade School for Girls. In 1903, she joined the newly organized Women's Trade Union League (WTUL), an organization of factory and upper-class women who worked together to improve working conditions.

O'Reilly exerted forceful leadership in shaping the league's goals and recruiting supporters. As vice president of the New York branch of the WTUL, and as a worker and a unionist, she helped to orchestrate the league's active efforts in the famous shirtwaist makers' strike of 1909. Two years later, after the tragedy of the Triangle Shirtwaist fire killed 146 women workers, she chaired the league's committee on fire protection and conducted an extensive survey of safety conditions and laws.

O'Reilly also helped to establish the National Association for the Advancement of Colored People (NAACP), joined the Socialist party, and worked for woman suffrage. During World War I, she represented the WTUL at the International Congress of Women at the Hague. She opposed American involvement in the war and later served on the WTUL's committee on social and industrial reconstruction.

In later years, poor health forced her to relinquish most of her activity in the labor movement. Besides possessing impressive organizational and administrative abilities, she was a dynamic speaker who skillfully galvanized public support for labor's cause.

Osborne, Sarah

ACCUSED WITCH

Born: ca. 1643
Watertown, Massachusetts

Died: May 10, 1692
Boston, Massachusetts

Along with the slave Tituba and Sarah Good, Sarah Osborne was one of the first three women accused of witchcraft in the Salem, Massachusetts witch-hunt of 1692. Before this frightening episode was over, 20 people were executed, nearly 200 were imprisoned, and 8—including Sarah Osborne—died in prison.

In 1662, she married Robert Prince of Salem Village and soon bore two sons. When he died in 1675, he left a substantial land holding in trust to his wife, with the provision that it be turned over to their two sons when they were older.

But Sarah, if not a witch, was certainly no angel. In 1677, she married Alexander Osborne, a young indentured servant whose services she had purchased for 15 pounds sterling, and the two of them tried to bilk her sons out of their rightful inheritance. Her neighbors—who were also her in-laws—did not take kindly to her attempts to cheat her sons or subvert traditional forms of inheritance, which provided for the transfer of property down the male line to sons.

In 1692, Tituba, who had been accused of practicing witchcraft by three young girls, in turn pointed the finger at Sarah Good and Osborne as fellow witches. At the time, Osborne was ill and often bedridden—hardly in the position to fly through the night on a stick, as Tituba claimed. On February 29, 1692, Osborne, along with Tituba and Good, was formally charged, and the next day the three of them were arrested and examined.

Unlike Tituba, Osborne and Good refused to confess to the crimes for which they had been charged. Both women languished in prison in chains. On May 10, 1692, Sarah Osborne died in Boston prison; Sarah Good was hanged that summer, and Tituba—the only one of the three to agree to her accusers' outlandish charges— was subsequently released and returned to bondage.

FURTHER READING

Boyer, Paul and Stephen Nissenbaum. *Salem Possessed: The Social Origins of Witchcraft.* Cambridge: Harvard University Press, 1974.
Demos, John. *Entertaining Satan: Witchcraft and the Culture of Early New England.* New York: Oxford University Press, 1982.

O'Sullivan, Mary Kenney

LABOR ORGANIZER AND FACTORY INSPECTOR

Born: January 8, 1864
Hannibal, Missouri

Died: January 18, 1943
West Medford, Massachusetts

Mary Kenney O'Sullivan was a lifelong champion of the working class. Born in the same town as Mark Twain, she attended a convent school and also a local public school until the fourth grade—"as far as any children of wage earners in Hannibal were expected to go," she explained later—then started working as an apprentice dressmaker.

When her father, a railroad worker, died, she became the chief support of her invalid mother. She found employment in a printing and binding company, and worked her way up to forewoman before the company went out of business.

After finding other work in the same industry, she became convinced that women must organize for better working conditions. After moving to Chicago, she joined a local women's branch of the American Federation of Labor (AFL) and quickly moved into a leadership position. With Jane Addams's help, she organized a union for women bookbinders and a residential club for working women.

In 1892, Kenney became the AFL's first woman general organizer. A year later she successfully lobbied for the first law in Illinois to regulate the employment of women and children and to set up a factory inspection department. Her marriage to John F. O'Sullivan, labor editor for the *Boston Globe,* and the births of four children did not slow down her labor work.

In 1903, she struck a historic blow for working-class women by organizing, along with William English Walling, the Women's Trade Union League (WTUL), an organization of factory and upper-class women who worked together to improve industrial conditions and unionize women in industry. She served as the national league's first secretary and vice president and actively worked with the Boston branch of the league. But she parted ways with the Boston chapter over her support for the 1912 Lawrence textile strike.

O'Sullivan ardently favored woman suffrage. During World War I, she joined the International League for Peace and Freedom because of her opposition to American entry into World War I. In 1914, she became a factory inspector for the Massachusetts Department of Labor and Industries, a position she held for 20 years.

Palmer, Bertha Honoré

SOCIAL REFORMER AND SOCIALITE

Born: May 22, 1849
Louisville, Kentucky

Died: May 5, 1918
Osprey, Florida

Known as the "Mrs. Astor of the Midwest," after the wealthy socialite Mrs. John Jacob Astor, Bertha Honoré Palmer marshaled her upper-class influence and civic spirit to become a highly effective social reformer in Chicago. She was born into affluence and attended exclusive private schools in Chicago and Washington, D.C.

In 1870, she married Potter Palmer, a rich businessman, and improved her social and financial status even more. With her eager support, he played a major role in rebuilding Chicago after fire destroyed most of the city in 1871, and she belonged to several exclusive social and literary clubs. She also helped introduce the new style of Impressionist art to America.

In the 1890s, she was a leading supporter of Jane Addams's Hull House and of the Chicago branch of the Women's Trade Union League (WTUL). She organized Chicago's millinery workers and fought for better educational opportunities for women. From 1892 to 1896, she served as a trustee of Northwestern University, a coeducational college. But Palmer was no feminist. She offered only lukewarm support for female suffrage and urged women not to sacrifice their femininity for their rights.

Her crowning social and civic achievement came in 1893, when she chaired the Board of Lady Managers for the World's Columbian Exposition in Chicago. She turned the Woman's Building, designed by architect Sophia Hayden, into one of the most spectacular displays at the exposition; the graceful, Italian-style building housed an array of exhibits showcasing women's accomplishments and work from around the world, including books, handicrafts, inventions, and other artifacts.

In 1900, she once again vaunted to prominence when President William McKinley appointed her the only woman on the United States Commission to the Paris Exhibition. In later years, she lived in Europe, then moved to Florida, where she ranched and farmed and helped to develop that region. An astute businesswoman, she more than doubled her family's fortune.

Palmer, Phoebe Worrall

EVANGELIST AND RELIGIOUS AUTHOR

Born: December 18, 1807
New York, New York

Died: November 2, 1874
New York, New York

Phoebe Worrall Palmer was a prominent 19th-century religious leader. She came by her religious calling from a childhood steeped in strict Methodist worship. Early on, she wrote poetry and was inspired by well-known Methodist ministers.

In 1827, at age 19, she married Walter Clark Palmer, a physician. After two sons died in childbirth, the couple decided to devote their lives to religious activities. Soon Phoebe Palmer was leading a weekly afternoon prayer meeting for women in New York City. Out of these meetings emerged the Perfectionist movement, a religious movement that rejected the Calvinist notion of predestination and believed that people could achieve religious salvation through their own efforts. Leading exponents of this movement attended Palmer's meetings.

Palmer traveled around the country to recruit followers and published articles in the *Guide to Holiness,* the main journal of the Perfectionist movement. In 1862, her husband bought the journal and appointed her editor-in-chief. In addition, she also published several books.

Throughout the 1850s and 1860s, the Palmers traveled around the United States to conduct revival meetings, and Phoebe Palmer did charity work as part of her quest for religious salvation. She visited prisoners, served as corresponding secretary for a relief agency, and was a founder of Five Points Mission, an early settlement house in New York City. The mission contained a chapel, classrooms, and 20 rent-free apartments for the poor.

Although Palmer did not endorse the women's rights movement, she paved the way for women to assume religious leadership. Following her example, scores of other women in the Perfectionist movement organized weekly gatherings in their homes. Palmer remained active in the movement until her death.

PUBLICATIONS
The Way of Holiness (1845)
Promise of the Father (1859)

FURTHER READING
White, Charles Edward. *The Beauty of Holiness: Phoebe Palmer as Theologian, Revivalist, Feminist, and Humanitarian.* Grand Rapids, Mich.: F. Asbury Press, 1986.

Park, Maud Wood

SUFFRAGE LEADER

Born: January 25, 1871
Boston, Massachusetts

Died: May 8, 1955
Reading, Massachusetts

Maud Wood Park was the first president of the League of Women Voters. Born in Boston, she attended the St. Agnes School in Albany, New York, and taught school in Boston. After saving enough money for tuition, she entered Radcliffe College in 1895—whereupon she discovered that only she and another student in her class supported woman suffrage. While attending Radcliffe, she became involved with Denison House, a settlement house in Boston's South End. There she met prominent social reformers and was inspired to join community-reform efforts.

In 1900, she was elected chairwoman of the Massachusetts Woman Suffrage Association (MWSA), and a year later became executive secretary of the Boston Equal Suffrage Association for Good Government. As a leader and cofounder of this progressive group, she promoted both woman suffrage and efforts to improve community life. Park helped to organize the first Boston Parent-Teacher Association, urged immigrant women to form civic clubs, and continued to work for woman suffrage. She also traveled around the country as cofounder of the College Equal Suffrage League (CESL) to convert college-age women to suffrage.

In 1919, the year that American women finally achieved the constitutional right to vote, Park became the first president of the newly organized League of Women Voters (LWV), a nonpartisan organization designed to inform women voters of their political rights. She immediately defined the league's mission as one of reform aimed at achieving protection for working women and children, more responsive public agencies, and community improvement.

Under Park's leadership, the league collaborated with other women's groups to secure passage of a child protection law and a law granting married women independent citizenship rights. Park represented a new generation of feminists—one more militant but also more pragmatic and politically adept at grassroots organizing than their feminist foremothers.

PUBLICATION
Front Door Lobby (autobiography, 1960)

Parks, Rosa

CIVIL RIGHTS ACTIVIST

Born: February 4, 1913
Tuskegee, Alabama

Often hailed as "the mother of the freedom movement," Rosa Parks refused to give up her seat on a crowded bus in Montgomery, Alabama, to a white man—and sparked a historic movement among African Americans for social and political equality.

She had grown up in a rural community in Alabama with a deep awareness of racial injustice. After marrying, she worked for integration and equal rights in the South. She became one of the first women to join the Montgomery chapter of the National Association for the Advancement of Colored People (NAACP) and was a member of the Montgomery Voters League, a group that helped blacks register to vote.

On Thursday, December 1, 1955, Parks struck a historic blow at racial injustice. Riding home from her job in downtown Montgomery, Parks was seated in the front of the "colored" section—the rows of seats in the back of the bus restricted to black passengers. When a white passenger got on and could not find a seat, the driver, who was also white, told

Parks and the other black passengers in her row to move. Rosa Parks, alone, refused to get up. The driver summoned the police, who ejected Parks and carted her off to jail.

Within days of her courageous act, Montgomery's black community organized a mass boycott against the Montgomery transit system. Boycotters walked, hitched rides, or carpooled to avoid riding on segregated city buses. The bus boycott lasted more than a year, and on December 20, 1956, 381 days after it had started, the Supreme Court ordered city officials to integrate Montgomery's buses.

After this victory, blacks in Montgomery and across the South organized a movement to dismantle segregation in all public facilities, including schools and libraries, and in the voting booth, where most blacks had been denied the constitutional right to vote. Parks, like other civil rights activists, endured malicious taunts and threats on her life because of her civil rights work. In 1957, she moved to Detroit, Michigan, where she continues to work for civil rights. She remains a towering example of courage and commitment to social justice.

PUBLICATION
Parks, Rosa, with Jim Haskins. *Rosa Parks: My Story.* New York: Dial, 1992.

Parton, Sara Payson Willis

AUTHOR, NEWSPAPER COLUMNIST

Born: July 9, 1811
Portland, Maine

Died: October 10, 1872
New York, New York

Better known by her pen name, Fanny Fern, Sarah Payson Willis Parton parlayed a sparkling wit and plucky spirit into a successful writing career. She was educated in Boston and at Catharine Beecher's seminary in Hartford, Connecticut. At age 26, she married Charles H. Eldredge, a bank cashier. They had three children, and Sarah Eldredge settled into a peaceful domestic existence.

When her husband died nine years later, she was left a widow without any means of support. She remarried but divorced three years later because her husband was abusive and autocratic. Once again forced to support herself and her children, she turned to teaching and sewing. Her earnings were so small that she could not even support her children and was forced to send her daughter to live with in-laws.

As a last resort, she turned to journalism, writing under the pseudonym "Fannie Fern." Several small Boston magazines carried her humorous pieces, and eventually newspapers also reprinted her columns. Launched on a successful journalistic career, Willis published several anthologies of her work, all of which sold astonishingly well. She also became a weekly columnist for the *New York Ledger*—and, as a result, one of America's first women columnists as well as the highest-paid newspaper writer of her day. She continued to publish collections of her writings, and also wrote two novels.

Though Fern's writings do not qualify as great literature, they offer a revealing glimpse into middle-class domestic life in the 1850s and 1860s. In her writing, moreover, Willis advocated greater social and intellectual equality for women. She condemned the double standard of morality for men and women, lamented how much time women spent on housework and child-rearing, and urged women to set goals for themselves beyond marriage and motherhood. She also spoke out against urban poverty and on behalf of children, urging parents to understand and respect them.

Finally, Willis took on organized religion; she condemned religious authorities for preaching to rather than truly helping their congregants. And she challenged prudish Victorian conceptions of sex and morality. Although she did not support woman suffrage at first, by 1858 she had been converted to the cause. She also helped to establish Sorosis, the women's club that launched a nationwide club movement among American women.

Fern had a dry, salty wit and enjoyed puncturing popular images of women as frail, delicate creatures. She claimed that she sweated, relished a good glass of ale, and on occasion, dressed in men's clothing to avoid the nuisance of petticoats. She railed against the idea that women should not voice their own opinions and once wrote: "But why a woman has not a right to love and hate persons and things as well and as strongly as a man; and why she has not a right, like him, to resent a manifest injustice . . . I have yet to learn."

MAJOR PUBLICATIONS
Ruth Hall (1855)
Fresh Leaves (1857)
Folly As It Flies (1868)
Ginger-Snaps (1870)

FURTHER READING
Warren, Joyce. *Fanny Fern: An Independent Woman.* New Brunswick, N.J.: Rutgers University Press, 1992.

Patterson, Mary Jane

EDUCATOR

Born: 1840 (exact date unknown)
Raleigh, North Carolina

Died: September 24, 1894
Washington, D.C.

In the years following the Civil War, Mary Jane Patterson, like many other African-American women, devoted herself to educating the first generation of black youth to know freedom. Born into slavery, she managed to secure her freedom and enrolled in Oberlin College in 1857, where she took the "gentlemen's," or classical, course, a more rigorous course of study than the "ladies'," or literary, course that most female students pursued. Among her classmates were Fanny Jackson (later Coppin), a future teacher, and Edmonia Lewis, a sculptor.

In 1862, Patterson graduated with a B.A. with highest honors. She taught first in Ohio and then in Virginia. In the mid-1860s, she became an assistant to Fanny Jackson at the Institute for Colored Youth in Philadelphia.

From there, she moved to Washington, D.C., where she was appointed principal of the Preparatory High School for Colored Youth. She was the school's first African-American principal and also the first African-American principal of a high school in Washington, D.C. Except for a one-year break, Patterson continued in this position until 1884, presiding over a student population that grew from fewer than 50 students to 172.

The records suggest that she was forced to step down in 1884 because school trustees decided that the growing student population needed a "male in charge." Patterson continued to teach at the school and also participated in organizations that benefited Washington's black citizens, including a rest home for elderly blacks and a girls' industrial school. Friends and colleagues praised her teaching and administrative abilities.

FURTHER READING
Brown, Hallie Quinn. *Homespun Heroines and Other Women of Distinction.* Ohio: Aldine, 1926.

Paul, Alice

FEMINIST

Born: January 11, 1885
Morristown, New Jersey

Died: July 9, 1977
Morristown, New Jersey

Alice Paul, a tough, dedicated feminist, led the final push to achieve woman suffrage in the United States. Her militant tactics, which included picketing the White House with signs reading "An Autocrat at Home Is a Poor Champion of Democracy Abroad" and staging hunger strikes in prison, galvanized public attention and transformed the suffrage movement from a genteel cause into a fierce crusade.

Paul was educated at Swarthmore College in Pennsylvania. From 1905 to 1906 she worked as a resident social worker in the College Settlement House in New York City. She received her master's degree in economics and sociology in 1907 and her Ph.D. in 1912 from the University of Pennsylvania. Ten years later, she obtained a law degree from Washington College of Law.

But her true work lay in the suffrage struggle. While studying in England from 1907 to 1909, she met the militant English suffragist Emmeline Pankhurst, who introduced Paul to the flamboyant tactics that she would later use. With Lucy Burns, Paul organized the first major suffrage parade in Washington—on the eve of Woodrow Wilson's inauguration as President in 1913. That same year, she and Burns established the Congressional Union, a branch of the National American Woman Suffrage Association (NAWSA), to secure woman suffrage through a constitutional amendment rather than through the state-by-state campaign favored by NAWSA. Friction with NAWSA officials over these differing strategies prompted Paul to break away and establish the Congressional Union as an independent organization. In 1916, the Congressional Union became the National Woman's Party (NWP), a militant suffrage organization that relied on picketing, parades, and hunger strikes to publicize its cause.

After the 19th Amendment, which granted woman suffrage, was ratified, Paul embarked on a campaign for "equal rights for women"—and again clashed with other women's rights activists who favored protective legislation to regulate women's working hours and conditions. This special legislation would apply only to women and not to men. Paul strenuously objected to any laws that did not apply to both sexes, and she spent the remainder of her life lobbying for an equal rights amendment (ERA) to the Constitution, which passed Congress in 1972 but was never ratified by the states.

During the 1930s and 1940s, she also worked for women's equality on a global scale and was a founding member of the World Woman's Party, which sent delegates to the founding meeting of the United Nations to include a provision for sexual equality in the preamble of the U.N. charter. Paul's life spanned the formative years of NAWSA, the struggle over the direction of the feminist movement in the wake of achieving female suffrage, and the present-day women's movement. Throughout her long and accomplished life, she remained committed to women's social and political equality.

FURTHER READING

Lunardini, Christine. *From Equal Suffrage to Equal Rights: Alice Paul and the National Woman's Party, 1910–1928.* New York: New York University Press, 1988.

Peabody, Elizabeth Palmer

TEACHER, AUTHOR, EDUCATIONAL REFORMER,
BOOKSTORE OWNER, PUBLISHER

*Born: May 16, 1804
Billerica, Massachusetts*

*Died: January 3, 1894
Boston, Massachusetts*

Elizabeth Palmer Peabody, champion of educational reform, was a leading figure in American intellectual life throughout the mid- to late 19th century. Her devotion to a life of the mind began in her childhood. Her father taught her Latin and inspired her to master 10 different languages, and her mother, a schoolteacher who believed that every child deserved a rigorous education, exposed the young Elizabeth to theology, philosophy, history, and literature. Her enlightened approach to educating the very young inspired her daughter's future pursuit of educational reform.

Elizabeth Peabody became a teacher in her teens, first in her mother's school and then in Boston. With her sister Mary Peabody (Mann), she opened a school in Brookline, a Boston suburb. Here, she came into contact with William Ellery Channing, a prominent minister who enrolled his daughter in her school. She and Channing developed a close friendship based on shared intellectual interests, and he introduced her to other thinkers, including Ralph Waldo Emerson.

In 1837, Peabody and Margaret Fuller became the first women to join the Transcendentalist Club, a loosely knit group of intellectuals who spurned traditional religious thinking and perceived a mystical unity between people and their natural surroundings. Often called a New England Renaissance, the Transcendentalist movement embraced fresh, new ideas about literature, philosophy, and social relations. Its followers celebrated the free flow of creative thinking, and Peabody eagerly shared their passion for new intellectual expression.

Through her involvement in the Transcendentalist movement, Peabody met Bronson Alcott, a visionary but eccentric educator. She enlisted as a teacher in his school in Boston, and the two pioneered a new way of educating very young children. Instead of drilling facts and figures, they used a Socratic method of questioning to help pupils discover their inborn talents and insights. This was a radical notion, for most people felt that children should be seen but not heard.

In 1840, Peabody opened a bookstore in Boston to carry foreign books, periodicals, and radical literature by American writers. She also published antislavery literature, three children's books by Nathaniel Hawthorne, whom she helped to discover, and the *Dial,* the journal of the Transcendentalists. She first published Henry David Thoreau's *Civil Disobedience,* a landmark book on nonviolent resistance that later inspired Mahatma Gandhi and Martin Luther King, Jr. In her bookstore, Margaret Fuller held her famous Wednesday evening Conversations for women, and there, too, the founders of Brook Farm, an experimental venture in communal living, planned their utopian community.

But Peabody's first passion lay in educational reform, and to this she devoted her time and energy. In 1860, she established the first kindergarten

in the United States, and published more than 10 books and 50 articles on educational reform between 1850 and 1884. In the years before the Civil War, she was also a fervent abolitionist, and later on she took up the cause of Native American rights. Contemporaries chided her almost comical devotion to intellectual causes—she could discourse for hours on the most obscure topics—but she was truly a gifted woman who astutely recognized and publicized new ideas for the larger public good.

PUBLICATIONS
Letters of Elizabeth Palmer Peabody, American Renaissance Woman. Rhonda, Bruce, ed. Middletown, Conn.: Wesleyan University Press, 1984.
Record of Mr. Alcott's School (3rd ed., 1874)

FURTHER READING
Tharp, Louise. *The Peabody Sisters of Salem.* 1950. Reprint. Boston: Little, Brown, 1988.

Peirce, Melusina Fay

DOMESTIC REFORMER

Born: 1836 (exact date unknown)
Burlington, Vermont

Died: date and location unknown

Fed up with spending all of her time doing household chores, Melusina Fay Peirce revolutionized housework—by forming a collective of homemakers who charged men for their household services. She was the daughter of an Episcopal minister and believed that her mother had died from excessive domestic toil. She attended the Young Ladies' School of Harvard professor Louis Agassiz, a famous botanist, in Cambridge, Massachusetts, where she met Charles Sanders Peirce, her future husband. They married in 1862, and Peirce settled down to be the wife of a Harvard professor.

Six years later, in 1868, she felt restless and resentful over the "costly and unnatural sacrifice" of her wider talents to full-time domesticity. She blamed her entrapment on the unpaid domestic labor she performed, and in a series of articles for the *Atlantic Monthly* she analyzed women's inferior economic role in industrial society. The solution she proposed was "cooperative housekeeping."

Peirce formulated—and put into effect in Cambridge—a plan by which 12 to 50 women organized a cooperative association to perform domestic work and charge their husbands for their services—cash on delivery. Using membership fees, the members purchased and equipped a building in which to perform their tasks. Peirce even provided a detailed description of the building's layout. She hoped that cooperative housekeeping would lead to two conditions vital to women's freedom—economic independence from men and collective power.

Although Peirce's cooperative lasted only from 1869 to 1871—most local men indignantly refused to patronize it—she had inspired others to rethink household arrangements in order to liberate women from a life of domestic drudgery. Throughout the 1870s, she, too, explored new ways to organize domesticity, and she continued to advocate cooperative housekeeping in lectures and articles.

In later years, she actively promoted women's education and culture. She supported the founding of Radcliffe College, the Boston Woman's Education Association, and the establishment of a women's orchestra. She also campaigned for better street cleaning and historic preservation. And she never stopped believing that cooperative housekeeping would grant women greater freedom and power over their lives.

PUBLICATIONS

Cooperative Housekeeping: How Not To Do It and How To Do It, A Study in Sociology (1880)
New York, A Symphonic Study (novel, 1918)

FURTHER READING

Hayden, Dolores. *The Grand Domestic Revolution.* Cambridge, Mass.: MIT Press, 1981.

Perkins, Frances

SOCIAL REFORMER, GOVERNMENT OFFICIAL

Born: April 10, 1880
Boston, Massachusetts

Died: May 14, 1965
New York, New York

Frances Perkins was the first woman to serve as a member of a U.S. President's cabinet. During the worst economic depression the nation has ever known, she presided over the Department of Labor, helping to put people back to work.

Perkins, who later married but fought in court to retain her maiden name, went to public elementary and high schools. She attended Mount Holyoke College and, after graduating in 1902, embarked upon a teaching career. She also did volunteer work at settlement houses. In 1910, she received a master's degree in economics and sociology from Columbia University, and became secretary of the New York Consumers' League, an organization that lobbied for better working conditions for New York's factory and saleswomen.

Through this organization she found her life's work—fighting for better working conditions for all employees. In 1918, she supported Alfred E. Smith's campaign for governor of New York State. When he won, he appointed her to the New York State Industrial Commission. She was the first woman to occupy this position. She also became active in Democratic party affairs and urged the party to support protective legislation for women and children and workplace safety standards.

In 1926, Perkins was promoted to chair the New York State Industrial Board (formerly the New York State Industrial Commission). For the next seven years, she helped improve workplace safety standards throughout the state. Under her watch, New York State passed a 48-hour work week, strengthened factory inspections, and granted all workers a day of rest.

When the stock market crashed in 1929, she advised Governor Franklin D. Roosevelt about emergency measures for easing the harsh impact on workers. After he became President in 1932, he appointed Perkins to be his secretary of labor. She helped draft some of the most important legislation of the New Deal, including provisions for creating new jobs. She was a staunch advocate for workers rather than employers, but she was less progressive when it came to working women. She opposed an equal rights amendment to the Constitution and urged married women workers during the Depression to give up their jobs to unmarried men.

Perkins left her post in 1945, shortly after Roosevelt died, and joined the Civil Service Commission, an agency that oversees government employees. For four decades, she fought for better working conditions, higher wages, and workplace safety standards, and she made her voice heard in the highest halls of government.

FURTHER READING

Colman, Penny. *A Woman Unafraid: The Achievement of Frances Perkins.* New York: Atheneum, 1994.

Martin, George. *Madam Secretary, Frances Perkins.* Boston: Houghton Mifflin, 1976.

Perry, Lilla Cabot

ARTIST

Born: January 13, 1848
Boston, Massachusetts

Died: February 28, 1933
Hancock, New Hampshire

A descendant of one of New England's oldest and most distinguished families, Lilla Cabot Perry first aspired to write poetry before turning to painting. In 1874, she married Thomas Sergeant Per-

ry, a Harvard professor. It may have been his brother-in-law, the artist John La Farge, who urged her to redirect her talents into painting.

In 1886, she began taking private lessons and then enrolled at the Cowles School of Art for further instruction. She earned enough money from painting portraits to finance a trip to Europe for herself and her husband and three daughters. In June 1887 the family sailed first class to Paris, where Perry studied at two art academies.

But her real artistic education came from living next door to the artist Claude Monet in the beautiful village of Giverny, France. For the next two decades, she and her family spent many summers in Giverny, where she could observe the great Impressionist master at work.

She also traveled and studied in Spain, and exhibited her paintings in Paris, Berlin, Dresden, and Munich. An extended visit to Japan in 1898 enabled her to experiment with a new Impressionist style that drew on Japanese and Chinese influences.

Perry won numerous awards for her art and was a founder of the Guild of Boston Artists. Like other Impressionist painters, she sought inspiration in nature and also painted portraits of women at tea, sharing private moments with their children, or playing a musical instrument. Among her favorite compositions was that of a woman standing alone in a room, lost in her own thoughts. Perry was one of the few women painters to join the Impressionist movement, and her art reveals the Impressionist love of luminous color, shadowing, and free-flowing brush strokes. Her paintings radiate a gauzy, light-filled effect.

Perry painted until the very end of her life. In her last years, she sought inspiration from the gentle, rolling New England landscape beyond her country home.

PUBLICATION

"Reminiscences of Claude Monet from 1889 to 1909," *The American Magazine of Art* (March 1927)

FURTHER READING

Levin, Gail, et al. *American Women Artists 1830–1930*. Washington, D.C.: National Museum of Women in the Arts, 1987.

Martindale, Meredith. *Lilla Cabot Perry: An American Impressionist*. Washington, D.C.: National Museum of Women in the Arts, 1990.

Peterson, Esther

FEDERAL GOVERNMENT OFFICIAL

Born: December 9, 1906
Provo, Utah

Esther Peterson was director of the Women's Bureau of the U.S. Department of Labor during President John F. Kennedy's administration. She also became the highest-ranking female government official when Kennedy appointed her assistant secretary of labor, as well as executive vice chair of the President's Commission on the Status of Women.

Peterson's background prepared her to be an advocate for women workers. After graduating from Brigham Young University in 1927, she taught physical education at an agricultural college in Utah before receiving her M.A. in physical education from Teachers College, Columbia University, in 1930.

Meeting her future husband, Oliver A. Peterson, was the turning point in her life and career. He introduced her to the issues and problems facing American workers and she quickly refocused her interests on labor and economics. From 1932 to 1939, she taught economics at the Bryn Mawr (Pennsylvania) Summer School for Women Workers in Industry and also worked temporarily for the International Ladies' Garment Workers Union and the American Federation of Labor. In 1939, she joined the executive board of the Amalgamated Clothing Workers of America as assistant director of education.

During the early 1950s, she and her husband lived in Europe, where she worked with a variety of labor organizations. In Paris, she helped to organize the first international school for working women and represented the American trade union movement at several international conferences.

From 1958 to 1961, back in the United States, she served as a legislative representative for the AFL-CIO. After Kennedy took office, he appointed her to the directorship of the Women's Bureau. In that position, she worked to increase the minimum wage and provide for better retraining among women returning to the work force.

In later years, she served as a special adviser to Presidents Lyndon B. Johnson and Jimmy Carter on consumer affairs issues, and has also been an advocate for senior citizens. In 1979, President Carter awarded her the Presidential Medal of Freedom.

Pinckney, Elizabeth Lucas

PLANTATION MANAGER

Born: ca. December 28, 1722
Antigua, West Indies

Died: May 26, 1793
Philadelphia, Pennsylvania

Elizabeth (better known as Eliza) Lucas Pinckney refined the cultivation of indigo, a plant used in creating dyes for fabrics. Her toil and perseverance enlarged her family's fortunes as well as the economy of South Carolina, which produced the crop for export to England. Born in the West Indies, Eliza Pinckney came to the colony of South Carolina as a child. Her father, a British military officer, inherited a plantation on Wappoo Creek in South Carolina and brought over his wife and two daughters, seeking a better climate for his wife's health.

Eliza Pinckney enjoyed a privileged childhood. Educated partly in England, she played the flute, was conversant with English literature, spoke French, and taught herself English philosophy and law. In addition, she taught two young slave women how to read, hoping to train them to educate the plantation's slave children. In 1741, she even spotted a hitherto unknown comet. Though she partook occasionally of the genteel social life in nearby Charleston, she devoted most of her energies to managing her father's three plantations. These were enormous land holdings whose vast fields were worked by scores of slaves, and she, not yet 17, became their mistress.

With her father's encouragement, and the labor of scores of slaves, she experimented with expanding the variety of crops at Wappoo, including ginger, cotton, and figs. From 1738 to 1744, she consulted experts and worked diligently to perfect the production of indigo. By 1744, she reported a successful crop, and within a few years Carolina planters were shipping thousands of pounds of indigo to England for sale.

On May 27, 1744, Eliza Lucas married Charles Pinckney, a lawyer, widower, and future chief justice of South Carolina. She bore four children, and divided her time between the family mansion in Charleston and a plantation on the Cooper River. She happily devoted herself to her children's education but also found time to cultivate a silkworm farm on the plantation to manufacture silk.

In 1753, upon her husband's appointment as commissioner for the colony, the family moved to London. There, Eliza Pinckney enjoyed a festive social life, befitting a government official's wife. They returned to South Carolina in 1758, and Charles Pinckney died a year later. Eliza Pinckney assumed management of his extensive land holdings. She spent her last years on her daughter's plantation, happily surrounded by her large and loving family. When she died of cancer in 1793, President George Washington made the unusual request to serve as one of her pallbearers. Through a combination of pluck and familial encouragement, Eliza Lucas Pinckney managed to carve out an unusual niche for herself—as an entrepreneur and landowner.

FURTHER READING

Williams, Frances Leigh. *Plantation Patriot: A Biography of Eliza Lucas Pinckney.* New York: Harcourt, 1967.

———. *A Founding Family: The Pinckneys of South Carolina.* New York: Harcourt Brace Jovanovich, 1975.

Plath, Sylvia

POET AND NOVELIST

Born: October 27, 1932
Boston, Massachusetts

Died: February 11, 1963
London, England

Sylvia Plath's haunting images have earned her poetry an enduring readership. From early on, she showed promise as a poet. An idyllic childhood in a seaside Massachusetts town ended for her at age eight when her father, whom she adored, died and Sylvia and her mother and brother moved in with her maternal grandparents. She attended high school in Wellesley, Massachusetts, and in 1950 entered Smith College on a scholarship.

During the summer of 1953, she spent a month in New York as a guest editor for *Mademoiselle* magazine. But, plagued by increasing self-doubt over her literary abilities and by an ever-present sadness because of her father's death, she went into a deep depression and returned to Wellesley for treatment. These personal ghosts would haunt her for the rest of her life—and provide rich inspiration for her poetry.

Plath graduated from Smith in 1955 and traveled to England to study on a Fulbright scholarship. There she met her future husband, the poet Ted Hughes, and they were married a year later. Hughes, highly successful in his own right, encouraged Plath's literary talents and also intimidated her. They returned to the United States, and she began teaching at Smith College.

In 1960, they moved back to London, and Plath gave birth to two children and worked on her poetry. In 1961, she published her first collection, *The Colossus,* and two years later a novel, *The Bell Jar.* Meanwhile, she and Hughes had separated. The resulting emotional turmoil unleashed her most powerful poetry. But the intense sadness and anger that drove her poetry also plunged her into emotional and spiritual crisis. Unable to conquer an overwhelming despair, she took her own life by asphyxiating herself in her kitchen oven.

Most of Plath's poetry has been published after her death. By the mid-1960s, her work had achieved an enormous following because of its vivid, soaring prose and explosive images of a woman probing her deepest feelings.

MAJOR PUBLICATIONS

The Colossus (1960)
The Bell Jar (novel, 1963)
Ariel (1966)
Crossing the Water (1971)
Winter Trees (1971)
Letters Home (a collection of Plath's correspondence, 1975)
The Journals of Sylvia Plath (1982)

FURTHER READING

Alexander, Paul. *Rough Magic: A Biography of Sylvia Plath.* New York: Viking, 1991.

Pocahontas

INDIAN HEROINE

*Born: ca. 1595 or 1596
Virginia*

*Died: March 1616 or 1617
London, England*

Generations of readers have grown up learning about the legendary Pocahontas, savior of Captain John Smith, the leader of the colony at Jamestown, Virginia. But the true story of Pocahontas is both more dramatic and more human than the heroic myths that have followed her into the history books.

The daughter of Powhatan, a great Indian chief in the Tidewater region of Virginia, she was actually named Matoaba, which contains the root meaning "to play, playful." "Pocahontas" was a nickname that may have meant "frolicsome"—an apt description of the young Indian woman who impressed John Smith and others with her frisky, winsome spirit.

Little is known about her until she saved John Smith, who had been captured by Powhatan's warriors, from certain death. According to Smith, "At the minute of my execution, she hazarded the beating out of her owne braines [sic] to [save] mine, and . . . so pre[v]ailed with her father that I was safely conducted to Jamestown." Her actions saved Smith's life and ushered in a period of more harmonious relations between the Indians and the settlers of Jamestown.

Shortly after Smith's return to Jamestown, in January 1608, Powhatan began to supply the colony with food. His agent of relief was none other than Pocahontas, who also served as her father's emissary to secure the release of some Indians captured by the colonists. According to Smith, she once even warned the colonists of a surprise attack planned by her father.

When Smith was forced to return to England in October 1609, Pocahontas's activities disappear from the records until 1613. In the spring of that year, Captain Samuel Argall of Jamestown, finding himself near Pocahontas's settlement, managed to lure her aboard his ship, whereupon he held her hostage; he hoped to ransom her in order to secure the freedom of some English settlers held by Powhatan's tribe and also improve relations between the colonists and Indians.

Pocahontas was sent to Jamestown, where she was treated graciously. Eager to learn English, she renounced the religious traditions of her people and was baptized into Christianity in the spring of 1614. She took Rebecca as her new English name. Meanwhile, an English colonist, John Rolfe, had become attracted to her and sought her hand in marriage. They were married in April 1614, and Powhatan granted them a tract of land. The couple had one son. Once again, Pocahontas, through her marriage, helped usher in more peaceful relations between the colonists and the Indians.

In 1616, Pocahontas and her husband and son sailed for England. There they visited John Smith and were also presented to the king and queen of England. Rolfe soon made plans to return to Virginia, but before their ship sailed Pocahontas contracted pneumonia or tuberculosis and died. She was buried near London.

Over the following century, the historical Pocahontas was quickly eclipsed by a growing legend perpetuated in stories, drama, and poetry. In these fanciful tales, she rescued John Smith out of her love for him. In reality, however, Pocahontas and Smith shared no such passion. He admired her playful spirit, and she seemed to regard him as an emissary to a culture she wished to learn more about.

FURTHER READING
Mossiker, Frances. *Pocahontas: The Life and the Legend.* New York: Knopf, 1976.

Pogrebin, Letty Cottin

JOURNALIST, AUTHOR

Born: June 9, 1939
New York, New York

Letty Cottin Pogrebin, a prolific author and journalist, is a founding editor of *Ms.* magazine, the premier journal of the contemporary American women's movement.

After graduating from Brandeis University in 1959 with a B.A. in English and American literature, she embarked upon a career in book publishing. She married Bert Pogrebin in 1963 and later

bore two daughters. By 1970, she was director of publicity and advertising, and also a vice president of a leading publisher in New York City. That same year, she published her first book, *How to Make It in a Man's World*, a humorous and practical guide to penetrating the male-dominated business world.

Inspired by a growing feminist movement, Pogrebin helped launch *Ms.* in 1971 and served on its editorial board. She also left book publishing to devote her energies to writing and feminist activism. She has campaigned for equal pay in the workplace, the establishment of state-supported child-care centers, and new forms of child-rearing that reject stereotypical modes of behavior. In 1971, she also helped found the National Women's Political Caucus, a political advocacy group. In addition, she has collaborated with the actress Marlo Thomas on *Free to Be . . . You and Me,* a record, book, and television special about nonsexist children's play.

While combating discrimination against all women, Pogrebin has also challenged discrimination against Jewish women within the international feminist movement. Writing in *Ms.* magazine in June 1982, Pogrebin declared that Jewish women have a two-front battle to wage: against sexism from their Jewish brothers and against hostility from their non-Jewish sisters. In *Deborah, Golda, and Me,* a highly personal account of her rediscovery of her Jewish identity, she explores the many ways in which her feminist politics and her Jewish ideals and values complement each other.

PUBLICATIONS
How to Make It in a Man's World (1970)
Getting Yours: How to Make the System Work for the Working Woman (1975)
Growing Up Free: Raising Your Child in the '80s (1980)
Family Politics: Love and Power on an Intimate Frontier (1983)
Among Friends: Who We Like, Why We Like Them, and What We Do About It (1987)
Deborah, Golda, and Me (1991)

Preston, Ann

PHYSICIAN, HOSPITAL ADMINISTRATOR

Born: December 1, 1813
West Grove, Pennsylvania

Died: April 18, 1872
Philadelphia, Pennsylvania

Ann Preston fought for women's right to practice medicine. She was raised in a Quaker family and community that supported the antislavery and women's rights movements. She attended a Quaker (Friends) school in West Grove and later a Friends' boarding school in Chester, Pennsylvania.

Active in the antislavery and temperance struggles, she taught school and continued to educate herself through reading and attending public lectures. By the early 1840s, she was concerned about the ignorance surrounding women's physiology and began to teach such classes to local women. She then apprenticed for two years to a Philadelphia doctor. After being rejected by several medical schools because she was a woman, she entered the newly opened Female (later Woman's) Medical College of Pennsylvania, founded in 1850 by Quakers.

Preston received her M.D. degree in 1851, then pursued postgraduate study until 1853, when she became an instructor at the college. Despite strong public opposition to women physicians, she helped found a women's hospital in affiliation with the college and arranged for Dr. Emeline Horton Cleveland to obtain advanced obstetrics training in Paris, in order to strengthen the hospital's surgery and obstetrics units. In 1863, Dr. Preston also started a nursing school.

Three years later, she became dean of the Woman's Medical College and fought for her students' right to obtain additional clinical training at Philadelphia's major hospitals. Responding to criticisms of immodesty and even immorality in wanting to educate male and female medical students

together, she insisted that women were entitled to receive all necessary medical training.

In later years, Dr. Preston also served as a consulting physician to Woman's Hospital and conducted a small private practice. Like Elizabeth Blackwell, Harriot Hunt, Mary Jacobi, and Rebecca Cole, she helped pave the way for women to enter the medical profession.

FURTHER READING
Abram, Ruth. *Send Us a Lady Physician: Women Doctors in America, 1835–1920.* New York: Norton, 1986.

Qoyawayma, Polingaysi

NATIVE AMERICAN EDUCATOR

Born: 1892 (exact date unknown)
Oraibi, Arizona

Died: exact date and location unknown

Half a century before other educators, Polingaysi Qoyawayma promoted Native American language and culture in her teaching. She was determined that her students not be forced to renounce their heritage, as she was forced to in her childhood.

As a young girl, she was sent from her Hopi village in Arizona to a white-run boarding school in California. There, like the other Native American students, she was forced to speak only English and to dress in Anglo clothes. Later she recalled the harsh treatment on the reservation where she lived and at the school she attended—how Hopi men cried when they had to cut their long hair to conform with Anglo fashion and how Native American students were humiliated by their white teachers.

When Qoyawayma began teaching Hopi and Navaho children in 1924, she was determined to preserve her students' heritage by incorporating their cultural traditions into her lesson plans. Despite the opposition of most educators and government officials, who had no respect for native cultures, she forged ahead, urging her students to keep alive their Indian heritage. She retired from teaching in 1954, a pioneer in promoting the culture and education of Native Americans.

PUBLICATION
No Turning Back (autobiography, 1964)

Rainey, Gertrude "Ma"

BLUES SINGER

Born: April 26, 1886
Columbus, Georgia

Died: December 22, 1939
Columbus, Georgia

Gertrude Pridgett Rainey, known affectionately to her audiences as "Ma" Rainey because of her intimate, homey manner, was one of the last great black minstrel entertainers. She helped to usher in a new style of singing called "the blues." Little is known about her early years except that she was baptized in the First African Baptist Church and that her grandmother may have been a stage performer after the Civil War.

Young Gertrude made her first stage appearance about 1900 at the Springer Opera House in Columbus, Georgia. She performed in a local talent show called "Bunch of Blackberries." Four years later, in 1904, she married Will ("Pa") Rainey, and the couple performed a song-and-dance act in black minstrel shows. They appeared with such troupes as the Rabbit Foot Minstrels, the Florida Cotton Blossoms, and Shufflin' Sam from Alabam'.

Rainey's popularity soared, and she soon received special billing. Her act took her through the back roads of southern villages, where she often performed in carnival or "tent" shows.

In these homely settings, lighted by simple gas lanterns, Rainey, a rotund woman dressed in flamboyant gowns and draped in shiny jewelry, sang about the sorrows of everyday rural black life. Her songs were gritty, homespun ballads about love, infidelity, heartbreak, suffering, and also about the few pleasures in life—music, dancing, sex, and a shot of whiskey now and then. Although she did not specifically touch on racial or political themes, her songs captured the fear and insecurity of life in a violent and segregated society and the hope for a better life up north. In the dimly lit setting, her rich, haunting voice lingered in the air like cigarette smoke.

Over the years, she performed in a variety of shows, sometimes writing her own lyrics and sometimes using those written for her. In 1923, she began recording phonograph records for the Paramount company, and her popularity spread to blacks up north who had never seen her perform. During the 1930s, she also owned and operated two theaters in Georgia.

Although Rainey never achieved the popularity of Bessie Smith, another blues singer, her music captured the pathos of African-American rural life and served as a vital link between earlier forms of African-American music and the distinct rhythms of 20th-century jazz.

FURTHER READING
Harrison, Daphne Duval. *Black Pearls: Blues Queens of the 1920s.* New Brunswick, N.J.: Rutgers University Press, 1988.
Jones, Hettie. *Big Star Fallin' Mama.* New York: Viking, 1994.
Lieb, Sandra R. *Mother of the Blues: A Study of Ma Rainey.* Amherst: University of Massachusetts Press, 1981.

Rankin, Jeannette Pickering

CONGRESSWOMAN, SUFFRAGIST, PACIFIST

Born: June 11, 1880
Grant Creek Ranch, Montana Territory

Died: May 18, 1973
Carmel, California

Jeannette Rankin achieved two firsts: She was the first woman elected to the U.S. House of Representatives and the only member of Congress to oppose American entry into World Wars I and II. She came from a family of accomplished women, including her mother, a schoolteacher, and her three sisters—a professor, a university administrator, and a lawyer. But Jeannette Rankin showed little predilection for higher education, though she graduated from the University of Montana in 1902 with a bachelor's degree in biology. She taught school briefly before becoming a seamstress.

In 1908, she returned to school at the New York School of Philanthropy and did social work in Montana and Washington. But the suffrage movement captured her allegiance, and she joined the National American Woman Suffrage Association (NAWSA) as a field secretary.

In 1916, she won a seat in the U.S Congress, representing the state of Montana. Her first significant vote as a representative was a vote against American entry into World War I. From this one act, she gained a reputation as a pacifist and subsequently opposed American involvement in all wars.

After losing a race for U.S. senator, she devoted her energies to pacifist activities and better health care and working conditions for women and children. In 1940, she was re-elected to Congress as a representative from Montana. On the day after Japanese bombers attacked U.S. ships in Pearl Harbor, she, alone, in both houses of Congress, voted against American entry into World War II.

Two years later, she was defeated for reelection and returned home to Montana. She traveled abroad to study pacifist techniques in other countries, such as India, where she met Mahatma Gandhi, the great exponent of peaceful nonresistance. She opposed the mounting military buildup of the Cold War, including U.S. involvement in Korea and Vietnam. In the late 1960s, opponents of the Vietnam War hailed Rankin as their leader, and they formed the Jeannette Rankin Brigade to demonstrate against the war.

Like other female pacifists of her generation, Rankin envisioned the world community of nations as an international domestic realm. She believed that women were obligated to spread the peaceful, nurturing values of the home not only to their own communities but throughout the world.

FURTHER READING
Josephson, Hannah. *Jeanette Rankin: First Lady in Congress.* Indianapolis, Ind.: Bobbs-Merrill, 1974.

Ray, Charlotte E.
LAWYER

Born: January 13, 1850
New York, New York

Died: January 4, 1911
Woodside, New York

Charlotte Ray was the first African-American woman lawyer. She came from a distinguished New York family, and her bloodline included Native American as well as white ancestors. Before the Civil War, her father, a preacher, was active in the Underground Railroad.

Ray attended the Institute for the Education of Colored Youth, a school in Washington, D.C. In 1869, she joined the faculty of Howard University, an African-American college also in Washington, D.C. She also enrolled in law school at Howard.

By all accounts, she had a keen, incisive mind for the law. In 1872, she graduated from the law school and was admitted to the Washington, D.C., bar. Because the D.C. bar had recently lifted barriers against admitting women, her application was not contested. She thus became the first African-American woman lawyer as well as the first female lawyer admitted to the D.C. bar.

She opened a law office in Washington, but prejudice against a black woman practicing law kept potential clients away. In 1879, she moved to New York City and taught school in Brooklyn. She died of acute bronchitis at age 60.

Reed, Esther DeBerdt

SOLDIERS' RELIEF WORKER

Born: October 22, 1746
London, England

Died: September 18, 1780
Philadelphia, Pennsylvania

Esther DeBerdt Reed started a long tradition of women's relief work. During the American Revolution, she organized a committee of wealthy women in Philadelphia to go door to door to request money for American soldiers. Her volunteers appealed to women of all ages, urging them to forgo luxuries such as fancy gowns and jewelry and contribute the equivalent sum to the cause. Less affluent women were also asked to contribute.

To win public support for her efforts, Reed wrote an article entitled "Sentiments of an American Woman." In it, she urged America's women to express their gratitude to the troops for defending their country, and she cited Joan of Arc, women from biblical times, and female monarchs as examples of women who had served their countries in heroic ways.

In the summer of 1780, under Reed's supervision, Philadelphia's women collected a large sum of money for the troops, then persuaded friends and relatives in other regions to do the same. Reed's article was published in newspapers throughout the colonies, inspiring other women to organize their own committees.

To her dismay, General George Washington spurned her offer of a monetary gift to each soldier, and suggested instead that Reed use the money to make shirts for the poorly clad troops. Reed—who wanted the soldiers to have a "reward for past Services & an incitement to future Duty"—reluctantly set about the task of organizing women to sew shirts.

She died before the work was completed, but other women took over, and by late December 1780 thousands of shirts, each embroidered with the name of the woman who had sewed it, were sent to the army.

Although Reed and her followers had wanted to do less traditional work, such as fund-raising, their efforts led to the creation of the Ladies' Association, the first women's organization in America. For the first time, women organized for a cause, and they achieved their goals and demonstrated their leadership abilities.

Rich, Adrienne Cecile

POET, WRITER

Born: May 16, 1929
Baltimore, Maryland

Adrienne Rich is a highly acclaimed, and provocative, poet and essayist. Her poetry deals with both personal and political issues, from sexuality and romantic love to her awakening as a feminist and lesbian activist. Even such seemingly personal subjects as family relations become powerful political statements in Rich's adroit hands.

She was raised in a southern Jewish household with a father "who encouraged me to read and write," as she later recalled. Initially, she was educated by her parents—mostly her mother—until she was nine. The elder Riches believed they could give their two daughters a better, more enlightened education than they would receive at schools away from home. To be sure, as a child Adrienne Rich was steeped in such world-famous poets as Tennyson, Keats, and Blake, and also wrote her own poetry. Later, after completing elementary and high school, she attended Radcliffe College, graduating Phi Beta Kappa in 1951. She also published her first book of poems, *A Change of World,* which received the Yale Younger Poets Award.

Settling down to marriage and motherhood, she taught poetry at City College of New York and also at Rutgers University in New Jersey. Her husband died unexpectedly in 1970, and over the following decade, Rich became a prominent creative voice for the women's movement and for an emerging gay and lesbian movement. Her most famous book, *Of Woman Born: Motherhood as Experience and Institution* (1976), is a brilliant analysis of how men have controlled the expectations and public image of motherhood.

Rich continues to speak out and experiment with new poetic modes. She is an eloquent, compelling thinker and writer who has immeasurably enriched American letters.

MAJOR PUBLICATIONS

Poems: Selected and New (1975)
Of Woman Born: Motherhood as Experience and Institution (1976)
On Lies, Secrets, and Silence: Selected Prose, 1966–1978 (1979)
Blood, Bread, and Poetry: Selected Prose, 1979–1985 (1986)
An Atlas of the Difficult World: Poems (1991)
What Is Found There: Notebooks on Poetry and Politics (1993)

Richards, Ellen Henrietta Swallow

CHEMIST, HOME ECONOMIST

Born: December 3, 1842
Dunstable, Massachusetts

Died: March 30, 1911
Boston, Massachusetts

Educated primarily at home by her parents, Ellen Swallow Richards early on showed an interest in household management—which she later parlayed into a career as a pioneer home economist. After attending a local academy and teaching school for several years, she entered Vassar College. There she dis-covered a love for science. In 1870, she entered the Massachusetts Institute of Technology (MIT) in Cambridge—the first female student to be admitted—and received a B.S. in 1873 as well as an M.A. from Vassar. She pursued further graduate study at MIT and assisted a professor who was doing pioneering research in analyzing public water supplies, but she never received a doctorate because she was a woman.

In 1875, she married Robert Hallowell Richards, another professor at MIT, with whom she shared a passion for science. They promoted each other's work—his in metallurgy, and hers in chemistry. Indeed, she was the first woman elected to the American Institute of Mining and Metallurgical Engineers.

Besides pursuing her own pioneering studies in household pollutants, for which she devised tests to determine impurities in wallpapers, fabrics, and cleaning fluids, she helped promote women's education in the sciences by teaching and organizing a Woman's Laboratory at MIT. She also helped to establish the Association of Collegiate Alumnae (later, the American Association of University Women) and tried to expand graduate educational opportunities for women.

But her most enduring contribution was her influence over the emerging home economics movement. She set up model kitchens in Boston and elsewhere to demonstrate nutritious recipes and sell scientifically prepared cooked foods, and she formulated nutritious menus for schools and hospitals. In the process, she paved the way for women to enter the new field of dietetics and organized the first college-level home economics department.

From these initial efforts, Richards went on to shape curriculum, training, and related studies in nutrition, sanitation, and hygiene for high school and college courses. She was the first president and guiding spirit of the American Home Economics Association, organized in 1908. Eager to apply science to the needs of daily life, she furthered women's advancement in the sciences and promoted healthier living through the guiding principles of home economics.

MAJOR PUBLICATIONS
Home Sanitation: A Manual for Housekeepers (1887)
Domestic Economy as a Factor in Public Education (1889)

FURTHER READING
Clarke, Robert. *Ellen Swallow: The Woman Who Founded Ecology.* Chicago: Follett, 1973.

Richards, Linda

PIONEER NURSING EDUCATOR

Born: July 27, 1841
near Potsdam, New York

Died: April 16, 1930
Boston, Massachusetts

Linda Richards became America's first accredited nurse and went on to develop comprehensive training programs in nursing. She grew up in Vermont, where she attended common schools and a local academy. By her teens, she had developed a reputation as a "born nurse," someone who had a natural ability to nurse the sick. During and after the Civil War, she began to consider nursing as a possible occupation, and she sought additional training. For a time, she worked at Boston City Hospital as an assistant nurse but found the nursing staff to be ill-trained and indifferent toward the patients.

In 1872, she entered Dr. Susan Dimock's newly organized nursing school at the New England Hospital for Women and Children in Boston. A year later, after training in all of the hospital's wards and mastering 12 lectures, she graduated with the first degree from this first American school of nursing.

She took a position as night superintendent at the Bellevue Training School in New York City, then became superintendent of the Boston Training School, later the Massachusetts General Hospital School of Nursing. There she reorganized and strengthened the program and, in the process, advanced the entire movement for better nursing education.

After additional study in England, including several private meetings with Florence Nightingale, she developed nursing programs in Boston and in Kyoto, Japan, where she established Japan's first nursing school. Upon her return in 1891, she established or improved existing nursing programs in hospitals in Philadelphia, New York, Hartford, and Boston. She then turned to the task of improving standards of nursing in mental hospitals before retiring in 1911 at age 70.

Despite initial resistance by physicians and hospital administrators who were willing to settle for inadequately trained nurses, she repeatedly won them over with her superior organizational and administrative abilities, and elevated nursing into a respected profession.

FURTHER READING
Baker, Rachel. *America's First Trained Nurse: Linda Richards.* New York: Julian Messner, 1959.

Robins, Margaret Dreier

LABOR REFORMER

Born: September 6, 1868
Brooklyn, New York

Died: February 21, 1945
Brooksville, Florida

Early in life, Margaret Dreier Robins rejected the frivolous pursuits of the debutante set and decided to dedicate her life to more useful ends. Born into an affluent and civic-minded family, she attended private schools and, though she did not go to college, she continued her education through a rigorous program of independent study.

At 19, she joined the women's auxiliary of Brooklyn Hospital, where she received her first exposure to poverty. She also joined a charity group that supervised mental hospitals and held an important post in the Women's Municipal League, a civic organization.

But her true work began in 1904 when she joined the newly formed Women's Trade Union League (WTUL), an organization of affluent and working-class women who together campaigned for better wages and working conditions for women in industry. Her marriage in 1905 to Raymond Robins, a settlement worker and self-made millionaire, helped strengthen her dedication to social reform. He shared her political ideals, and his wealth enabled them to devote their time and energy to their various causes.

In 1907, Robins became president of both the national WTUL and its Chicago chapter. In the 1910s, she was a key strategist for the WTUL's growing involvement in the great garment workers' strikes in New York, Philadelphia, and Chicago. Through her tireless efforts to raise money, organize support for the strikers, and secure legal counsel for imprisoned strikers, she turned the WTUL into a highly influential labor-reform organization. She was also active in other labor groups, including the American Federation of Labor, and she could always be counted on to march in protest against any number of injustices.

After World War I, Robins briefly served as president of the International Federation of Working Women, an organization that she largely created, and she also worked for the YWCA, the Red Cross, the League of Women Voters, and other civic and charitable organizations. Throughout her long and varied career, Robins remained a vigorous advocate for working women.

FURTHER READING

Payne, Elizabeth Anne. *Reform, Labor, and Feminism: Margaret Dreier Robins and the Women's Trade Union League.* Urbana: University of Illinois Press, 1988.

Robinson, Jo Ann Gibson

CIVIL RIGHTS ACTIVIST

Born: ca. 1912
Culloden, Georgia

Jo Ann Robinson was a principle organizer of the Montgomery bus boycott, the opening salvo of the American civil rights movement. Robinson, the daughter of prosperous farmers, graduated valedictorian of the all-black high school she attended in Macon, Georgia. She went on to earn a bachelor's degree from Fort Valley State College—the first person in her family to receive a college degree—and obtained a teaching position in the Macon public schools. She also married Wilbur Robinson and bore one son, who died in early childhood—a loss she never got over.

After moving to Atlanta, Georgia, she earned a master's degree in English at Atlanta University and, in 1949, joined the English faculty at Alabama State College in Montgomery, Alabama. She became a member of the Dexter Avenue Baptist Church, where the Reverend Martin Luther King, Jr., future civil rights leader, preached. She also joined the Women's Political Council, a black women's civic organization.

Robinson's own brush with discrimination on Montgomery's city buses inspired her to assume a key organizational role in the Montgomery bus boycott; she had been forced to give up her seat after sitting in a section of the bus reserved for whites.

After learning that such humiliating discrimination was routine, she urged the Women's Political Council to address the problem. When Rosa Parks was arrested for refusing to give up her seat to a white passenger, Robinson and other members of the Women's Political Council secretly deployed a plan for a bus boycott.

On December 5, 1955, about 50,000 blacks refused to take the city's buses and walked or hitched a ride to work throughthe system of car pools that Robinson and her co-organizers had devised. The boycott lasted over a year and, during the ensuing months, Robinson, like other activists, received death threats and had her home vandalized. But, ultimately, the boycott succeeded in integrating the city's transit system. It also launched the most far-reaching quest for equal rights for African Americans in this country's history.

PUBLICATION

Robinson, Jo Ann. *The Montgomery Bus Boycott and the Women Who Started It: Memoirs of Jo Ann Gibson Robinson,* edited by David J. Garrow. Knoxville: University of Tennessee Press, 1987

FURTHER READING

Crawford, Vicki L. et al. eds. *Women in the Civil Rights Movement: Trailblazers and Torchbearers, 1941–1965.* Brooklyn, N.Y.: Carlson, 1990.

Robinson, Rubye Doris Smith

CIVIL RIGHTS ACTIVIST

Born: April 25, 1942
Atlanta, Georgia

Died: October 7, 1967
Atlanta, Georgia

Hailed as "one of the few genuine revolutionaries in the black liberation movement," Rubye Doris Robinson quickly worked her way up the ranks to leadership within the Student Nonviolent Coordinating Committee (SNCC), the branch of the civil rights movement that recruited and organized students. The 1955 bus boycott by blacks in Montgomery, Alabama, first inspired young Rubye Smith's determination to achieve civil rights. She graduated from high school a year early and entered Spelman College in Atlanta, Georgia. In 1960, along with scores of other students, she joined the growing sit-in campaign to protest segregated seating in lunchrooms and attended the founding meeting of SNCC in Raleigh, North Carolina.

Smith's commitment to the civil rights movement only deepened with time and hardship, and she chose to go to jail twice rather than pay bail when arrested with other civil rights workers. She willingly participated in one of the most dangerous campaigns of the civil rights movement, the Freedom Rides. Together, black and white students rode interstate buses to challenge the legality of segregated interstate travel. At the end of one such trip, Robinson and nine other SNCC workers were brutally attacked by an angry white mob.

Robinson soon stood at the nerve center of SNCC's administrative and recruiting efforts. She coordinated the campaign to register black voters in Mississippi and established strategies and policies for SNCC. She also challenged the secondary roles that most women played in SNCC, and in 1966 was promoted to the position of executive secretary.

As SNCC gradually shifted from an integrated and nonviolent group to a black nationalist organization willing to use more aggressive tactics, Robinson cheered its new direction. She was a fighter, and she fought for civil rights until her unfortunate early death from cancer in 1967.

FURTHER READING

Branch, Taylor. *Parting the Waters: America in the King Years, 1954-63.* New York: Simon & Schuster, 1988.

Roosevelt, Eleanor

SOCIAL REFORMER, FIRST LADY

Born: October 11, 1884
New York, New York

Died: November 7, 1962
New York, New York

Revered as the "first lady of the world" because of her broad compassion and diligent efforts for international peace, Eleanor Roosevelt grew up in privileged, upper-class surroundings—hardly the setting to inspire her future role as crusader for the underdog. Her early years were filled with pain and loneliness; her mother, a cold and uncaring woman, died, and several years later her father, whom she adored, also passed away, leaving his daughter in the care of her maternal grandmother.

In 1899, at age 15, Eleanor Roosevelt enrolled in a private girls' school in London. The headmistress, Marie Souvestre, gave her the love, confidence, and stability that her own family could not provide. But her grandmother, critical of Souvestre's untraditional ways, pulled Eleanor out of the school after her second year, and she returned to the United States to prepare for her entrance into fashionable society. Her true interest, however, lay in charity work, and she joined the settlement-house movement and the National Consumers' League, an organization that campaigned for better working conditions for factory and saleswomen. Her lifelong commitment to social justice was born out of this early exposure to the problems and needs of the poor.

In 1905, she married her cousin Franklin Delano Roosevelt. Over the next decade they had six children, and Eleanor Roosevelt added the responsibilities of wife and mother to that of her volunteer work. While her husband, a young lawyer, pursued a political career, she dutifully organized social affairs to help his career along.

Gradually, however, she found her own political role. During World War I, she organized soldiers' relief activities, and in 1920 she joined the League of Women Voters. She also joined the Women's Trade Union League (WTUL) to work for protective legislation for working women, and she became a forceful voice for women within the Democratic party. At the Democratic National Convention in 1924, she fought for equal-pay and child-labor legislation and other issues of concern to women. She headed a female reform network that pressured the Democratic party to be more responsive to women's needs.

When her husband was elected President in 1932, Roosevelt wondered what role she would play. But she did not flounder for long. Because her husband, earlier stricken with polio, was unable to travel widely, she became his eyes and legs. From the coal mines of Virginia to the lumber camps of the Northwest, she toured the depression-scarred nation, becoming a vigilant advocate for the poor. Many of her ideas for relieving the nation's misery and improving people's lives found their way into her husband's New Deal policies.

She also promoted civil rights for African Americans and urged her husband to sign a law making lynching, which had been on the rise, a federal crime. In 1936, she became a syndicated newspaper columnist. Under the heading "My Day," she shared with readers her experiences and observations and urged them not to lose heart because of the nation's hard economic times. During World War II, she worked with the National Association for the Advancement of Colored People (NAACP) to combat discrimination in the armed forces and defense industry.

Her husband's death in 1945 did not diminish Roosevelt's activism. After World War II, she helped draft the charter of the United Nations and served as a U.S. delegate to the UN. In addition, she continued to fight for civil rights, campaigned for nuclear disarmament, supported the establishment of Israel, wrote a regular column for *McCall's* magazine, and traveled throughout the world representing the United States.

During the 1950s, Roosevelt denounced government persecution of former Communist sympathizers and worked more intensively for international peace. Her last public position, fittingly enough, was chair of the Commission on the Status of Women in the administration of President John F. Kennedy. When Roosevelt died, the entire world lost a friend—a courageous and compassionate crusader for peace and human progress.

MAJOR PUBLICATIONS

It's Up to the Women (1933)
This Is My Story (1937)
This I Remember (1949)
On My Own (1958)
The Autobiography of Eleanor Roosevelt (1958; reissued 1978, 1984)
You Learn by Living (1960)
Tomorrow is Now (posthumously published, 1963)

FURTHER READING

Cook, Blanche Wiesen. *Eleanor Roosevelt: 1884–1933.* vol. 1. New York: Viking, 1992.
Freedman, Russell. *Eleanor Roosevelt: A Life of Discovery.* New York: Clarion, 1994.
Goodwin, Doris Kearns. *No Ordinary Time: Franklin and Eleanor Roosevelt: The Homefront in World War II.* New York: Simon & Schuster, 1994.
Toor, Rachel. *Eleanor Roosevelt: Diplomat and Humanitarian.* New York: Chelsea House, 1989.

Rose, Ernestine Louise Siismondi Potowski

FEMINIST, REFORMER

Born: January 13, 1810
Piotrkow, Russian Poland

Died: August 4, 1892
London, England

The daughter of an Orthodox Jewish rabbi, Ernestine Rose began fighting for women's rights almost a decade before the organized women's rights movement began in the United States. In fact, Susan B. Anthony later called her one of the three pioneers of the movement. An only child, Ernestine Rose grew up with more freedom and education than was usual for young Jewish women of her day. Later she said, "I was a rebel at the age of five."

Her father taught her to read Hebrew, but she soon challenged Jewish teachings about the inferiority of women. At 16, when her father tried to marry her off without her consent, she went to court to obtain her independence and gain control over an inheritance left to her by her mother. The judges, so impressed by her oral skills, willingly granted her claim.

She left Poland and, after traveling through Europe, settled in England, where she supported herself by selling a household deodorant that she had invented. She also joined a radical political group. In 1836, she married William Ella Rose, a silversmith and jeweler, and they both immigrated to the United States.

In New York in 1840, Rose joined Paulina Wright (later Paulina Wright Davis) and Elizabeth Cady Stanton to work for legislation that would enable married women to keep property in their own names. She also joined the free-thought movement, lecturing and writing for the *Boston Investigator,* a free-thought journal.

By the 1850s, her primary cause was the women's rights movement. But, like other reformers of this era, she supported the antislavery and temperance movements as well. Although she did not attend the 1848 Seneca Falls convention, she later attended most of the national women's rights conventions. Called the "Queen of the Platform," she was one of the most skillful lecturers of the day and used her oratorical skills to promote woman suffrage.

During the Civil War, she helped found the Women's Loyal National League, and after the war she worked on behalf of working women and world peace. She also joined Stanton and Anthony in establishing the National Woman Suffrage Association (NWSA), one of two national women's rights organizations. Rose spent her last years in London, where she continued to work for various reform movements.

FURTHER READING

Suhl, Yuri. *Ernestine L. Rose: Women's Rights Pioneer.* New York: Biblio Press, 1990.

Rouse, Rebecca

REFORMER, RELIEF WORKER

Born: ca. 1799
New England

Died: date and location unknown

Rebecca Cromwell Rouse spearheaded one of the most extensive and effective soldiers' relief societies during the Civil War. Her prior work experience had readied her for the hard work of coordinating relief efforts for the Union soldiers of northern Ohio.

In 1821, she married Benjamin Rouse, a stonemason and one of the founders of the first Sunday school in Boston. They shared a passion for civic reform and moved to New York City in the late 1820s to work among the poor by distributing religious tracts in the city's tenement districts. In 1830, they carried their evangelical work to Ohio, where Benjamin organized 200 Sunday schools while Rebecca established the Female Baptist Sewing Society to raise money for a missionary society and poorhouse.

She also joined the temperance movement and helped establish an orphanage. In 1851, she supported Cleveland's seamstresses in their efforts to organize a protective union and cooperative store. By the late 1850s, she had emerged as one of Cleveland's most respected and influential reformers, and when a citywide meeting of women was called shortly after the Civil War began, she was chosen to lead the newly formed Ladies Aid and Sanitary Society.

Within two days, the society, under Rouse's direction, made and distributed blankets to 1,000 soldiers, and in almost as little time sewed 1,000 shirts for the troops. The society also recruited nurses and collected hospital supplies for a nearby military camp.

A few weeks into the war, the society's leaders decided to organize a soldiers' relief society for all of northern Ohio, and once again Rouse took charge of organizing and administering the new agency. She traveled up and down the state organizing local chapters and solicited money and free services from railroads, postmasters, and Western Union. She also tracked the distribution of supplies to the war front, to ensure that they reached their intended destination, set up a hospital in Kentucky, and treated wounded soldiers. She thrived at being in the line of fire and found joy and purpose in her work.

The end of war did not slow Rouse down. She continued to volunteer at the soldiers' relief home that her society had established. Three months after the war ended, her husband, Benjamin, wrote

to their daughter: "Mother is just as busy as she can be feeding soldiers on their [way to] return home . . . and taking care of the sick and wounded at the Soldier's home." He continued, "Mother wishes me to say she works so hard at the home days she's too tired to write you at night." Rebecca Rouse exemplified the eagerness with which women from both the North and South rose to the demands and challenges of war—and discovered from their wartime work new skills and inner resources.

FURTHER READING

Scott, Anne Firor. *Natural Allies: Women's Associations in American History.* Urbana: University of Illinois Press, 1991.

Rowlandson, Mary White

INDIAN CAPTIVE, AUTHOR

Born: ca. 1635
England

Died: after 1678
Connecticut

Mary Rowlandson survived a harsh captivity by hostile Native Americans and wrote a classic account of her ordeal. Her tale provides a revealing glimpse into a hitherto unknown aspect of frontier life. She was born in England and migrated to Salem, Massachusetts, in early childhood with her family.

In 1656, she married Joseph Rowlandson, a minister in Lancaster, Massachusetts, and they had four children, one of whom died in infancy. Mary Rowlandson would have remained an anonymous wife and mother but for a tragedy that struck her frontier village. During an Indian uprising against the English settlements throughout Massachusetts, a party of Indians attacked Lancaster in the early dawn hours of February 10, 1676. It was "the dolefullest day that ever mine eyes saw," Rowlandson later recalled. The attackers killed several settlers and set fire to their homes. About 36 surviving settlers took refuge in the Rowlandsons' house. The minister, away at the time, returned home to discover that 12 more settlers had been killed in his house and 24 taken captive—including his wife and 3 children.

Mary Rowlandson remained in captivity for three months. During that time, she endured many hardships, including separation from two of her children and the trauma of watching her young daughter, wounded in the attack, die in her arms. She endured forced marches, hard physical labor, and a meager diet. Occasionally, however, her captors showed kindness because she was a skilled seamstress.

Her religious faith as well as her quick thinking helped her survive her ordeal. She asked her captors to sell her back to her husband, and they complied, for the sum of 20 pounds. On May 2, 1676, she was released after her husband paid her ransom. Several weeks later, her two remaining children also arrived home safely.

Rowlandson and her family lived in Boston until 1677, when her husband accepted the pastorate of a church in Connecticut. He died on November 24, 1678, and she received an annual pension of 30 pounds from the town. Her narrative of her captivity remains a gripping account of a nightmare experienced by few other women of her time.

PUBLICATION
*The True History of the Captivity and Restoration of
Mrs. Mary Rowlandson* (1682)

Rowson, Susanna Haswell

NOVELIST, EDUCATOR, ACTRESS

*Born: ca. 1762
Portsmouth, England*

*Died: March 2, 1824
Boston, Massachusetts*

Susanna Rowson first came to America as a child. Because her father was a British government official, her family was persecuted during the American Revolution for sympathizing with the British Crown. The entire family was imprisoned for two years and later returned to London.

Self-taught, Susanna Rowson found work as a governess. In this position, she traveled throughout Europe with her employer's family and met the European aristocracy. In 1787, she married William Rowson, a merchant. When his hardware business failed in 1792, they both sought work as actors. They toured the eastern United States with several theater companies before settling in Boston. Rowson, while not a particularly talented actress, had an engaging personality and was a versatile performer. She sang, danced, played the harpsichord and guitar, and also wrote plays.

She retired from the stage in her mid-30s and opened a Young Ladies Academy in Boston. Her school was among the first in the United States to offer female students a comprehensive education beyond rudimentary reading and writing. Rowson also wrote some of the textbooks she used and was a columnist for several Boston journals.

But Rowson is best known as the author of *Charlotte Temple* (London, 1791; Philadelphia, 1794), a novel that became America's first best-seller. Although the plot was commonplace for its time—portraying the seduction and abandonment of an innocent schoolgirl by a British army officer—Rowson used the familiar material to condemn men's sexual power over women.

Despite her family's support for the British monarchy, Rowson became an ardent American patriot—and one of the first American women to express through her work her belief in women's equality.

PUBLICATION
Charlotte Temple (1791)

Ruffin, Josephine St. Pierre

CLUBWOMAN, SOCIAL REFORMER, EDITOR

*Born: August 31, 1842
Boston, Massachusetts*

*Died: March 13, 1924
Boston, Massachusetts*

Like other distinguished African-American women of her day, Josephine St. Pierre Ruffin dedicated herself to the betterment of her sex and race. She learned race pride at an early age. Rather than send her to Boston's segregated schools, her parents enrolled her in school in nearby Salem, Massachusetts. Later, she transferred to a school in Boston when it was no longer segregated.

This early lesson in race pride stayed with her when she married into a prominent black family and embarked upon social reform work. For a time, she and her husband lived in England to escape prejudice, but they returned to Boston after the Civil War erupted. During the war, Ruffin helped recruit black soldiers for the Union. In the postwar years, she joined numerous civic causes. She also helped to resettle southern blacks who were flocking to Kansas in search of a better life during the late 1870s.

But Ruffin mainly committed herself to the social and economic progress of African-American women. In 1894, she and her daughter organized the Woman's Era Club, one of the first major African-American women's groups. Ruffin served as president and edited the club's monthly journal, the *Woman's Era*. As president, she convened a conference of other African-American women's clubs, and out of this historic meeting was born the National Federation of Afro-American Women, a coalition of black women's clubs.

In 1896, the federation merged with the Colored Women's League of Washington to form the National Association of Colored Women. Ruffin served as first vice president. In addition, from 1899 to 1902 she served on the executive board of the Massachusetts State Federation of Women's Clubs. Through vision and determination, she had helped to launch a national black women's club movement. This movement, in turn, contributed immeasurably to improving economic and social conditions within black communities across the nation.

Ruffin was a powerful voice for the dignity and full social equality of African-American women. To the end of her life, she continued to participate in social welfare causes for blacks and whites. She had a broad, humane vision of social progress, born out of her fierce pride and dignity as an African-American woman.

FURTHER READING
Giddings, Paula. *When and Where I Enter: The Impact of Black Women on Race and Sex in America.* New York: Morrow, 1984.

Sacajawea

INDIAN INTERPRETER FOR THE LEWIS AND
CLARK EXPEDITION

Born: ca. 1786
central Idaho

Died: December 20, 1812
Fort Manuel, South Dakota

Sacajawea's name is synonymous with the opening up of the American West. She served as the interpreter for the team of Lewis and Clark as they explored the vast regions of the Louisiana Purchase. She was born about 1786 into the Lemhi band of Shoshoni, or Snake, Indians who lived in the eastern Salmon River region of what is now Idaho.

During a trip eastward with her tribe, she was captured by a war party of Hidatsa Indians and was either sold or gambled into slavery. By 1804, she had become enslaved to Toussaint Charbonneau, a French Canadian who lived with the Hidatsas. When William Clark and Meriwether Lewis, explorers dispatched by President Thomas Jefferson to examine the territory purchased from the French, hired Charbonneau as an interpreter, Sacajawea and her two-month-old son by Charbonneau accompanied the expedition.

Sacajawea acted as interpreter for the explorers, enabling them to make vital communication—and friendship—with Native American tribes along the way. She also scouted out wild edible plants for cooking and once rescued valuable instruments and records from being drowned in a storm. Of this incident, William Clark wrote that she exhibited "equal fortitude and resolution, with any person onboard at the time of the accedent [sic]."

She offered invaluable assistance by gaining the approval of the Lemhi Shoshones, whose help was vital to the explorers as they crossed the Rocky Mountains. And when she was reunited with her people, she urged her brother, now a chief, to provide guidance, horses, and other assistance across the Columbia River in the Northwest. There is, however, only one recorded example of any trail guidance that she provided. Her main contribution lay in being an interpreter and emissary to native peoples along the explorers' way.

Clark, who later helped her son secure an education and work, also assisted Sacajawea and Charbonneau in settling down in St. Louis, Missouri. But by the spring of 1811 they both wished to return to the western frontier, and they moved to Fort Manuel in what is now South Dakota. Sacajawea was described by a clerk at the fort as "a good and the best Women [sic] in the fort." She died of natural causes sometime in the winter of 1812.

Over the next century, a legend depicting Sacajawea as Lewis and Clark's main guide emerged. Novels, statues, and monuments honoring her, as well as the many mountain peaks, streams, and other geographical features named after her, attest to Americans' enduring fascination with Sacajawea.

FURTHER READING
Clark, Ella Elizabeth. *Sacajawea of the Lewis and Clark Expedition.* Berkeley: University of California Press, 1979.

Sampson, Deborah

REVOLUTIONARY WAR SOLDIER, LECTURER

Born: December 17, 1760
Plympton, Massachusetts

Died: April 29, 1827
Sharon, Massachusetts

Although her forebears included such distinguished Puritan leaders as Governor William Bradford, Miles Standish, and John Alden, Deborah Sampson's childhood was marred by poverty

and family upheaval. When her father abandoned his wife and children, Deborah was bound out as a servant in Middleborough, Massachusetts. There she attended school part-time and was also educated by her employer's children.

After her term of service ended, she taught school briefly in Middleborough and joined the First Baptist Church there. But she was excommunicated from the church two years later on suspicion of dressing like a man and enlisting in the army. In 1782, Sampson had turned up in Boston under the name of Robert Shurtleff, an enlistee in the 4th Massachusetts Regiment, part of the Continental troops fighting for American independence.

Above average in height, with strong features and considerable stamina, she was able to conceal her sexual identity, and she fought alongside her fellow soldiers. Not until she was hospitalized with a fever in Philadelphia was her true identity discovered. She was discharged in 1783 and returned to Sharon, Massachusetts, where she married, bore three children, and went on tour throughout New England and New York to lecture about her unusual military experiences. In later years, she received a small pension for her services as a soldier.

FURTHER READING
Freeman, Lucy and Alma Bond. *America's First Woman Warrior: The Courage of Deborah Sampson.* New York: Paragon House, 1992.

Sanger, Margaret

BIRTH-CONTROL ACTIVIST

Born: September 14, 1879
Corning, New York

Died: September 6, 1966
Tucson, Arizona

After watching her mother and scores of other women succumb to ill health from too many pregnancies and children to raise, Margaret Sanger made birth control her life's work. She was born Margaret Louise Higgins and was one of 11 children in a household that never had enough money for food. Although she resented her father for failing to support his burgeoning family, she respected his progressive ideas. He supported woman suffrage, dress reform, and other social causes.

Margaret Sanger attended public school and Claverack College, a private coeducational school in the Catskills, where she worked in the kitchen to pay for room and board. She taught first grade and then went to nursing school in White Plains, New York. She completed the training to become a practical nurse and intended to pursue additional training, but her marriage in 1902 to William Sanger, a young architect, put an end to those plans. Over the next eight years, she bore three children.

When the Sangers moved to New York City, she found work as a home nurse in the Lower East Side. She also made the acquaintance of rebels and socialists, and plunged into the social and political ferment of those pre–World War I years by joining the Industrial Workers of the World (IWW) and other radical organizations. Sanger soon became convinced that birth control was paramount to achieving social and economic equality; women, she believed, must be able to control their reproduction before they could achieve other rights. She wrote about female sexuality and traveled to Europe to study new methods of contraception.

In 1916, she and her sister opened a birth-control clinic in Brooklyn, New York—despite a New York State law that forbade distribution of birth-control information. Ten days later, the police shut down the clinic. Gradually, Sanger added a new argument for birth control. She claimed that birth control was necessary not only because it gave women greater reproductive freedom but because it would help control the birthrate among immigrant and lower-class women, thus preventing less "desirable" groups from overpopulating American society. In seeking support for birth control, Sanger appealed to popular prejudices against African Americans and immigrants, as well as to women's desire to regulate their reproduction.

In 1921, she organized the American Birth Control League, the forerunner of Planned Parenthood, and two years later she opened the first physician-staffed birth-control clinic in the United States. It served as a teaching facility and the model for a network of more than 300 birth-control clinics established by Sanger and her supporters. These clinics provided access to reliable contraceptive information and devices. Sanger also fought for legalizing birth control. Eventually, her efforts bore fruit: In 1936, the Supreme Court removed the legal ban against birth control.

After World War II, Sanger helped found the International Planned Parenthood Federation and served as the organization's first president. She also continued to seek new and better methods of contraception, including the birth control pill. In spite of her earlier appeal to people's prejudices to win support for birth control, Sanger remained a staunch advocate of reproductive freedom for women; she set women on the path to achieving control over their bodies.

PUBLICATIONS
My Fight for Birth Control (autobiography, 1931)
Margaret Sanger: An Autobiography (1938)

FURTHER READING
Chesler, Ellen. *Woman of Valor: Margaret Sanger and the Birth Control Movement in America.* New York: Summit , 1992.

Schlafly, Phyllis
ANTI-FEMINIST ACTIVIST

Born: August 15, 1924
St. Louis, Missouri

While struggling to make her way in the male-dominated realms of business and politics, Phyllis Schlafly has made a career out of urging other women to stay home as wives and mothers. She grew up during the Great Depression in a household in which her mother, a librarian, was the family breadwinner after her father lost his job.

Educated in a religious school, she attended Washington University in St. Louis, Missouri, supporting herself by working nights in a lab testing explosives. After attaining a fellowship to Radcliffe College, she earned a master's degree in government, and from 1945 to 1949 she worked as a financial analyst in a bank and became involved in Republican politics.

In 1949, she married Fred Schlafly and over the next several years she bore six children. During the 1950s, she ran for Congress twice, losing both races, and has attended every Republican Presidential convention as a delegate since then. She has also coauthored five books on strategic defense policy, urging the U.S. government to devise weaponry and take the offensive against Communism.

But in 1972 Schlafly embarked on a new—and highly visible—career when she waged her own campaign against the women's movement, which she described as "a bunch of bitter women seeking a constitutional cure for their personal problems." Characterizing feminists as "unkempt" and as "radicals" and "socialists," she developed a powerful grassroots lobby of followers who shared her opposition to an equal rights amendment to the Constitution. In the early 1980s, her "Stop ERA" campaign derailed passage of a constitutional amendment guaranteeing women equal rights under the Constitution.

Schlafly argues that women as a class are different from men and should not compete with them. She claims that an equal rights amendment is not necessary because existing legislation already protects women's rights. Essentially, however, she feels that a woman's true place is in the home as wife and mother. Her conservative perspective also condemns homosexuality, abortion, sexual relations outside marriage, and socialism.

PUBLICATIONS
The Power of the Positive Woman (1972)
Pornography's Victims (1987)
Who Will Rock the Cradle? (1990)

FURTHER READING
Felsenthal, Carol. *The Sweetheart of the Silent Majority: The Biography of Phyllis Schlafly.* Garden City, N.Y.: Doubleday, 1981.

Schneiderman, Rose

LABOR ORGANIZER, SOCIAL ACTIVIST

Born: April 6, 1882
Saven, Russian Poland

Died: August 11, 1972
New York, New York

With determination enough to match her fiery red hair, Rose Schneiderman rose up from exploited garment worker to militant labor activist. Born in a small town in Russian Poland, she migrated in 1890 with her parents and siblings to New York City's Lower East Side. Two years later, her father, a tailor, died, leaving his family destitute. For a time, Rose and her brothers lived in an orphanage because their mother could not afford their upkeep.

At 13, Rose began work, first as a department store cash girl earning $2 for a 70-hour work week, then as a capmaker in a factory. In 1903, after being introduced to socialist ideas, she and two other female capmakers organized fellow workers into a local affiliate of the Jewish Socialist United Cloth Hat and Cap Makers' Union. Their local grew in membership, in part because of Schneiderman's effective leadership. In 1905, during the capmakers' successful 13-week strike against employers, she led strike meetings and walked picket lines.

But Schneiderman's true immersion in union work came in 1907, when she joined the Women's Trade Union League (WTUL), an organization of women workers and upper-class women allies dedicated to improving factory women's working conditions and salaries. She considered the WTUL the "most important influence in my life." Schneiderman soon quit working as a capmaker and became a paid organizer for the WTUL. She also attended the Rand School of Social Science, a socialist night school for workers.

In addition, Schneiderman recruited members for the International Ladies Garment Workers' Union and helped to strengthen the union's presence in the women's clothing industry. She was one of the leaders of the "Uprising of the Twenty Thousand," the massive shirtwaist makers' strike that nearly paralyzed New York City's shirtwaist industry, and was a keynote speaker two years later after the tragic Triangle Factory fire, in which 146 shirtwaist makers died because of management's disregard for workers' safety.

In 1918, Schneiderman became president of the New York branch of the Women's Trade Union League, and in 1926 she also headed up the national WTUL. She held both positions until the 1950s, when the organization disbanded. During her long tenure, she focused on improving workers' education and was a founder of the Bryn Mawr Summer School for Women Workers. She also ran for the United States Senate as a candidate of the newly formed New York State Labor party and was an early advocate of woman suffrage.

Through her work for the WTUL, Schneiderman met Eleanor Roosevelt and became a close friend and advisor on labor issues for both the president and first lady. In 1933, President Roosevelt appointed her to the labor advisory board of the National Recovery Administration, a New Deal agency. She was the only woman on the board, and she worked to improve wages and working conditions for women in industry.

Continuing her work for the WTUL during the late 1930s, Schneiderman proudly watched two measures that she had worked for—a minimum wage law and an 8-hour workday—take effect in New York State. She lived the remainder of her life in New York City, the scene of so many battles she had fought to improve wages and working conditions for America's working women.

PUBLICATION
All for One (autobiography, 1967)

FURTHER READING
Lagemann, Ellen Condliffe. *A Generation of Women: Education in the Lives of Progressive Reformers.* Cambridge: Harvard University Press, 1979.

Scudder, Vida

SOCIAL REFORMER, SCHOLAR

Born: December 15, 1861
Madura, India

Died: October 9, 1954
Wellesley, Massachusetts

Vida Scudder, along with Jane Addams, was a pioneer settlement-house leader. She was born Julia Davida and spent her early years in Europe, where she developed a lifelong love of culture and scholarly pursuits. She attended private schools in Boston and graduated from Smith College in 1884. While doing graduate work at Oxford University in England, she became keenly aware of poverty and social injustice. When she returned to the United States to teach English at Wellesley College, she tried to incorporate political ideas into her lectures and writings.

Her growing interest in social reform inspired her to establish a college settlement house, a residential house staffed by college-trained professionals and students to assist workers and immigrants. The first college settlement opened in 1889 in New York's Lower East Side, an immigrant Jewish and Italian neighborhood, followed by a second settlement house in Boston's South End.

Soon, Scudder devoted her full attention to settlement work, embarking upon a lifelong quest to wed Christian precepts with socialist ideas. She worked to strengthen the role of settlement houses in arbitrating labor disputes between factory owners and their exploited employees. She also helped to organize the Boston Women's Trade Union League, and in 1911 she joined the Socialist party.

Although she supported American entry into World War I, she became a committed pacifist in later years. After retiring from teaching in 1928, she devoted her time to writing about the Franciscans, an order of Catholic priests who felt divinely inspired to engage in good works. She became dean of the Summer School of Christian Ethics at Wellesley and lectured in New York on Christian social thought. She continued to write and explore new pathways to social and spiritual progress.

Scudder imbued her social activism with an abiding spiritual faith. Indeed, she drew a direct link between spiritual growth and social reform, and throughout her last years she joined religious organizations that espoused these views.

MAJOR PUBLICATIONS
*The Church and the Hour: Reflections of a Socialist
    Church Woman* (1917)
The Franciscan Adventure (1931)
My Quest for Reality (autobiography, 1952)

Sedgwick, Catharine Maria

AUTHOR

*Born: December 28, 1789
Stockbridge, Massachusetts*

*Died: July 31, 1867
West Roxbury, Massachusetts*

The most popular American novelist before Harriet Beecher Stowe, Catharine Sedgwick helped to create an original American literary tradition, one that did not depend on European themes and settings. Throughout her prolific writing career, she also experimented with new literary forms.

As a child, she had few opportunities to acquire a formal education. She attended a local school, where she said later that she "learned to parse glibly," and also private academies in Albany, New York, and Boston. She acquired her love of reading from her father, who urged her to read the works of Shakespeare and Miguel Cervantes, author of *Don Quixote*.

Sedgwick fell into her writing career almost by accident. During a difficult period in her life, one of her brothers urged her to write a moral tract. But the religious work soon became a novel, and in 1822 she published *A New-England Tale*, a portrait of the people and villages of her native Berkshire Hill region—and a story uniquely American in setting and characters. Sedgwick went on to write five more novels, portraying contemporary society as well as America's colonial past.

She also wrote numerous moral tracts and instructive stories. Through her writing, she strove to champion the social, intellectual, and moral progress of American society, and urged reform of harsh urban living conditions and the growth of a more tolerant religious spirit. Although she abhorred slavery and supported protection of married women's property rights, she never joined the abolition or women's rights movements. Prison reform, however, was her chief cause, and from 1848 to her death she led the Women's Prison Association in New York City.

Sedgwick produced no single great work, but she deserves recognition for creating a new, indigenous form of American writing.

MAJOR PUBLICATIONS
A New-England Tale (1822)
Redwood (1824)
Hope Leslie (1827)

FURTHER READING
Foster, Edward H. *Catharine Maria Sedgwick*. Boston: Twayne, 1974.

Seton, Elizabeth Ann Bayley

DIRECTOR OF FIRST AMERICAN
ORDER OF NUNS

*Born: August 28, 1774
New York, New York*

*Died: January 4, 1821
Emmitsburg, Maryland*

Elizabeth Ann Seton, known to her followers as "Mother Seton," founded the first order of nuns in the United States. Raised by her stepmother, who taught her the Psalms, she attended a girls' finishing school and married William Magee Seton, a successful merchant. She bore five children and lived a genteel upper-class life, attending the theater and social affairs and doing charity work.

When her husband died while they were visiting Italy, she became aware of the teachings of Catholicism and, upon her return to the United States in 1805, she converted to the Catholic faith. Despite the disapproval of her Protestant family and friends, Seton adhered to her newfound faith and lived in near poverty as a boardinghouse matron. In 1808, she accepted an offer to run a Catholic girls' school in Baltimore, Maryland. When the school flourished, she decided to establish a religious community, a goal she had long harbored. In 1809, she took her vows as a nun and then set out for Emmitsburg, Maryland, the site of her new community, along with several female followers.

Mother Seton and her followers lived in harsh conditions: Rain and snow leaked into their rickety dwelling; they had to fetch water by hand from a spring and hike several miles to attend mass. But the little community flourished, and new members arrived.

The sisters nursed the sick and destitute, and the cornerstone of their work—their boardinghouse for girls—thrived. The sisters also provided free schooling to impoverished girls from a nearby parish, creating the first parochial school in the United States. In 1812, the community was officially recognized as the Sisters of Charity of St. Vincent de Paul by the Catholic hierarchy, and from this order sprang other orders in Philadelphia and New York. One hundred years after she died, Mother Seton was beatified as a saint, and numerous communities of Sisters of Charity can trace their origins to her foundation.

FURTHER READING

Celeste, Marie, ed. *Elizabeth Ann Seton: A Woman of Prayer*. New York: Alba, 1989.
Feeney, Leonard. *Mother Seton: Saint Elizabeth of New York*. Cambridge, Mass.: Ravengate Press, 1991.

Sexton, Anne Gray Harvey

POET

Born: November 9, 1928
Newton, Massachusetts

Died: October 4, 1974
Weston, Massachusetts

Like her friend and fellow poet, Sylvia Plath, Anne Sexton turned inner anguish and despair into compelling poetry. She spent her childhood in suburban Wellesley, Massachusetts, where she attended public school. After dropping out of a junior college to marry, she tried to settle in to the role of suburban homemaker. But inner demons gave her no peace. Upon giving birth to her second daughter, she had a mental breakdown and was hospitalized for several months.

In 1957, she enrolled in a poetry class in an adult-education program in Boston, and a year later she joined poet Robert Lowell's writing seminar at Boston University. Sexton discovered a gift for language and embarked upon writing poetry. Over the next decade, she published several volumes of poetry and garnered a number of awards, including a fellowship at the Radcliffe Institute for Independent Study in 1961, a Pulitzer Prize in 1967, and a Guggenheim Fellowship in 1969. During this time, she also taught at Harvard, Colgate University, and Boston University.

But the enormous success of her work could not ease her growing inner turmoil, nor help repair her broken marriage. In 1973 she was divorced, and a year later she committed suicide. Her best poems, paradoxically, bespeak an affirmation of life that could not rescue her from her demons: "I say Live, Live because of the sun / the dream, the excitable gift."

PUBLICATIONS
All My Pretty Ones (1963)
Live or Die (1966)

Love Poems (1969)
Transformations (1971)
The Book of Folly (1972)
The Death Notebooks (1974)
The Awful Rowing Towards God (1975)
45 Mercy Street (1976)
Anne Sexton: A Self-Portrait in Letters, edited by
    Linda Gray Sexton and Lois Ames (1978)

FURTHER READING
Sexton, Linda Gray. *Searching for Mercy Street: My Journey Back to My Mother.* Boston: Little, Brown, 1994.

Shaw, Anna Howard

MINISTER, WOMEN'S RIGHTS LEADER

Born: February 14, 1847
Newcastle-on-Tyne, England

Died: July 2, 1919
Moylan, Pennsylvania

As a minister, physician, and women's rights leader, Anna Howard Shaw dedicated her life to the advancement of women. During a hardscrabble childhood on the Michigan frontier, she decided that she wanted "to talk to people, to tell them things," as she later recalled, and she practiced preaching sermons to the trees around her family's roughhewn frontier home.

She had a smattering of formal education and taught briefly before being licensed to preach in front of a congregation. She continued her education at Albion College, a Methodist coeducational college, then decided to pursue formal training for the ministry at Boston University's divinity school. In 1878, she graduated with a certificate; she was the only woman in her class.

Shaw served as minister of two churches on Cape Cod and then enrolled in medical school in 1883 at Boston University. She wanted to help other women by becoming a physician. Three years later, she received her medical degree, but once again, seeking to find the most effective way to serve her sex, she changed professions—this time to lecture on behalf of women's rights and temperance. After meeting Frances Willard, president of the Woman's Christian Temperance Union (WCTU), Shaw assumed leadership of the Franchise Department of the WCTU.

Her friendship with Susan B. Anthony plunged her into full-time suffrage work, and in 1892, when Anthony became president of the National American Woman Suffrage Association (NAWSA), Shaw was chosen vice president. She rose to the presidency in 1904 but was not a skillful administrator, and after a difficult term of office she stepped down in 1915.

During World War I, Shaw, now in her 70s, chaired a national women's war preparedness committee and continued to promote woman suffrage. When the war ended, she helped rally public opinion for Woodrow Wilson's peace plan and for the League of Nations. She died during the ratification process of the woman suffrage amendment and did not live to see women's right to vote become codified in the U.S. Constitution.

PUBLICATION
The Story of a Pioneer (autobiography, 1915)

Short, Mercy

BEWITCHED SERVANT GIRL

Born: ca. 1675
Died: date and location unknown

Mercy Short, a Boston servant girl sent by her mistress on an errand to the Boston town jail in June 1692, there encountered several people accused of practicing witchcraft. When one of them, Sarah Good, asked Mercy for some tobacco, she threw a handful of wood shavings at the prisoner and exclaimed, "That's tobacco good enough for you!"

Shortly afterward, Mercy Short began to display the strange conduct that was considered characteristic of witches' victims. Her minister, Cotton Mather, took an interest in her case, and during the winter of 1692 to 1693 he observed as well as counseled her. Mather recorded his observations, and his notes provide evidence not of torment but of an exalted religious experience.

Mercy's "tortures," he wrote, "were turned into frolics, and she became as extravagant as a wildcat," indeed "excessively witty" and exhibiting behavior that belied her "ordinary capacity." Occasionally, she offered lengthy religious sermons.

Though Mather decided that she was bewitched, he used Mercy Short's example not as evidence that witchcraft was afoot but as a way of inspiring a similar religious fervor in others. Soon groups of up to 50 people at a time descended upon her room, praying and singing psalms and exhibiting symptoms similar to hers. They met in her room every night for almost a month.

Mercy Short's "bewitching" and her impact upon others who came under her influence constituted perhaps the first recognized religious revival in American history. Mather himself noted this in his diary: "[T]he souls of many, especially of the rising generation, have been thereby awakened unto some acquaintance with religion," and "some scores of young people"—including Mercy Short—flocked to join his church after being "awakened by the picture of Hell exhibited in her sufferings."

FURTHER READING
Boyer, Paul and Stephen Nissenbaum. *Salem Possessed: The Social Origins of Witchcraft.* Cambridge: Harvard University Press, 1974.

Demos, John. *Entertaining Satan: Witchcraft and the Culture of Early New England.* New York: Oxford University Press, 1982.

Robinson, Enders A. *The Devil Discovered: Salem Witchcraft, 1692.* New York: Hippocrene, 1991.

Simkhovitch, Mary Kingsbury

SETTLEMENT WORKER, SOCIAL REFORMER

Born: September 8, 1867
Chestnut Hill, Massachusetts

Died: November 15, 1951
New York, New York

Like other dedicated, talented women of her generation, Mary Simkhovitch played a vital role in improving living conditions for urban dwellers in the early 20th century. She came from a wealthy New England family in which the women enjoyed advanced educational opportunities, and attended a public high school and enrolled in Boston College. In 1890, she received her A.B. and was elected to Phi Beta Kappa.

Kingsbury taught high-school Latin for two years before embarking on graduate study in economic history and sociology at the Harvard Annex (later Radcliffe College). She also did volunteer work in Boston's low-income neighborhoods, where she learned firsthand about the need for better housing for urban workers.

After further study in Berlin and at Columbia University, she became head resident of the College Settlement House in New York City's Lower East Side. There she met the city's leading social reformers and became immersed in the political and cultural ferment of that district. In 1899, she married Vladimir Simkhovitch, a professor of economic history at Columbia University. Over the next five years, they had two daughters.

Meanwhile, in 1902, Simkhovitch organized Greenwich House, a settlement house, in New York City's Greenwich Village. She turned Greenwich House into a vital center for social reform activism. Under her leadership, the settlement sponsored numerous important studies on economics and community issues, such as racism, unemployment, inadequate housing, and immigration. Acting upon her beliefs that settlement houses must foster better community relations and neighborhood leaders, Simkhovitch helped to establish within Greenwich House a neighborhood theater, music school, and a network of neighborhood centers within local schools. Like other settlement leaders, she was a pioneer neighborhood organizer—seeking ways to improve urban neighborhoods and give residents more power over their lives.

She also joined various civic commissions to improve urban recreation centers, and she taught at Barnard College and Teachers College, Columbia University. In later years, she devoted her energies to improving public housing, and in 1934 she became vice chairman of the New York City Housing Authority. She helped to draft major legislation to create better public housing. During a long, productive life, Simkhovitch helped improve living and working conditions for thousands of Americans.

MAJOR PUBLICATIONS
The City Worker's World in America (1917)
Neighborhood: My Story of Greenwich House (autobiography, 1938)
Quicksand: The Way of Life in the Slums (1942)
Here Is God's Plenty: Reflections on American Social Advance (1949)

Smith, Bessie

BLUES SINGER

Born: April 15, 1894
Chattanooga, Tennessee

Died: September 26, 1937
Clarksdale, Mississippi

Hailed as the "Empress of the Blues," Bessie Smith was the greatest blues singer of her day and perhaps of all time. She exerted profound influence on subsequent generations of blues singers and jazz musicians. Louis Armstrong, the great trumpeter, declared, "She had music in her soul."

The young Bessie Smith grew up in poverty. Early on, she demonstrated a theatrical flair, and as a child she performed on the streets of Chattanooga for pennies while her brother played the guitar. At the age of 9 or 10, she made her singing debut at Chattanooga's Ivory Theater. Around 1910, Gertrude "Ma" Rainey heard her sing and proceeded to teach her the style of country blues. Rainey then invited Smith to join her touring company.

Over the next several years, Bessie Smith, like Rainey, traveled throughout the South singing with carnivals and tent shows and at oceanside bars and clubs. Later, she also performed in black vaudeville companies in Atlanta, Birmingham, Memphis, and other southern cities.

In 1923, she began to record with the Columbia Phonograph Company. That same year, she married Jack Gee, a Philadelphia policeman. From 1923 to 1930, Smith was at the peak of her fame. She made 160 recordings—some of which sold as many as 100,000 records in a week—and formed her own traveling show, which toured cities throughout the North and South. She also wrote many of her own songs.

Smith had a deep, rich contralto voice and a majestic and mesmerizing presence on stage. She sang about life's many trials—poverty, grief, unrequited love, and natural catastrophes—as well as about the small, unexpected joys of daily life. Her songs appealed to blacks struggling with poverty and racism and to those who had recently migrated North to new and unfamiliar surroundings. She set the standard and style of the blues tradition, and was the first singer to transform the blues from their country folk origins to an urban art form.

By the early 1930s, Smith's career had slowed down because of the collapse of the recording industry during the depression. She managed to make a living by performing in road shows and nightclubs, including Harlem's famed Apollo Theatre. She was on the verge of making more recordings when she was killed in an automobile accident in 1937.

FURTHER READING

Albertson, Chris. *Bessie*. New York: Stein and Day, 1970.

Jones, Hettie. *Big Star Fallin' Mama*. New York: Viking, 1994.

Moore, Carman. *Somebody's Angel Child: The Story of Bessie Smith*. New York: Crowell, 1969.

Smith, Eliza Roxey Snow

MORMON RELIGIOUS LEADER

Born: January 21, 1804
Becket, Massachusetts

Died: December 5, 1887
Salt Lake City, Utah

A fervent follower, and later a wife, of Mormon founder Joseph Smith, Eliza Roxey Snow Smith played a vital role in promoting women's influence within the Mormon church. Her own upbringing was religious but tolerant, and her parents encouraged their children to learn about all Christian denominations and choose their own religious faith. Eliza, who had revealed a pious spirit early on, began publishing religious verse while still in her teens.

She met Joseph Smith in 1831 and converted to the Mormon faith four years later. For a time, she boarded in Smith's household in Kirtland, Ohio, as a governess. When persecution mounted against the Mormons in Kirtland, she followed Smith and his worshippers to Nauvoo, Illinois.

There, the Mormon community flourished for a time, and Smith introduced the practice of plural marriage as a Mormon religious tenet. In 1841, Eliza Snow, who had long idolized him, secretly became one of his plural wives. After he was murdered in 1844 by an anti-Mormon mob in Nauvoo, she lived in the home of Brigham Young, Smith's successor as head of the Mormon church, and eventually married him.

Apart from her relationship with these two powerful men, Eliza Smith exerted notable influence in the Mormon church, both in Nauvoo and in Utah, where the Mormons resettled after being driven from Nauvoo. As secretary and, later, president of the Female (renamed Woman's) Relief Society, organized by Joseph Smith, she launched several women's activities, including women's cooperative stores to sell homemade Mormon goods, classes in hygiene, the first Mormon hospital, a women's newspaper, and various conferences and bazaars. All of these activities helped to strengthen women's visibility within the church.

In 1878, she also launched the Young Ladies' Mutual Improvement Association, the essential Mormon organization for women, and loyally defended the church's practice of plural marriage against detractors. A role model for other Mormon women, she urged female followers to practice virtue and serve as obedient "helpmeets" within the church. Although she said that she believed in women's equality, Smith spurned the organized women's rights movement, claiming that the Mormon church granted all of the rights that Mormon women needed. She remained active in church affairs until her death.

PUBLICATION
Poems, Religious, Historical and Political (2 volumes, 1856–77)

Smith, Emma Hale

EARLY MORMON WOMEN'S LEADER

Born: July 10, 1804
Harmony, Pennsylvania

Died: April 30, 1879
Nauvoo, Illinois

E mma Hale Smith bore the distinction—and the burden—of being married to the founder of the Mormon church, Joseph Smith. With him she shared the hardships and persecutions meted out to him and his followers by suspicious non-believers.

She grew up in a Methodist farm family and first met Joseph Smith in 1825 when he worked for a nearby farmer. Despite her father's opposition to the young man and his strange claims of magical powers, she eloped with Smith in 1827.

Three years later, Smith, who claimed that he communicated with angels and received divine revelations, published the Book of Mormon and founded the Mormon religion. Emma Smith served as his scribe, though initially she was dubious about the validity of his claims. Gradually, however, she overcame her lack of faith and transformed herself into a loyal follower. She edited a hymnbook and nursed sick congregants. In 1842, she became president of the Female Relief Society, the principal Mormon women's organization.

With Smith, she fled from one community to another as persecution mounted against the Mormons. Crossing the icy Mississippi River on foot when the Mormons were forced to leave Missouri, she smuggled the manuscript of her husband's Holy Scriptures in the hem of her skirts.

After settling in Nauvoo, Illinois, the Mormons entered a period of relative calm. Surrounding communities accepted the newcomers, and Smith's following grew as thousands of eager converts from England and the East Coast joined his community. There in Illinois, he began the practice of polygamy—marriage to more than one woman—and commanded Emma Smith to accept his actions as divinely ordained.

In 1844, Joseph Smith was murdered by an anti-Mormon mob. Heartbroken, Emma Smith remained in Nauvoo with her four sons and remarried a non-Mormon. But she continued to support a branch of the Mormon church that did not practice polygamy, organized by her oldest son, Joseph Smith III.

Smith, Lillian

WRITER, CIVIL RIGHTS REFORMER

Born: December 12, 1897
Jasper, Florida

Died: September 28, 1966
Atlanta, Georgia

Born into an affluent white family that supported segregation, Lillian Smith became a voice of racial reform and harmony in the South. She spent her early years happily playing with black friends until her parents taught her to regard them as social inferiors. She attended Piedmont College in Demorest, Georgia, for a year before dropping out to help her family during hard economic times. Smith found work as a principal of a rural school in Georgia and briefly taught music at a Methodist-sponsored school in China, where she first became aware of the destructive impact of racial and class bigotry.

In 1936, she and her lifelong partner, Paula Snelling, founded a little magazine. They called it *Pseudopodia,* later changing the name to *South Today.* It was the first white southern magazine to publish the work of black writers and scholars, and it also featured the work of aspiring women writers. While editing *South Today,* Smith educated herself in literature, psychology, anthropology, and philosophy, and reflected upon the social and moral damage wrought by segregation.

Deeply troubled by what she observed, she condemned bigotry in all of her writings, fiction as well as nonfiction. In 1944, she published her first novel, *Strange Fruit,* a story about interracial love and the social damage resulting from sexual and racial intolerance. The novel brought Smith national attention—and was banned by the U.S. Post Office for being "obscene." Eleanor Roosevelt's intervention overturned the ban.

Smith's most well-known book, *Killers of the Dream,* published in 1949, denounced segregation and the corrosive bigotry of southern whites. In 1954, Smith publicly supported the Supreme Court's famous decision to desegregate the nation's schools. Despite the public's hostility—including two fires set by arsonists to silence her—Smith held firmly to her convictions.

She was a friend of the Reverend Martin Luther King, Jr., and served for many years on the executive board of the Congress of Racial Equality (CORE) until that organization no longer supported nonviolence. To the end of her life, Smith remained a courageous—and mostly lone—voice for racial justice and equality among southern white women.

MAJOR PUBLICATIONS

Strange Fruit (novel, 1944)
Killers of the Dream (1949)
Now Is the Time (1955)
Our Faces, Our Words (1964)
How Am I to Be Heard: Letters of Lillian Smith, edited by Margaret Rose Gladney (1994)

Smith, Margaret Chase

U.S. SENATOR

Born: December 14, 1897
Skowhegan, Maine

Margaret Chase Smith was the first American woman to be elected to the United States Senate. With only a high school education, she became a teacher at age 19. But teaching did not suit her, and she went into office work.

In 1930, she married Clyde Smith, a businessman and publisher who was active in local and state politics, and embarked upon a political career. From 1930 to 1936, she served on the Republican State Committee in Maine, and when her husband was elected to the U.S. House of Representatives in 1936 she served as his assistant. When her husband, a U.S. congressman, died in 1940, she took his seat in Congress and soon established a power base for herself. In 1948, she ran for the United States

Senate and won. She was reelected in 1954, 1960, and 1966.

During the early 1950s, she courageously denounced the abusive tactics used by Wisconsin Senator Joseph McCarthy to expose Communist sympathizers. Although she did not call herself a feminist, she fought to grant permanent, rather than reserve, status to women in the military. By this action, she hoped to extend to military women equal benefits and opportunities for advancement.

In 1964, Smith sought the Republican nomination for U.S. president but lost out to challenger Barry Goldwater. After losing a fifth bid for the U.S. Senate in 1972, she taught at several American universities and lectured throughout the United States. She also wrote a nationally syndicated newspaper column.

PUBLICATIONS

Gallant Women (1968, book of portraits of famous American women, 1968)
Declaration of Conscience (autobiography, 1972)

FURTHER READING

Gould, Alberta. *First Lady of the Senate: A Life of Margaret Chase Smith*. Mount Desert, Maine: Windswept House, 1990.

Stanton, Elizabeth Cady

WOMEN'S RIGHTS LEADER

Born: November 12, 1815
Johnstown, New York

Died: October 26, 1902
New York, New York

Elizabeth Cady Stanton was the chief architect of the American women's rights movement. Although she was inspired by other women who had earlier espoused women's equality, it was her vision of women's absolute right to social and political equality that gave birth to an organized movement with specific goals and strategies. She was brilliant, uncompromising, stubborn, and far-sighted in her thinking.

From early on, Stanton was aware of women's second-class status in American life. She grew up witnessing the sad stories of women who had come to her father's law office seeking counsel when the law deprived them of their property or guardianship rights to their children. Even as a child, she rejected the idea that women were intellectually or socially inferior to men. She attended a private academy, where she studied math and classical languages, and went on to graduate from Emma Willard's Troy Female Seminary in 1832.

In her early adulthood, she became interested in the antislavery and temperance movements, and attended antislavery meetings. At one of these meetings, she met her future husband, Henry Stanton, a journalist and reformer, and in 1840 they were married. For their honeymoon, they sailed to England to attend the World's Antislavery Convention.

There, Elizabeth Cady Stanton met Lucretia Mott, the venerable Quaker reformer and abolitionist, and the two women were shocked to discover that female delegates to the convention—dedicated and hard-working volunteers like themselves—were seated apart from the men and were not allowed to address the convention. Outraged, the two women walked arm in arm through London, as Stanton later recalled, and "resolved to hold a convention as soon as we returned home, and form a society to advocate the rights of women."

But eight years would pass before they acted on their resolve. In the intervening years, both women became immersed in antislavery work and family responsibilities. Stanton, moreover, enjoyed living in Boston, where she eagerly partook of the cultural and political ferment sweeping the city. She joined reform groups, attended lectures, and met prominent thinkers and writers. In this intoxicating intellectual setting, she flourished.

But in 1847, when she and her husband moved to upstate New York, where the climate better suited his health, Stanton felt isolated. With three young children and Henry away on business much of the time, she felt overwhelmed by household cares, and became bitter and depressed. When she visited Lucretia Mott, who was staying nearby with friends, she poured out her frustration over tea, and five women, including Stanton and Mott, decided to organize a convention for women's rights. Finally, after eight years, she and Mott were acting on the idea they had first proposed in London.

The women issued a call, or announcement, in the *Seneca County Courier* for a two-day convention devoted to the question of women's rights. Stanton drafted a Declaration of Sentiments, which became the blueprint of the women's rights movement. Despite Mott's hesitation, she added a resolution proposing woman suffrage.

This convention, held on July 19, 1848, was the opening salvo of the women's rights movement; as the gospel of women's rights spread, more conventions and meetings were held across the country.

In 1851, Stanton met her future partner in the movement—Susan B. Anthony, who was attending an antislavery meeting in Seneca Falls. They forged a partnership that would last fifty years and endure numerous periods of estrangement. Although the Civil War interrupted their work of organizing meetings, writing articles, giving lectures, and circulating petitions, they quickly resumed their campaign after the war—expecting the country to reward its women for their vital wartime work by granting female suffrage.

Instead, Stanton, Anthony, and their followers faced a long and bitter battle. They soon found themselves at odds with former colleagues over differing strategies and priorities. In 1869, the clash erupted into a full-scale schism as two competing organizations emerged—the National Woman Suffrage Association (NWSA), organized by Stanton and Anthony, and the American Woman Suffrage Association (AWSA), formed by Lucy Stone and her followers. While AWSA had a more limited goal—merely to secure female suffrage—and appealed mainly to middle-class women, NWSA expounded a broader, more daring agenda, one that spoke to the needs of working-class women, advocated greater employment opportunities and equal wages for female workers, and championed birth control and divorce reform. Stanton's visionary thinking lay behind this highly progressive agenda.

For twenty years, the two organizations pursued their separate goals until in 1890 they merged as the National American Woman Suffrage Association (NAWSA). Stanton was elected president and Anthony vice president.

Meanwhile, as her seven children grew older, Stanton became increasingly independent from her family. She embarked on lecture tours, wrote articles, and continued to find ways to enlarge women's sphere. Defiantly, she challenged accepted ideas. "It is a settled maxim with me," she declared once, "that the existing public sentiment on any subject is wrong."

In perhaps her most controversial action, toward the end of her life she wrote the *Woman's Bible,* an astute point-by-point rebuttal of passages of the Bible that justified men's power over women. The work was a commercial success but raised a firestorm of criticism from religious leaders.

Undeterred, Stanton went on to publish her autobiography, *Eighty Years and More,* and offer her views on divorce, religion, and relations between men and women in numerous essays and articles. She died in her sleep, fittingly enough, after penning a letter to President Theodore Roosevelt urging him to support women's rights. Brilliant, courageous, and often exasperating, she was a warrior to the end for women's rights.

MAJOR PUBLICATIONS

History of Woman Suffrage (with Susan B. Anthony et al.; 6 volumes; first volume published in 1881)
"The Solitude of Self" (speech given at 1892 NAWSA convention)
Woman's Bible (1895)
Eighty Years and More: Reminiscences, 1815–1897 (1898)
Correspondence Between Elizabeth Cady Stanton and Susan B. Anthony, edited by Ellen DuBois (1981)

FURTHER READING

Banner, Lois W. *Elizabeth Cady Stanton: A Radical for Woman's Rights.* Boston: Little, Brown, 1980.
Cullen-Dupont, Kathryn. *Elizabeth Cady Stanton and Women's Liberty.* New York: Facts on File, 1992.

Starr, Ellen Gates

SETTLEMENT HOUSE WORKER

Born: March 19, 1859
Laona, Illinois

Died: February 10, 1940
Suffern, New York

With her dear friend Jane Addams, Ellen Gates Starr founded Hull House, one of the first settlement houses. Born on a farm, the young Ellen Gates Starr attended a one-room school and then enrolled in Rockford Seminary, where she met Addams, a fellow student. Forced to drop out after her first year because of financial problems at home, she became a teacher.

But teaching was not wholly satisfying, and Starr searched for other work. She wanted to promote art and other forms of human creativity in an increasingly impersonal and industrial society. She confided her concerns to Addams, who, in turn, confessed her own lack of vocational direction. During a trip to Europe in 1888, Addams told Starr about her hopes of establishing a settlement house, and Starr eagerly offered her assistance.

Upon returning to the United States, the two women searched through Chicago's West Side for a building, and in 1889 they opened Hull House. Reflecting a Victorian belief in the uplifting value of great art, Starr quickly launched a program of teaching arts and crafts and exposing neighborhood residents to great works of art and literature. She established reading clubs to study the works of Shakespeare, Dante, and Robert Browning, and decorated Hull House with reproductions of great art.

But Starr came to realize that such efforts were pointless when exploited workers had no time or energy left to enjoy art. She concluded that the working class needed, in her words, "a new life, a freed life." To this end, she shifted her energies to abolishing child labor. Joining the Illinois branch of the Women's Trade Union League (WTUL), an organization of upper- and working-class women who campaigned together for better working conditions, she supported textile and restaurant workers in strikes during the 1910s and 1920s. Eventually, she joined the Socialist party. In 1916, she ran as a Socialist candidate for the office of alderman.

Long possessed of a spiritual outlook, Starr spent her last years in a Catholic convent, speaking and writing about Catholic art and observance. But she had made her mark much earlier: She had lit the spark that ignited Jane Addams's burning desire to establish Hull House. Together, they set in motion an astoundingly effective and creative social-reform experiment to combat poverty and bring hope and renewal to Chicago's working classes.

FURTHER READING
Addams, Jane. *Twenty Years at Hull-House.* 1910. Reprint. New York: Macmillan, 1967.

Steinem, Gloria

FEMINIST, WRITER

Born: March 25, 1934
Toledo, Ohio

Gloria Steinem's name is synonymous with the resurgence of the American women's movement in the 1960s. In 1971, she helped establish *Ms.* magazine, one of the premier journals of the movement, and she has been a prominent advocate and activist for women's issues ever since. Her feminist commitment echoes that of her paternal grandmother, Pauline Steinem, who was a suffragist and one of two U.S. delegates to the 1908 meeting of the International Council of Women.

But Steinem's own fighting energy was bred during a difficult childhood. When she was 12, her parents divorced, and she became solely responsible for caring for her sick mother. After graduating Phi Beta Kappa from Smith College in 1956, Steinem spent two years in India on a research fellowship before embarking upon a career as a freelance journalist. One of her first well-known pieces, "I Was a Playboy Bunny," was a witty expose of the Playboy Club; to get her story, Steinem worked as a hostess at the club. Her account was a droll but devastating glimpse into the elusive world of the famous men's social club.

Soon, she was writing for *Vogue, Cosmopolitan,* and *Glamour,* among other magazines. She also worked as a screenwriter for a satirical weekly television news show, "That Was the Week." In 1968, Steinem became a contributing editor and political columnist for *New York* magazine, a gossipy, irreverent journal of arts and politics in New York City. Three years later, she helped found *Ms.* magazine, plunging into the feminist struggle. As a writer and speaker for the movement, she has lobbied for women's reproductive freedom, a constitutional equal rights amendment (ERA), and parental leave for both men and women, among other issues.

In 1971, she joined Betty Friedan, Bella Abzug, and Congresswoman Shirley Chisholm to establish the National Women's Political Caucus (NWPC), an organization that sponsors women candidates. Throughout the 1960s and 1970s, Steinem lent her support to other causes as well, including civil rights, opposition to American military involvement in Vietnam, and better working conditions and wages for all American workers. She has helped organize national as well as grassroots organizations, while continuing to guide *Ms.* magazine through changing currents in the women's movement. She offers a keen, iconoclastic perspective on political and cultural concerns.

MAJOR PUBLICATIONS
Outrageous Acts and Everyday Rebellions (1983)
Marilyn (1986)
Revolution from Within: A Book of Self-Esteem (1992)
Moving Beyond Words (1994)

FURTHER READING
Daffron, Carolyn. *Gloria Steinem: Feminist.* New York: Chelsea House, 1988.

Steward, Susan McKinney

PHYSICIAN, HOSPITAL FOUNDER, WOMEN'S RIGHTS ACTIVIST

---

*Born: 1847 (exact date unknown)
Brooklyn, New York*

---

*Died: March 7, 1918
Wilberforce, Ohio*

Susan McKinney Steward, the third African-American woman to become a doctor, dedicated her life to practicing medicine. She was the seventh of ten children born to a prosperous pig farmer. Early on, she showed an aptitude for music, especially for the organ. For two years, she taught music in the public school system in Washington, D.C., then enrolled in the New York Medical College for Women in 1867.

Three years later, she graduated valedictorian of her class and opened a practice in Brooklyn, her hometown. Her reputation spread and she eventually opened another practice in the nearby borough of Manhattan. Her patients included whites as well as blacks.

In 1874, she married William G. McKinney, an Episcopal minister, and they had two children. Marriage and motherhood did not curtail her professional life, however. In 1881, she helped to establish the Brooklyn Woman's Homeopathic Hospital and Dispensary and served on its medical staff until 1895. She also joined the staff of Elizabeth Blackwell's medical college of the New York Infirmary for Women and Children. To further her own medical education, she pursued postgraduate study at Long Island Medical College from 1887 to 1888.

Despite her busy practice, Steward found time to champion women's advancement in the medical profession and to join the woman suffrage and temperance movements and the black women's club movement.

Several years after her first husband died, she married Theophilus Gould Steward, a military chaplain. She practiced medicine at military bases where he served and also served as a resident physician at Wilberforce University in Ohio, where she died.

FURTHER READING
Seraile, William. "Susan McKinney Steward: New York State's First African-American Woman Physician," *Afro-Americans in N.Y. Life & History* 9 (July 1985).
Sterling, Dorothy, ed. *We Are Your Sisters: Black Women in the Nineteenth Century.* New York: Norton, 1984.

Stewart, Maria W.

WOMEN'S RIGHTS LECTURER, EDUCATOR

---

*Born: 1803 (exact date unknown)
Hartford, Connecticut*

---

*Died: December 17, 1879
Washington, D.C.*

Maria W. Stewart was the first American woman to lecture in front of an audience of both men and women—a once frowned-upon act. She was also the first African-American woman to lecture on women's rights. In ringing tones, sounding like an Old Testament prophet, she urged her audiences to abolish slavery and proclaimed the special role of black women—to "arise" and help improve their communities through educating themselves and their children. Stewart preached collective action among blacks, often prodding her audiences to work harder for their own advancement, and paved the way for other compelling African-American orators, including Sojourner Truth, Frances E. W. Harper, and Frederick Douglass.

Stewart was born to free black parents who died when she was five. She was raised in a clergyman's family and received a modicum of education in church-affiliated schools and through self-study. She worked as a domestic and in 1826 married James W. Stewart in Boston.

In 1831, she submitted a lengthy article to the *Liberator,* the journal founded by abolitionist William Lloyd Garrison, in which she urged blacks to "sue for your rights and privileges." She also warned whites that "our souls are fired with the . . . love of liberty and independence." Garrison subsequently reprinted her speeches, which also included fiery diatribes against slavery and racial injustice.

Stewart made her first speech in 1832 before the Afric-American Female Intelligence Society, a black women's social and educational group. She made three other public addresses before she was forced to leave Boston—her militant message and her audacity to speak in public had angered the city's black leaders. In 1833, she moved to New York City, where she became a public school teacher and joined black female literary and abolitionist organizations.

During the Civil War, she lived in Washington, D.C. She continued to teach and also worked as chief of housekeeping at the newly organized Freedmen's Hospital. In 1871, she opened a Sunday School for destitute children. She also raised money to purchase a building for the school. A gifted orator, Stewart put her words into practice by devoting her life to helping her fellow black Americans.

PUBLICATIONS
Productions of Mrs. Maria W. Stewart (1835)
Meditations from the Pen of Mrs. Maria W. Stewart (1879)

FURTHER READING
Giddings, Paula. *When and Where I Enter: The Impact of Black Women on Race and Sex in America.* New York: Morrow, 1984.
Richardson, Marilyn. *Maria Stewart: America's First Black Woman Writer.* Bloomington: Indiana University Press, 1987.
Sterling, Dorothy, ed. *We Are Your Sisters: Black Women in the Nineteenth Century.* New York: Norton, 1984.

Stone, Lucy
FEMINIST, ABOLITIONIST

Born: August 13, 1818
West Brookfield, Massachusetts

Died: October 18, 1893
Dorchester, Massachusetts

From early childhood, Lucy Stone, one of the founders of the organized women's rights movement, bristled against women's inferior station in American life. She bemoaned her mother's hard life and her father's preferential treatment of his sons. After attending local schools, she began teaching at 16 in a district school, earning less than half as much as the men who taught there. She supplemented her education with brief periods of study at nearby private schools, including Mt. Holyoke Female Seminary.

In 1843, despite her father's opposition and unwillingness to even loan her the tuition, she enrolled at Oberlin College. There she met Antoinette Brown Blackwell, a fellow student who would later become her sister-in-law. Together, they challenged the school's rules and restrictions against women students.

Stone graduated in 1847 and became a lecturer for the American Antislavery Society. But almost immediately she began advocating women's rights as well as abolition. When leaders of the American Antislavery Society objected, she replied, "I was a woman before I was an abolitionist. I must speak for the women." In her clear musical voice, she did indeed speak for the women, inspiring Susan B. Anthony and other future woman suffrage leaders.

In 1855, Stone married Henry Blackwell, brother of physicians Elizabeth and Emily Blackwell. He shared Stone's passion for promoting women's rights and urged her to continue her work. Stone, however, retired temporarily to give birth to their only child, Alice Stone Blackwell.

When the women's rights movement split into two factions after the Civil War, Stone reemerged to challenge the leadership of Elizabeth Cady Stanton and Susan B. Anthony. In 1869, she helped found the American Woman Suffrage Association (AWSA), a more conservative organization than Stanton and Anthony's National Woman Suffrage Association (NWSA), and served on its executive board. Stone also founded, financed, and edited the *Woman's Journal,* the newspaper of AWSA and later the main journal of the women's rights movement. She continued to lecture on women's rights as long as her health permitted. In 1893, she made her last public appearance at the World's Columbian Exposition in Chicago, where she and Anthony spoke on woman suffrage at a gathering of almost 500 European and American women.

PUBLICATION

Friends and Sisters: Letters Between Lucy Stone and Antoinette Brown Blackwell, 1846–1893, edited by Carol Lasser and Marlene Deahl Merrill (1987)

FURTHER READING

Kerr, Andrea M. *Lucy Stone: Speaking Out for Equality.* New Brunswick, N.J.: Rutgers University Press, 1992.

Stowe, Harriet Beecher

AUTHOR

Born: June 14, 1811
Litchfield, Connecticut

Died: July 1, 1896
Hartford, Connecticut

Harriet Beecher Stowe, one of the most prolific authors of the 19th century, wrote *Uncle Tom's Cabin,* the novel that aroused Northerners to the horror of American slavery. Indeed, when President Abraham Lincoln met Stowe during the Civil War, he jokingly said, "So this is the little lady who started this big war."

Stowe, daughter of the famous Congregational minister Lyman Beecher, was raised in a household filled with lively political and religious debates. Early on, she became keenly aware of new ideas and reform movements. At 13, she attended her sister Catharine Beecher's female seminary in Hartford, Connecticut, and later taught there.

In 1834, she published her first story, "A New England Sketch," in a regional journal, and two years later she married Calvin Ellis Stowe, a professor of biblical literature. With his encouragement, she continued to write, using her pen to convey her ideas on morality and on women's domestic roles. Like her sister Catharine, she believed that women were destined to be the nation's mothers and spiritual guardians.

That, in part, was her purpose in writing *Uncle Tom's Cabin,* which first appeared in serial form in the *National Era* and then in book form in 1852— to arouse readers to the immorality of slavery, especially to its evil impact on enslaved mothers and their children. She achieved astonishing success: The book became an instant best-seller in the North and abroad, and was duly banned in the South for perpetrating "vicious" lies about slavery. Throughout the 1850s, Northerners and Southerners hurled denunciations at each other, fueled in part by Stowe's novel and by events that forced the nation to confront the moral contradiction of slavery.

When Civil War finally erupted, Stowe ardently supported the Union cause, even after her son was seriously wounded in battle. She continued to write after the war, turning out numerous novels that portrayed 18th- and 19th-century New England life. She also wrote religious poetry and children's books, and contributed occasionally to the *Atlantic Monthly.*

But *Uncle Tom's Cabin* was her most powerful and enduring book, a tale that somehow prophesied the great conflagration between the North and South. "This is an age of the world where nations are trembling and convulsed," she wrote in the final chapter. "A mighty influence is abroad, surging and heaving the world."

MAJOR PUBLICATIONS
Uncle Tom's Cabin (1852)
A Key to Uncle Tom's Cabin (1853)
Men of Our Times (1868)
Old Town Folks (1870)

FURTHER READING
Bland, Celia. *Harriet Beecher Stowe: Author and Abolitionist.* New York: Chelsea House, 1993.
Boydston, Jeanne et al., eds. *The Limits of Sisterhood: The Beecher Sisters on Women's Rights and Women's Sphere.* Chapel Hill: University of North Carolina Press, 1989.
Hedrick, Joan D. *Harriet Beecher Stowe: A Life.* New York: Oxford University Press, 1994.
Rugoff, Milton. *The Beechers: An American Family in the Nineteenth Century.* New York: Harper and Row, 1981.

Swisshelm, Jane Gray Cannon

JOURNALIST, REFORMER, WOMEN'S RIGHTS ACTIVIST

Born: December 6, 1815
Pittsburgh, Pennsylvania

Died: July 22, 1884
Pittsburgh, Pennsylvania

Jane Swisshelm was a prominent antislavery and women's rights journalist in the mid-19th century. Reared in a strict Presbyterian family, she attended local schools and at age 14 became a schoolteacher.

In 1836, she married James Swisshelm, a farmer's son. He expected deference and submission from the strong-willed Jane, and their marriage followed a long, rocky path. Though she had aspired to be an artist, she said later, "I put away my paintbrushes to cook cabbages," and faithfully discharged her domestic duties. She also worked as a corsetmaker to supplement the family income.

Swisshelm embarked on a newspaper career by writing articles for a local paper opposing capital punishment. Soon, she also contributed articles in which she condemned slavery and advocated

women's rights to a Pittsburgh antislavery journal. After this journal folded, she started her own antislavery paper, the *Saturday Visiter.* She used the paper as a forum to voice her unbending opposition to slavery and to promote temperance and women's rights. In 1848, her editorials in support of married women's property rights may have helped win passage of a Pennsylvania law that protected married women's property from grasping husbands.

Swisshelm finally divorced her husband in 1857, relinquished editorial control of her newspaper, and moved to St. Cloud, Minnesota, where she promptly took control of another publication, the *St. Cloud Visiter.* She turned that paper as well into a forceful antislavery journal. She also lectured about abolition and women's rights.

During the Civil War, she worked as a Union army nurse, writing letters home to her newspaper to describe the appalling conditions in military hospitals. After the war, she started another paper, the *Reconstructionist,* to express her support for the radical Republicans' program of Reconstruction. Ill health forced her to curtail her activities, but she continued to lecture for woman suffrage and supported the prohibition of liquor.

PUBLICATION
Half a Century (autobiography, 1880)

Tekakwitha, Kateri (Catherine)

RELIGIOUS LEADER

Born: ca. 1656
Auriesville, New York

Died: April 17, 1680
Sault St. Louis, Canada

The daughter of an Algonquian Indian mother, who was Christian, and a Mohawk Indian father, Tekakwitha was baptized on Easter Sunday, April 18, 1676. When Jesuit missionaries built a community near her home, she came under their influence and converted to Roman Catholicism, incurring the wrath of her Native American brethren. Forced to flee, she took refuge in the mission of St. Francis Xavier, Sault St. Louis, in Canada.

There she became the leader of a female cult, one that sought religious inspiration through intense self-deprivation and torture. Her followers whipped each other, deprived themselves of food and sleep, wore no clothing in the middle of winter, and recited rosaries until they were hoarse. This intense physical pain was intended to deepen their spirituality.

At first, the Jesuit priests and other male members of the mission watched with a mixture of envy and fascination, but they soon grew alarmed by the bizarre activities they witnessed. Kateri, however, became ill and died, and her female following disbanded. But Kateri's memory has lived on, and visitors continue to pray at her grave for her blessing. In 1932, the Catholic church began the process of declaring her a saint—the first Native American to claim such a distinction.

Terhune, Mary Virginia Hawes

NOVELIST, DOMESTIC ADVICE WRITER

Born: December 21, 1830
Dennisville, Virginia

Died: June 3, 1922
New York, New York

Known to her many readers as Marion Harland, Mary Terhune was perhaps the most prolific writer of her age. Contemporaries regarded her as a model woman; although she pursued her literary career with astounding success, she never neglected her duties as wife, mother, and benevolent reformer.

She was born into affluence. Her father urged her to read and think for herself, and even hired tutors for both his sons and daughters, while her mother impressed upon her the value and satisfaction of being a homemaker.

She began writing essays as a child and published her first pieces anonymously in a local newspaper at age 14. From then on, she never stopped writing. In 1856, she married Edward Payson Terhune, a Presbyterian minister, and they had six children over the next two decades—two of whom followed their mother's path into a literary career.

After seeking her husband's permission, Mary Terhune pursued her writing career while raising her children and doing the charity work expected of a minister's wife. During the 1850s and 1860s, she wrote more than two dozen novels and short stories, mostly set in the antebellum South. Similar in plot and structure, they were sentimental, even pious, in tone, featuring heroines who reveled in their domestic roles.

Although Terhune urged women to acquire an education and equip themselves for paid work, if necessary, she was no advocate of women's rights. In her later novels, she dismissed the women's rights movement and urged women to dedicate themselves to marriage and motherhood. She believed that women's highest calling was domesticity.

By the 1870s, Terhune had changed her literary focus to household advice. Over the next 20 years, she wrote about 25 books on household concerns, from cooking to etiquette. She also edited two magazines, *Home-Maker* and *Housekeeper's Weekly,* and her syndicated columns appeared in 25 daily newspapers. In addition, she wrote another dozen books on travel and colonial history, and published biographical profiles of Charlotte Brontë, William Cowper, and others. A writer to the end, she published her last book when she was 89.

SELECTED PUBLICATIONS
Common Sense in the Household (1871)
Home of the Bible (1896)
Marion Harland's Autobiography (1910)
Looking Westward (1914)

Terrell, Mary Eliza Church

COMMUNITY LEADER AND CLUBWOMAN,
TEACHER, SUFFRAGIST

Born: September 23, 1863
Memphis, Tennessee

Died: July 24, 1954
Annapolis, Maryland

Daughter of the South's first black millionaire, Mary Church Terrell spent her childhood mostly untouched by the vicious reality of racial discrimination. She attended public schools up north and enrolled at Oberlin College in Oberlin, Ohio. As the only black student in her class, she felt compelled to excel academically to prove that blacks were not intellectually inferior.

After graduating from Oberlin in 1884, she returned briefly to Memphis. Over her father's objections—he wanted her to spend her days in genteel social pursuits—she moved north to join the faculty of Wilberforce University in Xenia, Ohio. In 1887, she moved to Washington, D.C., to teach high school Latin. After a two-year tour of Western Europe—and thoughts of living abroad because European society was far less bigoted—she felt obligated to return to the United States, she later said, to "promote the welfare of my race."

Her marriage to Robert Heberton Terrell in 1891 ended her teaching career because married women were not allowed to teach in the Washington, D.C., public schools. But Terrell continued to devote her energies to community work. For more than 11 years, she served on the Board of Education for the District of Columbia—the first African-American woman to do so—and in 1896 she was elected president of the newly organized National Association of Colored Women, a national federation of black women's clubs.

Terrell also embarked upon a public-speaking career. She lectured about women's rights and black affairs and wrote articles on black history and life for newspapers and magazines. After World War I, she served on the executive committee of the Women's International League for Peace and Freedom. When American women gained the right to vote, Terrell, a suffragist, worked for the Republican National Committee, recruiting black women's allegiance.

As a member of the National Association for the Advancement of Colored People (NAACP), she protested repeatedly against lynching and discrimination, unafraid to take her cause to the highest halls of government. To the end of her life, she strove to combat racial injustice. At 85, she was the first African-American woman to join the American Association of University Women, and shortly before she died she led picket lines to end segregation in the coffee shops of Washington, D.C. With dignity and determination, she fought for justice for her people.

PUBLICATION
A Colored Woman in a White World (autobiography, 1940; reprinted 1968)

FURTHER READING
Giddings, Paula. *When and Where I Enter: The Impact of Black Women on Race and Sex in America.* New York: Morrow, 1984.

Thanadelthur

INDIAN INTERPRETER

Born: date unknown

Died: February 5, 1717
York, Canada

Thanadelthur's remarkable story exemplifies the important role that some Native American women played in promoting trade relations between white settlers and Indian tribes. Her early life remains a mystery. In the spring of 1713, still a young woman, she was captured by Cree Indians in a raid upon her Chipewyan settlement. More than a year later, she and another captive managed to escape, hoping to make their way back to their people before the harsh winter set in.

But cold and hunger forced them to turn around. Although her companion perished in the woods, Thanadelthur somehow found her way to the campsite of the Hudson Bay Company on Ten Shilling Creek. She was weak from hunger and cold. Nursed back to health, she showed her gratitude by helping the fur traders find more sources of fur.

She also helped mend relations between the warring Crees and Chipewyans. During one such peace-seeking mission, she forced the two sides to talk. Dispatched by the company commander, James Knight, she had joined the mission as an interpreter. She quickly realized the significance of her role and exerted decisive leadership. When the delegation, which included several Cree Indians, ran into harsh weather and potential danger, most of the participants wanted to turn back. But Thanadelthur pressed on alone, and returned with two Chipewyan representatives. She then served as chief negotiator between the warring sides, goading them to talk. William Stuart, Knight's personal representative, described her role: "She made them all Stand in fear of her, she Scolded at Some and pushing of others . . . and forced them to ye peace." Stuart admired her "Devillish Spirit" and "Carriage and Resolution" and credited her actions for the mission's success.

Thanadelthur and several Chipeywans returned to live at the Hudson Bay Company's fort in York, Canada. There, she advised the company commander of ways to expand the company's trade to gold and other minerals. She soon became one of his chief advisers. Though she married another Chipeywan, she would not let her marriage interfere with any trade missions that she undertook for the company.

But in the harsh winter of 1717, she became gravely ill. As she fought to stay alive, she gave final instructions to the "English boy" who was to accompany her on a trade mission to her people. On February 5, 1717, she died. The company commander, who had come to regard her as a valued adviser, wrote: "I am almost ready to break my heart . . . She was one of a Very high Spirit and of the Firmest Resolution that ever I see any Body in my Days and of great Courage & forecast."

FURTHER READING
Van Kirk, Sylvia. *Many Tender Ties: Women in Fur-Trade Society in Western Canada, 1670–1870.* Norman: University of Oklahoma Press, 1980.

Thomas, Marlo
ACTRESS

Born: November 21, 1943
Detroit, Michigan

Marlo Thomas, actor and producer, has spent the last two decades promoting women's rights and children's welfare. She came from an acting background—her father was the comedian and TV star Danny Thomas—and attended the University of Southern California. From 1966 to 1971, she starred in "That Girl," a television situation comedy about an aspiring actress.

In addition, she has produced or starred in numerous television movies and has won four Emmy awards and the prestigious George Foster Peabody Broadcasting Award. She has also served on two Presidential commissions on the status of women and children and has used her performing talents to promote political and economic measures benefiting women and children. In her award-winning book and television special *Free to Be . . . You and Me,* she expresses her hope that by doing away with gender restrictions on child-rearing people will break away from traditional stereotypes in all aspects of their lives. She is a member of the Ms. Foundation and the National Women's Political Caucus.

PUBLICATIONS
Free to Be . . . You and Me (1972)
Free to Be . . . A Family (1987)

Thomas, Martha Carey

EDUCATOR AND FEMINIST

Born: January 2, 1857
Baltimore, Maryland

Died: December 2, 1935
Philadelphia, Pennsylvania

M. Carey Thomas, as she preferred to be known, was one of the nation's first female college presidents. She was raised in the Quaker faith and attended Quaker schools. Her parents encouraged her to read and think for herself, but while her mother supported women's rights, her father was less certain when it came to giving his daughter a higher education.

After opposing her desire to attend college, he agreed to send her to Cornell. She completed her A.B. degree in 1877 and once again sought his consent for additional education, this time in Germany. But no German university would grant a Ph.D. to a woman, so Thomas completed her degree at the University of Zurich in 1882.

In 1885, Bryn Mawr, a new Quaker women's college, was established in Pennsylvania, and Thomas, passed over for the presidency because of her sex, was appointed dean and professor of English. Nine years later, she was promoted to the presidency and remained in that office until 1922.

Thomas was a high-handed president who often made decisions without consulting others, and harbored bigoted attitudes; she was disinclined to admit black students or hire and promote Jewish professors. But, unlike her predecessor, she established impressively high academic standards for the college. Determined to elevate Bryn Mawr to the intellectual caliber of the most prestigious men's colleges, she fashioned a curriculum that required extensive coursework in math and the classics, with few electives.

In later years, she became active in the women's rights movement. In 1908, she served as the first president of the newly formed National College Women's Equal Suffrage League, and played an active role in the National American Woman Suffrage Association (NAWSA). By 1920, she had joined the more radical National Woman's party (NWP).

She endorsed the party's opposition to sex-based protective legislation, such as laws limiting female workers' hours, because she regarded such preferential treatment as a barrier to complete equality. While Thomas held uncompromising views on sexual equality, she was also an elitist: As a college administrator and feminist, she hoped to cultivate a select group of women from the nation's leading women's colleges to assume leadership and rise above what she called the "thousands of ordinary college graduates."

MAJOR PUBLICATIONS
"Should the Higher Education of Women Differ from That of Men?" *Educational Review* (January 1901)
"The Future of Women in Independent Study and Research," *Educational Review* (February 1903)

FURTHER READING
Horowitz, Helen Lefkowitz. *The Power and Passion of M. Carey Thomas.* New York: Knopf, 1994.

Tituba

SLAVE AND ACCUSED WITCH

Born: date and location unknown

Died: date and location unknown

Tituba's name is forever entwined with the mystery and drama of the Salem witch-hunts. Born in the West Indies, and later bought by the Reverend Samuel Parris of Salem, Massachusetts, Tituba taught a small group of local girls some of the rituals and folklore of African voodoo. In the evenings, after her chores were done, she held her small audience spellbound with her tales of ritual and prophecy and her demonstrations of herbal healing and fortune-telling. These seemingly innocent spectacles, however, set off one of the most frightening and bizarre episodes in American history—the Salem witch trials.

When three members of her circle—Elizabeth Parris, 9-year-old daughter of Tituba's master; 11-year-old Abigail Williams; and 12-year-old Anne Putnam—began to display weird behavior, the person they accused of bewitching them was Tituba. They claimed that she appeared as a specter and tormented them by pinching and pricking them with pins. Their strange accusations sparked a collective nightmare in which nearly 200 people were imprisoned, 20 were hanged or stoned to death, and 8 died in prison—men as well as women.

But, oddly enough, Tituba was spared—because she admitted to being a witch and cleverly went along with the ludicrous line of questioning put forth by her inquisitors at court. In addition, she named Sarah Good and Sarah Osborne as fellow witches. When asked by one magistrate what she rode upon in her witchly travels, she replied, "I ride upon a stick or pole, and Good and Osborne behind me." The magistrates reserved their greatest fury for defendants who denied any association to witchcraft, and who attempted to answer their ridiculous charges with logical answers.

Though Tituba was spared the gallows, she languished in prison throughout the 16 months that the Salem witch trials lasted. She was declared innocent on May 9, 1693. When her master refused to pay the prison fees required to release her, she was sold to a slave trader in Virginia.

The Salem witch-hunt continues to fascinate historians and lay readers alike. It is a story of economic conflict, for many of the accused came from influential and affluent backgrounds, while their accusers were farmers fearful of being displaced by a growing merchant class. The witch trials also illuminate the ways in which women found limited power within a patriarchal society—and illustrate how easily paranoia can replace rationality in human affairs.

FURTHER READING

Boyer, Paul and Stephen Nissenbaum. *Salem Possessed: The Social Origins of Witchcraft.* Cambridge: Harvard University Press, 1974.

Demos, John. *Entertaining Satan: Witchcraft and the Culture of Early New England.* New York: Oxford University Press, 1982.

Robinson, Enders A. *The Devil Discovered: Salem Witchcraft, 1692.* New York: Hippocrene, 1991.

Tompkins, Sally

CONFEDERATE HOSPITAL SUPERVISOR

Born: November 9, 1833
Poplar Grove, Virginia

Died: July 25, 1916
Richmond, Virginia

Sally Tompkins came from a distinguished Virginia planter family. She spent her early years on the family plantation, where friends and relatives gathered for lavish entertainments and where she developed a skill for nursing. Shortly before the Civil War erupted, her father died, and the family moved to Richmond. There, after the outbreak of war, she organized the Robertson Hospital to treat wounded Confederate soldiers. She supervised the nursing staff, composed primarily of other planter women, and the rest of the hospital staff.

At a time when nearly as many soldiers died from infection in germ-ridden military hospitals as on the battlefield, Robertson Hospital, with a capacity of 25 beds, could boast the highest cure rate of any Confederate hospital. Tompkins's rigid insistence on sanitary precautions accounted for the hospital's astounding success. Her facility's sterling record was all the more impressive because military leaders often sent the most seriously wounded soldiers there.

Indeed, when the surgeon general attempted to close the hospital and move its patients to newer, bigger military hospitals, President Jefferson Davis commissioned Tompkins a cavalry captain to keep her facility open.

It was said that Tompkins ruled her hospital with "a stick in one hand and a Bible in the other." She was a devout Episcopalian who conducted prayer services every evening and tolerated no nonsense from her patients or staff. Patients who violated her rules against alcohol could find themselves booted out of bed and thrown out onto the street. She also had a remarkable ability to raise the morale of discouraged soldiers.

After the war, Tompkins remained in Richmond, working occasionally as a nurse and pursuing charity work. For the rest of her life, she enjoyed the love and respect of Confederate veterans and other loyal adherents to the Lost Cause.

FURTHER READING
Woodward, C. Vann, ed. *Mary Chesnut's Civil War.* New Haven: Yale University Press, 1981.

Truth, Sojourner

FORMER SLAVE, ABOLITIONIST,
WOMEN'S RIGHTS ADVOCATE

*Born: ca. 1797
Hurley, New York*

*Died: November 26, 1883
Battle Creek, Michigan*

Sojourner Truth was born a slave, but she lived much of her life in the fashion of a prophet, preaching and arousing her nation's conscience. Her birth name was Isabella Hardenburgh. In 1827, just one year before slavery was abolished in New York State, she escaped. After she rescued one of her children, who had been sold to a planter in Alabama, she worked as a domestic in New York City and joined a religious commune.

In 1843, she felt inspired to travel and preach, and she renamed herself Sojourner Truth. She soon joined the abolitionist movement and went on the lecture circuit. Her unique gift of language and her compelling presence rendered her one of the movement's most effective speakers.

Truth also lent her powerful voice to the cause of women's rights. Indeed, she was one of the few African-American women to play a visible role in the antebellum women's rights movement. In 1851, she made an unforgettable speech at the third women's rights convention in Akron, Ohio. Responding to the previous speaker, a minister who had declared that women needed protection rather than equal rights, Truth demolished his argument. "I have ploughed, and planted, and gathered into barns, and no man could head me! And a'n't I a woman? . . . I have borne thirteen children, and seen them most all sold off to slavery, and when I cried out with my mother's grief, none but Jesus heard me! And a'n't I a woman?" When she finished, the audience sat mesmerized, tears streaming down the cheeks of some.

During the Civil War, Truth helped recruit black soldiers for the Union cause and worked as a nurse and teacher in refugee camps for newly liberated slaves. In the postwar years, she continued to promote women's rights but devoted much of her energies to helping ex-slaves. She urged the federal government to help resettle the former slaves out west, where they could own their own farms.

Indeed, in the 1870s thousands of blacks migrated to Kansas and Missouri in part because of her encouragement. She visited some of these newly formed African-American communities in the Midwest and exhorted them to "be clean! For cleanliness is godliness." But Truth still aimed her message mostly at white audiences, urging them to support black rights and woman suffrage.

With regal dignity and an abiding spiritual faith that sustained her through so many trials, Sojourner Truth was a towering voice of conscience and reform. She strode through a crucial period in American history, serving her people and her country with courage and compassion.

PUBLICATION
Narrative of Sojourner Truth (as told to Olive Gilbert, 1850)

FURTHER READING
Ortiz, Victoria. *Sojourner Truth: A Self-made Woman.* Philadelphia: Lippincott, 1974.
Krass, Peter. *Sojourner Truth.* New York: Chelsea House, 1988.

Tubman, Harriet

FORMER SLAVE, ABOLITIONIST,
CIVIL WAR SCOUT AND NURSE

Born: ca. 1820
Dorchester County, Maryland

Died: March 10, 1913
Auburn, New York

Though she was born into bondage, Harriet Tubman, stubborn and fiercely independent, could never submit to slavery. Five years after marrying a free black, John Tubman, she made her break for freedom in 1849 and escaped to Philadelphia. There she worked as a hotel servant and contrived a plan to rescue other slaves.

From 1850 to 1860, Tubman made approximately 19 trips back to Maryland to rescue slaves and guide them up north to freedom along the Underground Railroad. Traveling at night and mostly during the dark winter months, she risked her own life—for slave catchers and planters had put a bounty on her head—to bring some 300 slaves out of bondage, including her own parents. She received assistance from abolitionists and other antislavery sympathizers, but Tubman had mostly to rely on her own ingenuity and physical prowess to accomplish her mission. She used disguises, learned how to trip up slave catchers on her trail, and knew the most remote backroads and byways out of Maryland.

During the Civil War, Tubman served the Union army as a spy and scout, continuing to rescue slaves. The information that she gleaned from spying helped Union military officials make several successful raids into coastal areas of South Carolina, Georgia, and Florida. In perhaps her most spectacular escapade, she helped Union soldiers raid South Carolina and destroy stockpiles of Confederate weapons and cotton, liberating hundreds of slaves in the process.

After the war, Tubman returned to a small farm that she had purchased in Auburn, New York, and opened a boardinghouse for orphaned black children and elderly blacks. Though she had never had the opportunity to acquire an education, she strongly supported efforts to educate former slaves. She also attended women's rights meetings. Tubman lived her final years in her boardinghouse in Auburn. She was widely esteemed for her earlier courageous exploits and her devotion to the betterment of her people.

FURTHER READING
Bentley, Judith. *Harriet Tubman.* New York: Franklin Watts, 1990.
Bisson, Terry. *Harriet Tubman.* New York: Chelsea House, 1991.

Wald, Lillian D.

SETTLEMENT LEADER, SOCIAL REFORMER,
NURSE

Born: March 10, 1867
Cincinnati, Ohio

Died: September 1, 1940
Westport, Connecticut

Lillian Wald accomplished two major advances in social reform: She pioneered the field of public-health nursing, and she established the Henry Street Settlement, a hub of cultural and educational activities for residents of New York City's Lower East Side. Born into a Jewish family with roots in Germany and Poland, she enjoyed a childhood surrounded by books and music. She attended a private school in Rochester, New York, and at 16 applied to Vassar College but was told she was too young to be admitted.

After enjoying a carefree social life, she claimed that she felt the "need of serious, definite work." Choosing nursing, she enrolled in 1889 in the New York Hospital training school for nurses, then supplemented this training, which she felt to be inadequate, with medical training at the Woman's Medical College in New York. When, in 1893, she was asked to organize home nursing classes for immigrant families on the city's Lower East Side, she found her "definite" work, as she said later—public-health nursing.

With a friend and fellow nurse, she moved into a tenement apartment to establish a neighborhood health clinic. Other nurses soon joined them, and they found larger quarters on Henry Street in the Lower East Side, a neighborhood of Jewish and Italian immigrant families.

By 1913, the Henry Street Visiting Nurses Service included 92 nurses who made 200,000 house calls annually throughout New York City. They also established first-aid stations and convalescent facilities. Similar programs sprang up around the country, and Wald was soon recognized as the founder of a new public-health nursing movement.

But the Henry Street Settlement was more than just a health-care facility. It quickly expanded into a neighborhood center for civic, social, and educational reform. Like other settlement houses, it offered academic and vocational training, as well as cultural entertainment, and housed programs and projects to improve tenement housing and create more parks and playgrounds.

All of Wald's activities and projects reflected her desire to improve the quality of urban life. She spearheaded attempts to eradicate tuberculosis, the scourge of tenement dwellers living and working in unsanitary conditions, abolish child labor, and also prevent war. The establishment of the federal Children's Bureau in 1912 resulted from her efforts to promote children's welfare. During World War I, she fought government attempts to curtail civil liberties and coordinated the work of public and private nursing agencies during the deadly influenza epidemic of 1918. But, always, her work on behalf of the Henry Street Settlement was her first priority.

Although her major achievement lay in creating the field of public-health nursing, her vision and commitment reached far beyond this innovative program to seek ways to improve the quality of life for all urban dwellers. In 1933, 40 years after she had established the Henry Street Settlement, she resigned and retired to Westport, Connecticut, where she died.

PUBLICATIONS
The House on Henry Street (autobiography, 1915)
Windows on Henry Street (autobiography, 1934)

FURTHER READING
Daniels, Doris. *Always a Sister: The Feminism of Lillian D. Wald.* New York: Feminist Press, 1989.
Siegel, Beatrice. *Lillian Wald of Henry Street.* New York: Macmillan, 1983.

Walker, Alice Malsenior

WRITER, POET, LECTURER

Born: February 8, 1944
Eatonton, Georgia

Writer Alice Walker uses her literary gifts to capture the lives and struggles of African-American women. She regards her writing as a way of "paying homage to the people I love, the people who are thought to be dumb and backward but who taught me to see beauty." On paper, Walker has a genius for wresting beauty and dignity out of the most meager of lives.

Perhaps part of this genius comes from her own impoverished background. She is the eighth child of sharecropping parents who never earned more than $300 a year. But her fertile imagination was nourished early by a love of reading and by listening to her parents spin tales about their ancestors. When Walker was in high school, her mother managed to save enough money to buy her a typewriter—a gift that symbolized to

Walker her mother's admonition to "go write [my] ass off."

Walker graduated from her local high school in 1962, the valedictorian of her class. She enrolled in Spelman College in Atlanta, Georgia. But she found Spelman's "puritanical atmosphere" too confining and transferred to Sarah Lawrence College in Bronxville, New York. She spent the summer following her junior year in Africa, an experience that inspired her first collection of poetry, *Once,* published in 1968.

After graduating from Sarah Lawrence College in 1965, Walker went south to Georgia and Mississippi, where she helped blacks register to vote. There she met and married Melvyn Rosenman Leventhal, a civil rights attorney, and began to write in earnest. She wrote both essays and short stories and, in 1967, published her first novel, *The Third Life of Grange Copeland.* Over the next decade, Walker wrote several more novels and collections of poetry, but not until 1982, when she published her third novel, *The Color Purple,* did she finally gain widespread critical and popular acclaim. This novel, written in the form of a series of letters, chronicles the struggles of Celie, a young, sexually abused black woman living in the rural South, as she overcomes her traumatic past and awakens to her desires and goals in life. The novel, made into a movie in 1984, established Walker's reputation for vividly bringing to life the hopes, struggles, and dreams of African-American women.

Walker describes her writing as "womanist" because she strives to express "the spirit that we see in black women." In all of her writing—her essays, poetry, and fiction—she captures that tough, vibrant spirit and creates characters who are not soon forgotten.

MAJOR PUBLICATIONS
Meridian (1976)
The Color Purple (1982)
In Search of Our Mothers' Gardens: Womanist Prose (1983)
Living by the Word (1988)
The Temple of My Familiar (1992)

FURTHER READING
Bradley, David. "Telling the Black Woman's Story." *New York Times* (January 8, 1984), 24–37.
Christian, Barbara. "Alice Walker: The Black Woman Artist as Wayward." In *Black Women Writers (1950–1980): A Critical Evaluation,* edited by Mari Evans. New York: Anchor, 1984.
Gentry, Tony. *Alice Walker.* New York: Chelsea House, 1993.
Tate, Claudia, ed. *Black Women Writers at Work: Conversations,* pp. 175–87. New York: Continuum, 1983.

Ward, Nancy
CHEROKEE LEADER

Born: ca. 1738
Chota, Tennessee

Died: ca. 1822
near Benton, Tennessee

Nancy Ward, later known as the "Pocahontas of the West," played a long and vigorous role in peace-making between the Cherokee nation of Tennessee and the oncoming colonial settlers. At an early age, she married Kingfisher of the Deer Clan and bore one son and daughter. She first distinguished herself in 1775 during a battle between the Cherokee and Creek Indians. When her husband was killed in battle, she took his place and helped the Cherokees triumph.

For her bravery, she was chosen Agi-ga-u-e, or "Beloved Woman" of her tribe, and assumed leadership of the influential Woman's Council, a governing body composed of a representative of each Cherokee clan. She also sat on the Council of Chiefs. Thereafter, Nancy (the Anglicized version of her Indian name Nanye'hi) devoted her energies to securing peace for both the Cherokees and the oncoming colonial settlers.

After marrying again, this time to Bryant Ward, a white trader, Nancy Ward developed a steady friendship with white colonists settling the river valleys of eastern Tennessee. During the American Revolution, she alerted the settlers of a planned pro-British Cherokee attack and personally intervened to save one female settler from being killed by Cherokee warriors. Her popularity with settlers spared Chota, her Cherokee village, from being decimated by colonial troops.

After the war ended, she emerged as a leader of the now-defeated Cherokees, urging friendship rather than warfare between her people and the new American nation. At two separate peace conferences, she served as a principle negotiator for the Cherokees. In addition, to expand the Cherokees' economy, she introduced dairy production, cattle raising, and new methods of farming. Though she urged her people not to give up more land to the advancing tide of settlers, her voice was drowned out by new Cherokee leaders who chose to relinquish land for peace.

Forced to leave Chota after white settlers invaded its boundaries, Nancy Ward established a small inn in southeastern Tennessee, near the present town of Benton. There she died in 1822 and was buried on a nearby hill. Thirteen years later, the Cherokees relinquished all claim to their homeland and were forcibly removed to Indian Territory (now Oklahoma). The long, brutal march they made came to be known as the Trail of Tears because of the hardships they suffered along the way.

Warren, Mercy Otis

POET, PATRIOT, HISTORIAN

*Born: September 14, 1728
Barnstable, Massachusetts*

*Died: October 19, 1814
Plymouth, Massachusetts*

The daughter of a farmer who was also a merchant, lawyer, and county judge, Mercy Otis Warren came of age in a household fully engaged in political affairs. She received no formal education,

but she occasionally sat in on her brothers' private lessons and had access to her uncle's library.

At age 26, she married James Warren, a merchant and farmer, and was soon drawn into the growing revolutionary ferment. Her husband, father, and brother all strongly opposed the British Crown, and her home frequently served as a meeting place for Massachusetts's colonial patriots, including John and Samuel Adams.

Warren, who had earlier composed poetry for pleasure, turned her literary talents to political satire. In 1772, she published her first play, *The Adulateur,* anonymously in the Boston newspaper the *Massachusetts Spy.* It was followed by *The Defeat.* Both plays cast Thomas Hutchinson, the royal governor of Massachusetts, as a villainous ruler of a mythical country who wanted to destroy "the ardent love of liberty in [America's] free-born sons." Warren wrote other plays that championed American independence, as well as poetry that expressed her revolutionary fervor.

In later years, her husband's political opponents denounced her for opposing the ratification of the U.S. Constitution—she believed that it gave the federal government too much power—and for supporting the French Revolution. For years, she labored on a three-volume work on the American Revolution, *History of the Rise, Progress and Termination of the American Revolution,* which she published in 1805. Unlike John Adams and other Federalists who supported a strong central government, she favored a government that left more power in the hands of the people.

Adams, for one, was not pleased with her portrayal of him in her history; she declared that he had "forgotten the principles of the American revolution" and accused him of being proud and ambitious at the expense of his political principles. "History," he complained in response, "is not the Province of the Ladies."

Although Warren did not make women's rights an intellectual priority, she lamented the lack of educational opportunities for women in the new nation, believing they were capable of participating in a wider sphere. Spirited, independent-minded, and liberty-loving, she was a true American patriot—and one of the nation's first historians.

PUBLICATIONS

Observations on the New Constitution (1788)
History of the Rise, Progress and Termination of the American Revolution (1805)

Washington, Margaret Murray

EDUCATOR, CLUBWOMAN

Born: March 9, 1861
Macon, Mississippi

Died: June 4, 1925
place of death unknown

Although she was most well known as the wife of Booker T. Washington, Margaret Murray Washington deserves recognition in her own right for her educational and community service to her fellow African Americans.

Little is known about her early life beyond her mixed parentage. Her mother was black, and her father, who died when Margaret was seven, was an Irish immigrant. After sporadic schooling in her early years, in 1881 she entered Fisk University's preparatory school, where she was a model student, associate editor of the school newspaper, and president of a campus literary society.

She graduated in 1889, after completing both the preparatory and college-level requirements, and began teaching at Tuskegee Institute. A year later, she was promoted to the position of "lady principal" by Booker T. Washington, founder of the school. In 1892, they were married.

She continued to teach at Tuskegee and eventually became dean of women. Beyond her official responsibilities as educator and wife of the school's president, she formed a mothers' club for the rural black women who lived near Tuskegee. Every Saturday, she invited the mothers for coffee and cake and an uplifting talk while their children played in another room. She advised the women on health, hygiene, nutrition, and morality. By 1904, these meetings drew nearly 300 women.

She also lectured throughout the South on similar topics and was an active member of the black women's club movement, presiding over several state and national boards. In 1920, she urged her reluctant black sisters to work with white women on the Commission on Interracial Cooperation (CIC). In addition, she helped form the International Council of Women of the Darker Races to instill pride in black history and culture, and served as its first president.

The motto of the National Association of Colored Women (NACW), of which Washington was secretary, was "Lifting as We Climb." Washington was part of a generation of African-American women who dedicated their energies to serving their communities; like her sisters, she took this motto to heart, enlarging her spirit and consciousness as she helped her people.

FURTHER READING

Neverdon-Morton, Cynthia. *Afro-American Women of the South and the Advancement of the Race, 1895–1925*. Knoxville: University of Tennessee Press, 1989.
"Short Sketch of the Life of Mrs. Margaret Murray Washington," in *Lifting As They Climb*, ed. by Elizabeth Lindsay Davis. Washington, D.C.: National Association of Colored Women, 1933.

Wells-Barnett, Ida Bell

JOURNALIST, LECTURER, CLUBWOMAN

Born: July 16, 1862
Holly Springs, Mississippi

Died: March 25, 1931
Chicago, Illinois

Ida Wells-Barnett led a courageous one-woman crusade against lynching—risking her own life to abolish this heinous crime against American blacks.

Though she was born into slavery, she enjoyed educational opportunities after emancipation that her parents never had. She attended a high school for former slaves and in later years augmented her education by attending summer school at Fisk University. At 14, she became both breadwinner and mother to her four younger siblings when her parents and three other siblings perished in a yellow fever epidemic.

She taught school and also began to write articles for small, local black-owned newspapers, using the pen name "Iola." When the school board in Memphis, where she lived, fired her for criticizing the inferior schooling available to the city's black children, she became a full-time journalist and eventually assumed part ownership of Memphis's black newspaper, the *Memphis Free Speech*.

Wells-Barnett used her journalistic platform to denounce an upsurge of lynchings against southern blacks and to urge Memphis's black citizens to move out west, where they would escape this deadly racism and find more economic opportunity. She investigated the circumstances surrounding the lynchings and published her findings. She contended that although southern whites claimed that lynching punished black men who had sexually threatened white women, they were actually using lynching as a tool of terror against blacks who had managed to amass some property. While she was visiting the East Coast in 1892, her newspaper office was mobbed and destroyed, and she was unable to return to Memphis for fear of her life.

From New York, she embarked on a one-woman crusade against lynching. Up and down the East Coast, she lectured and established anti-lynching societies and black women's clubs. During a trip to Britain in 1893, she even established an anti-lynching organization there.

In 1895, she married Ferdinand Lee Barnett, a black lawyer and newspaper editor who shared her desire to combat racism. She traveled less frequently after marrying and focused her energies on helping the black community of Chicago, where she and her young family lived. She organized social and educational activities, and from 1913 to 1916 she served as a probation officer for the Chicago municipal court.

In 1910, she attended the founding meeting of the National Association for the Advancement of Colored People (NAACP)—though she believed the organization was not vocal enough in pressing for black rights. She also founded the first African-American woman suffrage group, the Alpha Suffrage Club of Chicago, and worked with Jane Addams to prevent city officials from segregating Chicago's black children in school.

Wherever an opportunity arose to improve living conditions and educational opportunities for Chicago's African-American community, Ida Wells-Barnett was there, urging city officials "to set the wheels of justice in motion" and secure equal rights and equal protection under the law for the city's blacks. She was passionate, courageous, and vigilant in demanding justice for African Americans.

PUBLICATION
Crusade for Justice (autobiography, published posthumously in 1970)

FURTHER READING
Van Steenwyk, Elizabeth. *Ida B. Wells-Barnett: Woman of Courage.* New York: Franklin Watts, 1992.

Wheatley, Phillis
POET

Born: ca. 1754 (exact date unknown)
West Africa

Died: December 5, 1784
Boston, Massachusetts

From bondage to literary renown—this is the remarkable story of an African-American woman who spent most of her life enslaved but whose spirit soared high and free. Brought to Boston from West Africa aboard the slave ship *Phillis*, the young girl, who was only seven or eight, was sold to a Boston merchant, John Wheatley, and his wife, Susanna. They named her after the ship that had borne her to New England, and trained her to be a household servant.

Although she was a slave, the Wheatleys treated her well. She had her own room, and her household duties were not arduous. More important, the Wheatleys' children taught her to read and write. She was a quick student; within a year and a half, she could read and comprehend the most difficult passages of the Bible.

With her owners' blessing, she joined the Old South Meeting House and soon channeled her creative and intellectual abilities into a deeply religious outlook, which she expressed through poetry. She published her first poem when she was 13, and six years later published a book of verse, *Poems on Various Subjects, Religious and Moral.* In her poetry, she expressed her deep love of learning and virtue and her belief in Christian redemption.

Still enslaved to the Wheatleys, Phillis attracted a wide circle of admirers, including an English countess who was active in evangelical and antislavery causes. When Wheatley visited England in 1773, the countess introduced her to other poets and dignitaries, and her following grew even larger.

Upon her return from London, the Wheatleys freed Phillis. She married John Peters in 1778, but he was a ne'er-do-well who could not make a living. Wheatley bore three children, only to be deserted by her husband. She worked in a boardinghouse to support herself, snatching time to write when she could. Inexplicably, her public— once so lavish with praise for her work—now spurned her, and Wheatley died alone and impoverished. But her poetry survived and has enjoyed a splendid rebirth of interest in the late 20th century.

PUBLICATION
The Collected Works of Phillis Wheatley, John C. Shields, ed. (1988)

FURTHER READING
Richmond, Merle. *Phillis Wheatley.* New York: Chelsea House, 1988.

Whitman, Narcissa Prentiss

MISSIONARY

Born: March 14, 1808
Prattsburgh, New York

Died: November 29, 1847
Waiilatpu, Oregon

Narcissa Prentiss Whitman sacrificed her life for a cause that had become her burden rather than her salvation. Raised in a highly religious family, she attended a Presbyterian academy and then taught while "awaiting the leading of Providence." That moment came in 1834 when she heard the Reverend Samuel Parker, a recruiter for missionaries, speak about a project to spread Christianity to Native Americans in the Far West.

Already determined to dedicate her life to missionary work, the young woman volunteered her efforts, but the agency sponsoring the project refused to enlist "unmarried females," and so she married Marcus Whitman, a physician and fellow missionary. In 1836, they joined a wagon train and embarked upon the long, hard journey out west. She and another woman on the train became the first white American women to cross the Continental Divide, blazing the way for thousands of other women who would soon journey west. They set up their mission in Waiilatpu, Oregon, among the Cayuse Indians.

While her husband conducted religious services, practiced medicine, and supervised the construction of buildings and farms, Narcissa Whitman taught in the mission school and trained Native American women in domestic skills. At first, she derived great satisfaction from her work. But troubled times set in after her young daughter accidentally drowned and the rigors of missionary life became overwhelming. Language and cultural barriers, and the unwillingness of the Cayuse to adopt a foreign religion, turned her into a bitter, disillusioned, and haughty missionary.

Her unhappy life as a missionary came to a violent end in 1847 when a measles epidemic, brought by white settlers to Oregon, killed numerous Indian children who did not respond to the Whitmans' nursing. Although the children died of natural causes—they had no immunity to measles—the Cayuse accused Marcus and Narcissa Whitman of practicing witchcraft and killing their children. On a cold autumn day, the Cayuse rose up and murdered the Whitmans and 12 other whites and took 47 prisoners. The Whitmans were buried near Walla Walla, Washington, and scores of visitors stop at their graves each year.

PUBLICATIONS
My Journal, 1836, Lawrence Dodd, ed. (1982)
The Letters of Narcissa Whitman, Ye Galleon Press (1986)

FURTHER READING
Jeffrey, Julie Roy. *Converting the West: A Biography of Narcissa Whitman.* Norman: University of Oklahoma Press, 1991.

Willard, Emma Hart

EDUCATOR

Born: February 23, 1787
Berlin, Connecticut

Died: April 15, 1870
Troy, New York

Although Emma Willard came of age at a time when women were expected to obey their husbands and devote themselves to family duties, her father, a farmer and Jeffersonian liberal, encouraged her to develop her intellect. He discussed English political philosophy with her and even interrupted her domestic duties to engage her in intellectual conversations.

At 13, she taught herself geometry and, two years later, enrolled at the Berlin Academy—a highly as-

sertive act for a young girl who had earlier dismissed formal education as unsuited to her lowly station in life. Soon she was teaching younger students at Berlin, and in 1805 she began conducting classes in her parents' home. Eager to improve her teaching abilities, she also attended classes in nearby Hartford,

In 1807, she became head of a female academy in Middlebury, Vermont. Two years later, she married John Willard, a physician and champion of female education. When his practice failed, she opened a school in her own home, calling it the Middlebury Female Seminary. Denied admission to Middlebury College for additional education, she taught herself academic subjects in order to instruct her students better, for she hoped to give them a rigorous classical and scientific education equal to that available to male students.

Her school prospered, and she next sought to establish a state-supported system of schools for young women. Although such luminaries as John Adams, Thomas Jefferson, and James Monroe endorsed her plan, New York State legislators vetoed it.

But in 1821, with the assistance of a community council in Troy, New York, she opened the Troy Female Seminary to train young women as teachers. She offered training in both domestic skills and academic subjects, including science and math classes more advanced than those offered in many men's colleges: trigonometry, astronomy, chemistry, botany, mineralogy, and physiology.

Troy Female Seminary was the first school of higher learning for women, and it was a resounding success. Although Willard argued that her school would better prepare women for marriage and motherhood—and therefore help to strengthen the moral fiber of the new republic—many of her students went on to teach or to establish other women's schools. Among Troy's most distinguished alumnae was Elizabeth Cady Stanton, a chief architect of the organized women's rights movement.

Despite personal misfortune, including her husband's death and a brief but disastrous second marriage, Willard continued to teach at Troy and crusade for better educational opportunities for women. Though she did not support the organized women's rights movement, she was a passionate advocate of equal educational opportunities for women. Her vision and commitment made possible the establishment of better schools for American women.

PUBLICATION

An Address to the Public; Particularly to the Members of the Legislature of New-York, Proposing a Plan for Improving Female Education (1819)

FURTHER READING

Solomon, Barbara. *In the Company of Educated Women: A History of Women and Higher Education in America.* New Haven, Conn.: Yale University Press, 1985.

Willard, Frances Elizabeth Caroline

TEMPERANCE LEADER, FEMINIST

Born: September 28, 1839
Churchville, New York

Died: February 17, 1898
New York, New York

From a rough-and-tumble childhood on the Wisconsin frontier to leader of one of the most powerful women's organizations of the 19th century—this was the remarkable path taken by Frances Willard, founder of the Woman's Christian Temperance Union (WCTU). She received her first schooling from her mother, then attended a district school over her father's opposition. Later she recalled how resentful she felt that her brother could vote, but because of her sex she could not.

In 1859, she graduated from the North Western Female College in Evanston, Illinois. Altogether, her formal education had amounted to less than four years. For the next several years she taught at various schools and colleges for women, but she derived little satisfaction from this work. A two-year

trip to Europe rekindled her energies and ambitions, and she returned to the United States eager to serve "the class that I have always loved and that has loved me always—the girls of my native land and my times."

To this end, she became president of the Evanston College for Ladies, a Methodist institution; and in 1873—now a well-known educator—she helped to establish the Association for the Advancement of Women, an organization that promoted women in professional life. A year later, she joined a new temperance organization in Illinois, and was a delegate at the convention that gave birth to the Woman's Christian Temperance Union (WCTU). She was elected corresponding secretary of the WCTU, and in 1879, after steadily moving up the leadership ranks, she became its president.

Willard infused new life into the WCTU. Under her leadership, the organization adopted new goals and strategies, evolving from a prayer society opposed to the consumption of alcohol to a comprehensive movement for social change. Willard espoused a "Do Everything" policy, urging members to help improve all aspects of women's lives. Her vision was yet another expression of women's belief in their role as caretakers of their communities. In 1884, she offered an explanation of her philosophy, reflecting as well the goals of other women's volunteer activities during this era: "Were I to define in a sentence, the thought and purpose of the Woman's Christian Temperance Union, I would reply: 'It is to make the whole world homelike.'"

Inspired by her vision, WCTU members worked not only for temperance but for a variety of causes. They created boys' and girls' clubs, tea parties for mothers, homes for alcoholic women, and evening schools for working women. They also campaigned for better working conditions in factories, more humane prisons, health education in public schools, and public drinking fountains. But, as Willard realized even before she became president, the WCTU had no real power to effect these changes until women could vote. As president, she made female enfranchisement a prime goal.

Willard also joined the American Woman Suffrage Association (AWSA) and, in 1891, became president of the World's WCTU. In addition, she helped to establish the General Federation of Women's Clubs, a national network of white women's organizations. But it was the WCTU that was truly her life's work. She remained president of the organization until her death, using the club to serve, as she had said so many years before, "the class that I have always loved."

MAJOR PUBLICATIONS

Woman and Temperance (1883)
Glimpses of Fifty Years: The Autobiography of an American Woman (1889)
A Woman of the Century (1894)

FURTHER READING

Bordin, Ruth. *Frances Willard: A Biography.* Chapel Hill: University of North Carolina Press, 1986.

Williams, Eunice

INDIAN CAPTIVE

Born: September 17, 1696
Deerfield, Massachusetts

Died: November 1785
Kahnawake, Canada

Eunice Williams, a descendant of a leading New England family, was seven when she was captured in 1704 during an Indian raid on Deerfield, Massachusetts, where she and her family lived. Kahnawake Indian warriors from Canada joined forces with the French and descended upon the settlers. Eunice's infant sister and six-year-old brother, as well as the family's slave, Parthena, were killed in the raid, and her mother died during the long, forced march up to Canada.

Eventually, Eunice's surviving sister and brothers, along with their father, John Williams, a minister, were freed by ransom and returned home. But Eunice, who had been adopted by Iroquois Indians, converts to Roman Catholicism, chose to stay with her new family. She stopped speaking English, and refused to return to Deerfield—even after her father journeyed twice, in 1713 and again in 1714, to retrieve her.

By then, she had converted to Catholicism and had married an Iroquois Indian named Arosen, also Catholic. Eventually, she and her husband visited Deerfield, but by then Williams had long cast her allegiances and fate with her adopted Indian community.

FURTHER READING

Demos, John. *The Unredeemed Captive: A Family Story from Early America.* New York: Knopf, 1994.

Williams, Fannie Barrier

LECTURER, CIVIC LEADER, CLUBWOMAN, JOURNALIST

Born: February 12, 1855
Brockport, New York

Died: March 4, 1944
Brockport, New York

A founder of the National Association of Colored Women, a national federation of African-American women's clubs, Fannie Barrier Williams spent her life helping to improve social and economic conditions for her race. She came from a free northern family of modest means; for many years, her family were the only black residents in their small township of Brockport, but they encountered little discrimination and her father was respected in the community. Fannie Barrier Williams attended local schools with white children and graduated from the State Normal School in Brockport in 1870.

Not until she went South during Reconstruction to teach former slaves did she face racism, and she was seared by the ordeal. She wrote later, "I have never quite recovered from the shock and pain of my first bitter realization that to be a colored woman is to be discredited, mistrusted and often meanly hated." She returned north to Boston, where she studied at the New England Conservatory of Music, and then attended the School of Fine Arts in Washington, D.C.

There she met S. Laing Williams, a young lawyer, and in 1887 they were married. Fannie Williams's career of public service began in 1893 when she lectured on the "Intellectual Progress of the Colored Woman of the United States since the Emancipation." Soon she found herself in demand as a speaker, and she used the lecture platform to advocate solidarity and collective action among African Americans to advance their needs. She lectured around the country and also wrote for several newspapers, including the *Chicago Record-Herald* and the *New York Age*.

Williams became a leader in the black women's club movement, both on the national level and in local organizations in Chicago, where she lived. In 1893, she helped found the National League of Colored Women (NLCW) and, three years later, presided over its merger with another black women's federation to form the National Association of Colored Women. For her, the club movement represented "the struggle of an enlightened conscience against the whole brood of social miseries, born out of the stress and pain of a hated past."

Less publicly and with some success, she urged employers to hire black women applicants for skilled positions, and in her lectures and writings she promoted the dignity and advancement of black women. In later years, she supported the woman suffrage movement and urged her black sisters to join the fight for equal rights. Along with Mary Church Terrell, Ida Wells-Barnett, Lugenia Hope, and other talented, dedicated black women, she made the welfare of her people the beacon of her work.

PUBLICATIONS

"A Northern Woman's Autobiography," *Independent* (July 14, 1904)

"The Club Movement Among Colored Women in America," in Booker T. Washington, ed., *A New Negro for a New Century*. Chicago: American Publishing House, 1900

FURTHER READING

Davis, Elizabeth Lindsay, ed. *Lifting as They Climb*. Washington, D.C.: National Association of Colored Women, 1933.

"Fannie Barrier Williams," in Bert James Loewenberg and Ruth Bogin, eds. *Black Women in Nineteenth Century American Life*. University Park: Pennsylvania State University Press, 1976.

Wilson, Dagmar

CHILDREN'S BOOK ILLUSTRATOR AND LEADER OF WOMEN STRIKE FOR PEACE

Born: ca. 1916

New York, New York

Dagmar Wilson founded Women Strike for Peace (WSP), a loosely knit organization of women around the nation who, in the early 1960s, marched, picketed, and lobbied the U.S. government to end nuclear-weapons testing and work for nuclear disarmament and world peace. Wilson, who had been outraged by the arrest of the British philosopher Bertrand Russell for taking part in anti-nuclear-bomb demonstrations, contacted several friends about efforts to promote peace, and in September 1961 their efforts and ideas crystallized into a movement.

On November 1, 1961, 50,000 women in 60 cities around the country marched against the resumption of nuclear testing by the U.S. government and for world peace. From there, the movement expanded into a comprehensive effort to outlaw the tools of war. Members lobbied Congress, picketed stores selling war toys, demonstrated in front of the White House, circulated petitions for peace, educated themselves on the dangers of nuclear fallout, and through leaflets and press campaigns kept the public informed of their efforts. They also dispatched representatives to international conferences on disarmament and appealed directly to President John F. Kennedy and Soviet premier Nikita Khrushchev.

Wilson, the daughter of a foreign correspondent, developed a political awareness early on. She attended a progressive school in London, where, as she later said, "We always seemed to be questioning the traditional ways of doing things." She also spent four years at the Slade School of Fine Art, University College, London. In addition, she sat in on discussions between her parents and other journalists, wondering why these people who seemed to know so much were not running the country.

Wilson was not comfortable with the mantle of leadership in Women Strike for Peace. She regarded the organization as a grassroots effort, and herself as an "ordinary housewife. I symbolize something." She believed that people must speak up for their beliefs: "When your destiny appears to be decided in ways opposite from the way you want it to go, you've got to get out there and concern yourself with it."

In addition to her work for WSP, Wilson has taught art and worked as a children's book illustrator and graphic artist. A wife and mother, she once defined success: "Having the freedom to pursue my craft without having to prostitute myself. Having combined professional recognition and private appreciation for my activities. Having made a small contribution to effecting social change in founding a peace movement and by holding my ground before the 'inquisitors' [House Un-American Activities Committee], I like to think that I have made a small mark on history for good."

FURTHER READING
"Close-up of a 'Peace Striker,'" Schuster, Alvin. *New York Times Magazine.* May 6, 1962, p. 324.

Winnemucca, Sarah

NATIVE AMERICAN LEADER

*Born: ca. 1844
Humboldt Sink, Nevada*

*Died: October 16, 1891
Monida, Montana*

Next to Pocahontas and Sacajawea, Sarah Winnemucca is the most famous Native American woman in American history. Repeatedly, she spoke out against the injustices that her people had suffered at the hands of whites. She was the daughter of a Piute chief and lived for a time at a Mormon trading post as a companion to the daughter of a stage company agent. There she refined her command of English and embraced Christianity without entirely relinquishing the spiritual beliefs of her tribe.

In 1860, as more white settlers converged on Nevada, the Piutes were herded onto reservations and were cruelly exploited by government agents. Any form of protest or resistance on their part brought swift, and ruthless, retaliation; after Piute men stole some cattle, soldiers from a nearby army post raided their camp, murdered several Indian women and children, and set fire to their homes. Sarah Winnemucca lost her baby brother in this massacre. Her hatred of the agents only intensified, and she became an interpreter for her people. Ten years later, she visited an army general in San Francisco to protest these and other wrongs committed against her people.

During a forced march from Nevada to Washington Territory in the bitter winter of 1878, she beseeched military officials, with little success, to ease the hardships of the journey for her people. Several years later, she went on a lecture tour to publicize the travail of that journey and other wrongs committed against the Piutes. In 1880, she even testified before President Rutherford B. Hayes and Secretary of the Interior Carl Schurz. Although they promised to allow the Piutes to return to Nevada and to secure individual land allotments, they never carried through on this promise.

After marrying Lieutenant L. H. Hopkins in 1881, Winnemucca lectured again about her people's plight and published *Life Among the Piutes,* a slender volume summarizing her lectures. In later years, she opened a school for Piute children on her brother's ranch in Nevada. Although she was not able to secure better treatment for her people, she had displayed astonishing courage in publicly voicing her anger at their plight, and her forceful words aroused the public's sympathy, if not action, on their behalf.

PUBLICATION
Life Among the Piutes (1883)

Winthrop, Margaret

WIFE OF JOHN WINTHROP, FIRST GOVERNOR OF THE MASSACHUSETTS BAY COLONY

Born: ca. 1591
England

Died: June 14, 1647
Boston, Massachusetts

Margaret Winthrop was an abiding helpmeet to her husband during his tumultuous tenure as governor of the Massachusetts Bay Colony. She was born into a family of modest means but royal influence; her father was an official of the royal court.

Her early life and education remain obscure. On April 29, 1618, she married John Winthrop and moved into his father's manor house in Suffolk, England. As mistress of the manor, which included her husband's father and John Winthrop's four children from previous marriages, as well as the two children she bore, Margaret Winthrop gained valuable administrative skills that would serve her well in the new colony. Although the manor house was isolated from markets and main roads, it still managed to draw many visitors who stayed for weeks at a time. Winthrop quickly learned how to make her large household self-sufficient as well as hospitable.

In the years before John Winthrop sailed to the New World, his duties as attorney at the Court of Wards and Liveries kept him in London, and his visits to the manor were few and brief. During these long periods of separation, Margaret and John Winthrop conducted a lengthy correspondence in which they affirmed their love for each other. Wrote Margaret: "I have many reasons to make me love thee, whereof I will name two, first because thous lovest God, and secondly because that thou lovest me."

Throughout their 30-year marriage, they shared a tender love and regard for each other, even across the vast distance of the Atlantic Ocean. Margaret, like other married women of her day, deferred to her husband, calling herself his "faythful and obedient wife," but the unequal relationship between husband and wife was leavened by mutual love and respect.

In 1630, eager to construct a "new world" of Puritan righteousness but saddened by leaving his wife behind, John Winthrop sailed to America to establish the Massachusetts Bay Colony. A year and a half later, in the fall of 1631, Margaret Winthrop joined him in Boston, having brought much-needed supplies for the new colony. The voyage across the ocean was an ordeal; while at sea, her infant daughter died.

For 16 years, she presided as first lady of the fledgling colony. Though she did not publicly participate in the political and religious controversies that marred her husband's tenure as governor, she was distressed by "all these troubles among us," as she wrote in one letter. She died in the summer of 1647, after a brief illness. Her husband called her "a woman of singular virtue, prudence, modesty and piety . . . beloved and honoured of all the country."

FURTHER READING
Moseley, James G.. *John Winthrop's World: History as a Story, the Story as History*. Madison: University of Wisconsin Press, 1992.

Wolcott, Marion Post

PHOTOGRAPHER

Born: June 7, 1910
Montclair, New Jersey

Died: November 24, 1990
Santa Barbara, California

From 1938 to 1942, as the country slowly climbed out of a devastating economic collapse, Marion

Post Wolcott criss-crossed the rural South to photograph people and places ravaged by the depression. Her photographs provide a stark and stunning visual record of the poverty and despair wrought by economic disaster, as well as of the enduring power of the human spirit.

Wolcott grew up in the small New Jersey town of Bloomfield, where farmers still used horse-drawn carts to peddle their produce at the Saturday morning markets in nearby Newark. Wolcott's father was a family physician, and her mother was a registered nurse. But despite their shared professional interests, they were as opposite in temperament and outlook as two people could be. While her father turned a stern, humorless gaze to the world, her mother enjoyed the company of artists and other free spirits. Eventually, they divorced, and Wolcott's mother moved to Greenwich Village in New York City and joined Margaret Sanger's crusade for legalized contraception.

As a child, Marion Post—nicknamed "Sis"—attended boarding schools and also a coeducational progressive school in Greenwich, Connecticut. There she discovered an interest in the arts. After graduation, she took classes at the New School for Social Research in New York City and at Vassar College. She also taught elementary school.

Like her mother, her politics were highly progressive. She supported educational reform and civil rights for African Americans. And she felt most truly alive when she was creating art—primarily sculpture and photography. But teaching remained her primary work—until she started taking pictures of the artists and actors with whom she socialized. Soon she began seeking assignments from magazines such as *Parents, Vogue,* and *Woman Today,* and embarked upon more serious study of photographic techniques.

In 1936, she moved to Philadelphia to work for the *Evening Bulletin.* She was the only woman photographer on a staff of nine, and her co-workers made her life miserable until she warned them, "Look, you bastards, I'm staying, so get used to me."

Although they finally accepted her, she found the work to be unsatisfying and looked for another position.

In the summer of 1938, she began working for the Farm Security Administration, a New Deal government agency. She was responsible for documenting through photographs the human and economic problems of the depression in order to rally public support for the New Deal. But her pictures went beyond mere documenting to present a kind of visual poetry of human hardship and survival.

Starting in July 1938, at a salary of $2,300 a year plus expenses, she traveled alone by car through the back roads of the South, stopping in such hardscrabble towns as Maidsville and Caples, Bluefield, Mohegan, Granville, and Elkins to take pictures. She ate in honky-tonk restaurants and slept in rundown hotels. It was often a lonely life, as she recalled later, a "kind of numbness. . . . One never has the same feeling of belonging as one does when with former acquaintances and friends." She produced some 15,000 photographs, focusing her lens on everything from rundown buildings to a card game in progress to a tenant farmer's ravaged hands or worn work shoes. Her camera caught the wistful expression on a young black girl's face as well as the grim countenance of a poor white sharecropper.

Her brief but prolific career ended when she married Lee Wolcott in June 1941. Remembering the unsettled years of her own childhood, when her mother shuttled her to various boarding schools, she decided that the itinerant life of a photographer was not suitable for raising a family. She put away her camera and devoted herself to her husband and children. In later years, she exhibited her work in galleries and museums. Although Wolcott's career as a professional photographer was all too brief, she gave the world an enduring visual record of human suffering and strength.

FURTHER READING

Hendrickson, Paul. *Looking for the Light: The Hidden Life and Art of Marion Post Wolcott.* New York: Knopf, 1992.

Woodhull, Victoria

FEMINIST, POLITICAL ACTIVIST

Born: September 23, 1838
Homer, Ohio

Died: June 10, 1927
London, England

Victoria Woodhull stunned the women's rights movement and late-19th-century American society with her provocative ideas and flamboyant style. She and her sister Tennessee Claflin spent a colorful childhood following their feckless parents around as they tried to make a living—not always by honest means. Such a peripatetic life afforded little opportunity for schooling, but both girls acquired another kind of education— from their father, who demonstrated his ability to deceive people out of their money.

The sisters joined forces with one of their brothers to create a traveling medicine show that offered a phony elixir of life for sale as well as their services as spiritualists. In 1853, Victoria married Canning Woodhull, a physician. She bore two children during their 12-year marriage before divorcing him and marrying Colonel James Harvey Blood, a Civil War veteran.

In 1868, Woodhull—claiming to follow the advice of the spirit of an ancient Greek orator who had appeared before her— moved to New York City, where she and her sister became Wall Street speculators. The railroad baron Cornelius Vanderbilt offered financial advice, but the women had enough innate business savvy to turn their venture into a resounding succes.

Soon the sisters shifted their prodigious energy to politics, and both became persuasive—and provocative— spokeswomen for the women's rights movement. In their journal, *Woodhull & Claflin's Weekly*, which they established in 1870, they espoused their controversial beliefs on dress reform, legalized prostitution, and world government. In 1871, they published Karl

Marx's *Communist Manifesto,* the blueprint of communism (which had been published in Europe in 1848)— their journal was the first American publication to feature this historic document. They also became muckrakers by exposing fraud on Wall Street.

Woodhull, the more flamboyant of the two, also voiced radical ideas about women's rights. She condemned loveless marriages and advocated free love, a movement that challenged organized religion's authority and wanted to abolish legal marriage because it stifled the dictates of the heart.

She claimed that the U.S. Constitution protected the practice of free love. Both women and men had the undeniable right to begin or end any intimate relationship, including marriage, because they were free and independent individuals. "I have an inalienable, constitutional and natural right to love whom I may . . . to change that love every day if I please," she declared.

Woodhull's opinions greatly embarrassed the women's rights movement because free lovers were lambasted in the popular press for their rejection of the marriage institution. Woodhull herself earned the dubious title of "Mrs. Satan" and "Queen of Prostitutes."

In reality, however, she had made an important contribution to the women's rights movement. With the legal imagination of a constitutional scholar, she argued that the 14th Amendment, which guaranteed citizenship rights to all persons born or naturalized in the United States, and the 15th Amendment, which prohibited states from denying the right to vote because of race, already granted to women (as citizens) the right to vote. She urged Congress to pass an act explicitly confirming that the U.S. Constitution granted the ballot to all U.S. citizens, including women. Woodhull claimed that women's right to vote was part of the inalienable right of citizenship protected by the U.S. Constitution.

But her flamboyant words often overshadowed the logic of her message. She was a fiery orator with a fiery message. In 1871, she addressed a meeting of the National Woman Suffrage Association, declaring, "We mean treason; we mean secession. . . . We are plotting revolution; we will . . . [overthrow] this bogus Republic and plant a government of righteousness in its stead."

A year later, she made good on her words by running for President of the United States as a candidate of the newly organized Equal Rights party.

Personal problems and scandals, as well as opposition to her ideas, isolated Woodhull from mainstream suffragists. She was wrongfully accused of being married to two men at once. In response to these accusations, she exposed a romantic liaison between the venerated preacher Henry Ward Beecher and Elizabeth Tilton, a married woman in his congregation. She printed her exposé in a special edition of her newspaper—and was promptly arrested and jailed for violating a federal law against distributing obscene literature through the mail. Although she was eventually acquitted, the long, drawn-out episode, with accusations flung at her by the press and Beecher's supporters, undermined her public credibility.

She and Claflin spent their last years in London, where Woodhull continued to espouse her controversial views in public lectures. She was a brilliant, provocative woman who was light years ahead of her time, and she and her sister added zest and drama to the women's rights movement.

FURTHER READING

Brough, James. *The Vixens! A Biography of Victoria and Tennessee Claflin.* New York: Simon & Schuster, 1980.

Johnston, Johanna. *Mrs. Satan: The Incredible Saga of Victoria Woodhull.* New York: Popular Library, 1967.

Wright, Frances

WRITER AND REFORMER

Born: September 6, 1795
Dundee, Scotland

Died: December 13, 1852
Cincinnati, Ohio

Frances Wright was a passionate seeker of new ways to improve people's lives. Her enlightened ideas about women's status, sexual relations, and educational reform were far ahead of her time. She was born into a liberal, free-thinking family, but her parents died when she was very young, and she and her sister went to live with an uncle who taught at Glasgow College. There, she availed herself of the vast intellectual resources of the college's library. In her early twenties, she published poetry and drama, and made her first trip to the United States in 1818. She became an ardent supporter of the young country, and published her glowing reactions in *Views of Society and Manners in America.*

But she condemned the institution of slavery as a moral blight on this new Eden, and in 1825 she embarked upon a plan to bring about the gradual abolition of slavery. Purchasing land near Memphis, Tennessee, she also bought several slaves and established a plantation, which she called Nashoba, to prepare the slaves for freedom. She promised them eventual emancipation, which they would earn by working. An overseer and schoolteacher also joined the tiny community.

The plantation never prospered and, in fact, almost went bankrupt while Wright was visiting Europe. Undismayed, she freed the slaves, arranged for their resettlement in Haiti, along with housing and employment, and proceeded to publish her views on religion and sex. Amidst accusations that Nashoba had been a "free love" colony, where people were free to have sexual relations with whomever they wished, she decried all organized religions, the institution of marriage, and prohibitions against interracial sex—perhaps the most controversial aspect of her thinking.

Some people called her a dangerous lunatic, while others dismissed her as a harmless eccentric. Undeterred by the condemnation, she lectured throughout the East and Midwest before settling in New York City. There she continued to speak and write, endorsing equal educational opportunities for men and women, legal rights for married women, more liberal divorce laws, and legalized birth control. To these visionary and provocative ideas, she added one more progressive proposal: the establishment of a system of free state-supported boarding schools, where all children would learn academic and vocational skills.

In 1830, Wright returned to Europe, where she married a French physician, then came back to the United States and briefly campaigned for the 1836 Democratic Presidential ticket. After offering a new round of lectures on the evils of contemporary society, she ended her public speaking career. Like Victoria Woodhull, she was a highly original thinker who offered ideas too advanced for her time—ideas that still merit serious attention.

PUBLICATION
Views of Society and Manners in America (1821)

Yezierska, Anzia
WRITER

Born: ca. 1880
Plotsk, Russian Pale of Settlement

Died: November 21, 1970
Ontario, California

Anzia Yezierska was a prolific writer who gave poignant voice to the struggles that immigrant Jewish women faced in "making for themselves a better person," in her words. She spent her early childhood in Plotsk, a shtetl, or small town, on the Vistula River in the Polish part of Russia. Her father, Reb Baruch Yeziersky (the masculine form of the name), was a talmudic scholar who smoldered with the faith of the Old Testament prophets. While he occupied himself with questions of the soul, his wife, Pearl, like other East European Jewish wives, worried about keeping her family free from starvation and safe from marauding Russian cossacks.

Along with thousands of other Jews in the Russian Pale, the Yezierskys fled economic hardship and religious persecution by emigrating to America. Around 1890, when Anzia was about 10, the family settled in the Lower East Side of New York City. For Anzia, as she later wrote, America meant "free schools, free colleges, free libraries, where I could learn and learn and keep on learning." The young girl eagerly enrolled in school. But financial troubles at home soon forced her to drop out and work in a factory. Gradually, in the sweatshops and on the streets, she began to learn English, and almost immediately she started to write, mostly at night, after the long workday.

Stifled by her parents' Old World ways, the young woman fled from her family and lived in a succession of furnished rooms and settlement houses while she supported herself by day in the sweatshops and attended school at night. Though she stayed in touch with her family—they lived only a few blocks away—she felt utterly alone, caught between two worlds. She knew she could never settle for her mother's selfless, traditional way of life, but she did not know what she wanted instead. She trained and worked as a home economics teacher, but her true goal was to write—to "get it out of . . . my heart or die," as she said later.

She wrote mostly about young Jewish women like herself, who had great potential and a burning desire to make something of their lives but who felt imprisoned by poverty and their Old World past. Undaunted by the scores of rejections she received, she continued to peddle her stories among the magazines of her day. For years she lived in relative obscurity until an anthology of her stories, *Hungry Hearts,* was sold to Hollywood. Anzia's star had finally risen. She was hailed by the press as a "sweatshop princess," a creative genius fresh out of the ghetto.

Meanwhile, she married and abruptly left her husband, then inexplicably married again. This second marriage was no more successful; after several futile attempts to reconcile herself to full-time domesticity, Yezierska deserted her husband and young daughter to devote herself to her writing—an audacious act for a Jewish woman, who was expected to devote her life to marriage and motherhood. A brief but passionate friendship with the philosopher John Dewey followed, but that, too, ended abruptly and mysteriously.

During the early 1920s, a period of intense interest in the immigrant experience, Yezierska was much sought out for her life story. In newspaper interviews and later in her semifictional autobiography, *Red Ribbon on a White Horse,* she failed to mention her college education and teaching, her two marriages, and her daughter. Instead, she portrayed herself as an immigrant fresh out of the ghetto and sweatshop. For the rest of her life, she would regard herself as an outsider, an immigrant Jew, unable to find a niche in an alien setting.

As interest in immigrant culture gradually waned, she slipped into obscurity but continued to write. In 1950, she published *Red Ribbon on a White Horse,* and in the l960s she shifted her literary focus from immigrants to the elderly. Drawing again on the theme of the outsider, she wrote poignant autobiographical tales about growing old in a society that has no use for its elderly. She died in l970, in a nursing home in Ontario, California, near her daughter's home. Her stories continue to attract readers who seek a vivid glimpse into the world of the East European immigrant Jewish woman.

Major Publications
Bread Givers (1925)
Red Ribbon on a White Horse (1950)
The Open Cage: An Anzia Yezierska Collection,
   edited by Alice Kessler-Harris (1979)

Further Reading
Levitas, Louise. *Anzia Yezierska: A Writer's Life.*
   New Brunswick, N.J.: Rutgers University Press,
   1989.

Zaharias, Mildred Ella (Babe) Didrikson

ATHLETE

Born: ca. June 26, 1911
Port Arthur, Texas

Died: September 27, 1956
Galveston, Texas

Babe Didrikson, as she was known to her fans, put women's professional golf on the map. She was the daughter of Norwegian immigrants and acquired the nickname "Babe" from childhood friends who likened her athletic prowess to that of the famed baseball player Babe Ruth. After achieving star status on her high school basketball team, she joined the women's basketball team of a Dallas-based business and soon led her teammates to a national championship. By 1932, she was also reaching new heights as a high jumper and javelin thrower, and won gold medals at the 1932 Olympics in the javelin and hurdles.

In 1938, she married George Zaharias, a wrestler and promoter whom she had met when they played together in a men's golf tournament. She had aspired to be a professional golfer, but with only two professional golf tournaments open to women, she was forced to play in men's tournaments.

Although she continued to play basketball and also tried her hand at baseball, it was in golfing that she broke barriers for professional women golfers. In 1948, after playing for a decade, she and five other women formed the Ladies Professional Golf Association, the first such organization. Immediately, the new group embarked on a round of nine tournaments, opening up the sport to other professional female golfers. Didrikson played professional golf and scored victories until she died of cancer in 1956. She turned golf into a professional sport for women, and paved the way for other professional women athletes to compete in all sports.

Publications
"I Blow My Own Horn," *American Magazine* (June
   1936)
This Life I've Led (autobiography, 1955)

Further Reading
Johnson, William and Nancy P. Williamson. *Whatta-*
   gal! The Babe Didrikson Story. Boston: Little,
   Brown: 1977.
Lynn, Elizabeth. *Babe Didrikson Zaharias.* New
   York: Chelsea House, 1989.
Sanford, William R. and Carl R. Green. *Babe*
   Didrikson Zaharias. New York: Crestwood
   House, 1993.

MUSEUMS AND HISTORIC SITES RELATED TO THE HISTORY OF AMERICAN WOMEN

Alabama

Civil Rights Memorial
400 Washington Street
Montgomery, AL 36104

Honors men and women who died in the struggle for racial equality in the United States. Some of the women commemorated include Viola Liuzzo and four children killed in the bombing of the 16th Street Baptist Church in Birmingham—Denise McNair, Carole Robertson, Cynthia Wesley and Addie Mae Collins. Dedicated in 1989, the monument is located in the plaza of the Southern Poverty Law Center.

Scott and Zelda Fitzgerald Museum
919 Felder Avenue
Montgomery, AL 36106
205-264-4222

Residence of the novelist and his wife, also a writer, in the early 1930s; Zelda Fitzgerald wrote *Save Me the Waltz* here. Includes family memorabilia.

Helen Keller Birthplace and Shrine
Keller Lane
Tuscumbia, AL 35674
205-383-4066

Furnishings and memorabilia of Keller, who overcame blindness, deafness, and muteness; site includes the pump at which she learned her first word, "water."

Lurleen B. Wallace Museum
725 Monroe Street
Montgomery, AL 36130
205-242-3183

Memorabilia of Wallace, late wife of Governor George Wallace; she served as first woman governor of Alabama in the late 1960s. Includes library of state history.

Weeder House Museum
300 Gates Avenue
Huntsville, AL 35801

Birthplace of 19th-century artist and poet Marie Howard Weeder; restored house, built in 1819, includes Weeder's furnishings, memorabilia, and a collection of her watercolors.

Women's Army Corps Museum
Fort McClellan, AL 36205
205-848-3512

Displays of uniforms, artifacts, and photographs tracing the history of the Women's Army Auxiliary Corps (WAAC) and the Women's Army Corps (WAC) from their creation during World War II until they were abolished in 1978; includes library of books and scrapbooks.

California

Hearst Mansion
Hearst San Simeon State Historical Monument
750 Hearst Castle Road
San Simeon, CA 93452
805-927-2020

Items related to Phoebe Hearst, clubwoman and philanthropist; Julia Morgan, architect; and Marion Davies, movie actress.

Hoover Institution on War, Revolution and Peace

Stanford University
Stanford, CA 94305
415-723-1754

Home of First Lady Lou Henry Hoover's geology works, writings, translations, and speeches.

Grace Hudson Museum and Sun House

431 South Main Street
Ukiah, CA 95482
707-462-3370

Includes works by early-20th-century Native American painter Grace Carpenter Hudson, as well as Indian artifacts and historical photographs collected by her husband, ethnologist John W. Hudson.

Oakland Museum

1000 Oak Street
Oakland, CA 94607
510-238-3401

Costume and textile collections, plus large holdings on women in the West. Hosts exhibits on women's history topics.

Women's Heritage Museum

870 Market Street #547
San Francisco, CA 94102
415-433-3026

Large collection of artifacts relating to women's history. Sponsors traveling exhibitions on California women's history.

Colorado

Molly Brown House Museum

1340 Pennsylvania Street
Denver, CO 80203
303-832-4092

Residence (built 1889), furnishings, and memorabilia of Molly Brown, a survivor of the *Titanic* sinking in 1912; her life inspired the stage and screen musical *The Unsinkable Molly Brown.*

Mother Cabrini Shrine

Golden, CO 80401
303-526-0758

Roman Catholic shrine honoring St. Frances Xavier Cabrini (1850–1917), first American citizen to be canonized (1946).

Connecticut

Connecticut State Library and Museum

231 Capitol Avenue
Hartford, CT 06106
203-566-3056

Home to a large woman suffrage collection, including records, banners, sashes, and buttons of the Connecticut State Woman Suffrage Association.

Prudence Crandall Museum

Canterbury Green
Canterbury, CT 06331
203-546-9916

Former home of Crandall, who founded one of the first schools for African Americans, in the early 19th century; includes furnishings, memorabilia, and library of items on women's and African-American history.

Museum of American Political Life

University of Hartford
200 Bloomfield Avenue
Hartford, CT 06117
203-768-4090

Displays include materials on woman suffrage and women in political campaigns.

Katharine Ordway Preserve

165 Good Hill Road
Weston, CT 06883
203-227-9410

Former home and gardens, now a nature preserve, of a prominent amateur naturalist and philanthropist who died in 1979. Ordway was the major benefactor of the Nature Conservancy, which administers the preserve.

Harriet Beecher Stowe House

73 Forest Street
Hartford, CT 06105
203-525-9371

Home of Stowe (1811–96), author of *Uncle Tom's Cabin* and other works; includes furnishings, books, and memorabilia.

Delaware

Winterthur Museum

Route 52
Winterthur, DE 19735
302-888-4600

Collections and exhibitions on domestic life of women, including decorative and household arts, costumes, and furnishings from the colonial era through the 19th century.

District of Columbia

Bethune Museum and Archives

1318 Vermont Avenue, N.W.
Washington, D.C. 20005
202-332-1233

Museum has exhibits on the life of Mary McLeod Bethune, an early-20th-century educator and founder of Bethune-Cookman College, Florida. Displays focusing on the role of the African-American woman in shaping the society and heritage of the United States are also featured.

Hillwood Museum

4155 Linnean Avenue, N.W.
Washington, D.C. 20008
202-686-8500

Mansion and gardens that once belonged to Marjorie Merriweather Post, noted philanthropist. Includes early-20th-century furnishings and items from her collection.

National Museum of American History

Smithsonian Institution
14th Street and Constitution Avenue, N.W.
Washington, D.C. 20560
202-357-2700

This museum is the home of extensive collections that document the roles of women in the making of America. Includes collections about fashion, domestic life, furnishings, women's political history, women and reform politics, entertainment, nursing, and the peace and settlement house movements.

National Museum of Women in the Arts

New York Avenue and 13th Street, N.W.
Washington, D.C. 20005
202-783-5000

Displays artwork by women from the 16th century to the present, including paintings, sculpture, and ornamental silver.

Sewall-Belmont House

144 Constitution Avenue, N.E.
Washington, D.C. 20002
202-546-3989

History and artifacts belonging to Alice Paul, early-20th-century suffragist, along with material about the National Woman's Party, the struggle for woman suffrage, and the equal rights amendment.

Textile Museum

2320 S Street, N.W.
Washington, D.C. 20008

Extensive holdings and displays on textiles and women's role in their making.

Vietnam Women's Memorial

West Potomac Park
Washington, D.C. 20008

Located on the Mall, near the Lincoln Memorial and the Vietnam Veterans Memorial, the sculpture was dedicated in November 1993 and honors women in the U.S. armed forces who died in the Vietnam War.

Florida

Bethune-Cookman College

Fine Arts Building
640 Dr. Mary McLeod Bethune Boulevard
Daytona Beach, FL 32114
904-255-5062

College established by Mary McLeod Bethune, early-20th-century black educator.

Marjorie Kinnan Rawlings State Historic Site

Route 3, Box 92
Hawthorne, FL 32640
904-466-3672

Cross Creek, the home (from the early 1930s) of Rawlings (1896–1953), author of *The Yearling* and other works; includes furnishings and memorabilia.

Georgia

Juliette Gordon Low Birthplace/ Girl Scout National Center

142 Bull Street
Savannah, GA 31410
912-233-4501

Includes furniture, artworks, and memorabilia of Low, who founded the Girl Scouts of America in 1912, and her family.

Oak Hill and Martha Berry Museum

Berry College
Rome, GA 30161
706-291-1883

Oak Hill (built in 1847) was the plantation home of Berry, who began teaching local children in a log cabin on the property in 1902. Berry became known internationally as an educator; her school later became Berry College. Martha Berry Museum, formerly her house, includes furnishings and personal memorabilia.

Harriet Tubman Historical and Cultural Museum

340 Walnut Street
Macon, GA 31201
912-743-8544

Tubman Museum includes exhibits on historical and cultural contributions of noted African-American men and women, including Tubman herself.

See additional listing for Tubman *under* New York.

Hawaii

The Bishop Museum

1525 Bernice Street
Honolulu, HI
808-847-3511

Collection and history exhibits of Bernice Pauahi Bishop, Polynesian educator and philanthropist; include diaries, books, and other personal possessions.

Queen Emma Summer Palace

2913 Pali Highway
Honolulu, HI 96817
808-595-3167

Home of Queen Emma and her husband, King Kamehamea IV, rulers of Hawaii in the mid-19th century; includes furnishings, photographs, and memorabilia of Queen Emma and her family.

Illinois

Jane Addams/Hull House Museum

800 West Halsted Street
Chicago, IL 60607
312-996-2793

Restored settlement house, founded by social worker Addams and Ellen Gates Starr in 1889. The home of many famous women reformers and pioneers in social work, labor reform, and health-care reform. Includes furnishings, photographs, documents, and memorabilia relating to Addams and the immigrant population she served.

Mother Theresa Dudzik Museum

1250 Main Street
Lemont, IL 60439
708-257-6606

Memorabilia of Dudzik, 19th-century founder of the Franciscan Sisters, a Catholic religious order.

Chicago Historical Society

Clark Street at North Avenue
Chicago, IL 60614
312-642-4600

Has displays of costumes, household technology, furniture, and decorative arts.

Frances E. Willard House

1730 Chicago Avenue
Evanston, IL 60201
708-864-1397

Residence of Willard (1839–98), the most important president of the Woman's Christian Temperance Union, serving from 1879 to her death in 1898; includes furnishings and memorabilia. The Woman's Christian Temperance Union was the largest women's organization in the late 19th century and pursued many other reform aims, including women's right to vote.

Monument to Women Statuary Gardens

Nauvoo, IL 62354

Thirteen life-size sculptures in this restored Mormon community depict women in traditional activities (such as courting and teaching children); gardens are located behind the Visitors Center on Main Street.

Indiana

Conner Prairie Museum

13400 Allisonville Road
Fishers, IN 46038
318-776-6000

Living history of 19th-century pioneer life, including the lives of pioneer women.

Limberlost State Historic Site

200 East 6th Street
Geneva, IN 46740
219-368-7428

Restored home of Gene Stratton Porter, early-20th-century popular novelist and naturalist. Includes furnishings, photographs, and memorabilia.

Gene Stratton Porter State Historic Site

State Route 9
Rome City, IN 46784
219-854-3790

Cabin and gardens of novelist/ naturalist Porter (see previous entry); includes furnishings, photographs, and memorabilia.

Madame Walker Urban Life Center

617 Indiana Avenue
Indianapolis, IN 46202
317-236-2099

Restored former headquarters of Madame C. J. Walker's cosmetics company in the early 20th century. Walker (1867–1919), an African American, was the first self-made, black female millionaire in the United States.

Iowa

Mamie Doud Eisenhower Birthplace

709 Carroll Street
Boone, IA 50036
515-432-1896

Birthplace of Mamie Doud (1896–1979), wife of army general and President Dwight D. Eisenhower; includes furnishings, photographs, letters, and memorabilia.

Laura Ingalls Wilder Park and Museum, Inc.

Burr Oak, IA 52131
319-735-5436

Restored 19th-century hotel and period furnishings pay tribute to Wilder, author of the *Little House* books.

See additional listings for Wilder *under* Minnesota, Missouri, *and* South Dakota.

Kansas

Martin and Osa Johnson Safari Museum

111 North Lincoln Avenue
Chanute, KS 66720
316-431-2730

Osa Johnson and her husband, Martin, were pioneering wildlife photographers in the early 20th century. Museum includes photographs, manuscripts, books, films, and memorabilia, as well as exhibits of their trips to the South Seas between 1917 and 1937.

Carry A. Nation Home

211 West Fowler Avenue
Medicine Lodge, KS 67104
316-886-3417

Furniture and memorabilia of Nation (1846–1911), a leading temperance crusader.

Kentucky

Nancy Hanks House

Lincoln Homestead State Park
Springfield, KY 40069
606-336-7461

Restored cabin home of Abraham Lincoln's mother before her marriage to Thomas Lincoln; part of complex that includes buildings from Lincoln's childhood.

Mary Todd Lincoln House

578 West Main Street
Lexington, KY 40507
606-233-9999

Restored home of Mary Todd from 1832 until her marriage to Abraham Lincoln in 1849. Includes furnishings and personal articles of Todd and the Lincoln family.

Cora Wilson Stewart Schoolhouse

Morehead State University
Morehead, KY 40351

First of a series of "moonlight schools" opened by Stewart for adults in the early 1900s (so-called because classes were held only on moonlit nights, so that students would be able to see their way to the building). A pioneer in adult education in the United States, Stewart enrolled students between 18 and 86 in her schools, which are credited with virtually eliminating illiteracy in Kentucky in the first half of the 20th century.

Louisiana

Beauregard-Keyes House

1113 Chartres Street
New Orleans, LA 70116
504-523-7257

Home of Civil War Confederate general Pierre Beauregard was restored by popular novelist Frances Parkinson Keyes in the mid-20th century. Includes her furnished bedroom and study with memorabilia, as well as Beauregard furniture and other family items.

Melrose Plantation

Melrose, LA 71452
318-379-0055

A freed slave named Marie Therese Coincoin and her sons established Melrose Plantation in 1796. During the next 37 years they erected eight buildings on the property, which have been restored and are open to the public.

Maine

Sarah Orne Jewett House

5 Portland Street
South Berwick, ME 03908
603-436-3205

Lifelong home of Jewett, a late-19th-century writer who wrote *The Country of the Pointed Firs,* and was novelist Willa Cather's mentor. Includes family furnishings and memorabilia.

Nordica Homestead Museum

Holley Road
Farmington, ME 04938
207-778-2042

Birthplace and childhood home of early-20th-century opera singer Lillian Nordica. Includes furnishings as well as costumes and memorabilia from Nordica's career.

Margaret Chase Smith Library Center

Norridgewock Avenue
Skowhegan, ME 04976
207-474-7133/7134

Displays on the life and career of Smith, a mid-20th-century political leader who served in the U.S. Senate and House of Representatives a total of 36 years.

Cordelia Stanwood Homestead Museum and Birdsacre Sanctuary

State Route 3
Ellsworth, ME 04605
207-667-8460

Home of a pioneering ornithologist in the early 20th century; includes furnishings and memorabilia. More than 100 species of birds make their home in the adjacent 130-acre wildlife preserve.

Maryland

Clara Barton National Historic Site

5801 Oxford Road
Glen Echo, MD 20812
310-492-6245

Home (1891–1912) of the founder of the American Red Cross. Furnishings, memorabilia, and research library with transcripts of Barton's diaries and manuscripts.

See additional listing for Barton *under* Massachusetts.

Barbara Fritchie House
154 West Patrick Street
Frederick, MD
301-698-0630

Reconstructed home of a legendary supporter of the Union during the Civil War. Fritchie is supposed to have waved the Union flag defiantly from her window when Confederate general Thomas "Stonewall" Jackson marched his troops through Frederick in 1862. Her act was commemorated in the poem "Barbara Fritchie" by John Greenleaf Whittier.

Shrine of St. Elizabeth Ann Seton
U.S. Highway 15
Emmitsburg, MD 21727
301-447-6606

In 1975, Seton (1774–1821) became the first native-born American to be canonized by the Roman Catholic Church. She founded the American branch of a religious order, the Sisters of Charity, in the early 19th century and opened the first parochial school in the United States. Complex of buildings includes a museum containing her personal effects and the chapel where she is buried.

Massachusetts

Abigail Adams Birthplace
North and Norton Streets
Weymouth, MA 02191
617-335-1067

Abigail Smith Adams (1744–1818) was the wife of President John Adams and the mother of President John Quincy Adams. House, built in 1685, includes Smith family furnishings.

Clara Barton Birthplace
68 Clara Barton Road
North Oxford, MA 01537
508-987-5375

Memorabilia and furnishings of Barton, founder of the American Red Cross, and her family; includes library of Barton's books.

See additional listing for Barton *under* Maryland.

Emily Dickinson House
280 Main Street
Amherst, MA 01002
413-542-8161

Restored lifetime residence of the 19th-century poet; includes furnishings and memorabilia.

Mary Baker Eddy Historical House
277 Main Street
Amesbury, MA 01913
508-388-1361

One of several residences of Mrs. Eddy, the founder of Christian Science (1879), which have been restored and include original furnishings and memorabilia. There are three other Eddy homes in Massachusetts:

Mary Baker Eddy Residence
12 Broad Street
Lynn, MA 01902
617-450-3790

Mary Baker Eddy Historical House
133 Central Street
Stoughton, MA 02072
617-344-3904

Mary Baker Eddy Historical House
23 Paradise Road
Swampscott, MA 01907
617-599-1853

See also additional listing for Eddy *under* New Hampshire.

Lowell National Historical Park
169 Merrimack Street
Lowell, MA

Commemorates women workers in Lowell textile mills and has historical displays of early to mid-19th-century factory work.

Maria Mitchell Science Center
1 Vestal Street
Nantucket Island, MA 02554
508-228-2896

Restored birthplace and home of the astronomer Mitchell (1818–89); includes furnishings, personal items, and an observatory.

The Mount
Plunkett Street
Lenox, MA 01240
413-637-1899

Partially restored mansion and gardens designed by novelist Edith Wharton (1862–1937) and built for her in 1902; includes photographs and documents relating to Wharton's life.

Rebecca Nurse Homestead
149 Pine Street
Danvers, MA 01923
508-774-8799

Nurse was hanged as a witch in 1692 during the Salem witch trials. Restored cottage includes 17th- and 18th-century furnishings and artifacts.

Orchard House
399 Lexington Road
Concord, MA 01742
508-369-4118

Home of novelist Louisa May Alcott (1832–88); she wrote *Little Women* and other books here. Includes furnishings and memorabilia.

Plimoth Plantation
137 Warren Avenue
Plymouth, MA 02360
508-746-1622

A living history of the Plymouth Colony, originally founded in 1620, includes women's work in the settlement as of 1627. Collections and exhibits include artifacts of Pilgrim and Native American societies.

Arthur M. and Elizabeth Schlesinger Library on the History of Women in America
3 James Street
Cambridge, MA 02138
617-495-8647

Thousands of documents—manuscripts, books, periodicals, diaries, papers of women's rights organizations—and photographs are housed in this library at Radcliffe College, named for a prominent American historian (1888–1965) and his wife. Public exhibits featuring women writers, artists, and historical figures vary by season.

Old Sturbridge Village
1 Old Sturbridge Village Road
Sturbridge, MA 01566
508-347-3362

A resurrected early-19th-century village, peopled with women and men, emphasizing family and work roles in farm and community life.

Michigan

Henry Ford Museum & Greenfield Village
20900 Oakwood Boulevard
Dearborn, MI 48124
313-271-1620

Extensive costume, textile, furnishings, decorative arts, and household technology holdings and information on women's work. Periodic exhibitions on women's topics.

Minnesota

Minnesota Historical Society
History Center
345 West Kellogg Boulevard
St. Paul, MN 55102-1906
612-296-6126

Displays and exhibits include information on women's role in the cultural, economic and agricultural history of Minnesota, especially the St. Paul area.

Laura Ingalls Wilder Museum and Tourist Center
Walnut Grove, MN 56180
507-859-2358

Memorabilia—quilts, furniture, toys—belonging to Wilder, the author of the *Little House* series.

See additional listings for Wilder *under* Iowa, Missouri, *and* South Dakota.

Mississippi

Kate Freeman Clark Art Gallery
Holly Springs, MS 38635
601-252-2943 (Chamber of Commerce)

More than 1,000 paintings by an early-20th-century artist (1876–1957) who was born in Holly Springs and studied art in New York City. Considered the world's largest collection of work by a single artist.

Missouri

Harry S. Truman National Historic Site

U.S. Highway 24 and Delaware Street
Independence, MO 64050
816-833-1400

Housed in Bess Truman's childhood home, this collection shows her involvements with her husband's career, along with many original furnishings and possessions.

Laura Ingalls Wilder–Rose Wilder Lane Museum and House

Route 1, Box 24
Mansfield, MO 65704
417-924-3626

Home of Wilder, her husband, Almanzo, and their daughter, Rose, from 1894 onward. Wilder wrote the *Little House* series here beginning in the 1930s. Displays memorabilia of Wilder and her daughter, including five *Little House* manuscripts, family photos, Pa's fiddle, clothing, and other artifacts.

See additional listings for Wilder *under* Iowa, Minnesota, *and* South Dakota.

Nebraska

Willa Cather Childhood Home

3rd Avenue and Cedar Street
Red Cloud, NE 68970
402-746-3285 (Historical Center)

Restored home of Cather family from 1884 to 1904 includes Willa Cather's attic room. Tours are available through the Historical Center (see next listing).

Willa Cather Historical Center

338 N. Webster Street
Red Cloud, NE 68970
402-746-3285

Interpretive exhibits on the life of novelist Cather (1873–1947); also houses an archive of related documents.

New Hampshire

Mary Baker Eddy Historic House

Stinson Lake Road
Rumney, NH 03266
603-786-9943

Eddy, founder of Christian Science, lived here in the early 1860s. Includes furnishings and memorabilia.

See additional listings for Eddy *under* Massachusetts.

New York

Susan B. Anthony Memorial Inc.

17 Madison Street
Rochester, NY 14608
716-381-6202

Anthony's "home headquarters" for her adult life. Includes her personal belongings as well as photographs and documents of her associates in the struggle for women's rights.

Baseball Hall of Fame

25 Main Street
Cooperstown, NY 13326
607-547-7200

Permanent exhibition on the women's baseball leagues of the 1940s and 1950s.

Jane Colden Native Plant Sanctuary

Knox's Headquarters State Historic Site
State Route 94
Vails Gate, NY 12584
914-561-5498

Garden named in honor of Colden (1724–66), the first woman botanist in America.

Fashion Institute of Technology

227 West 27th Street
New York, NY 10001
212-760-7673

Collections and exhibits on fashion history, changes in manufacture and technology, the fashion industry, and women in advertising.

Lower East Side Tenement Museum

97 Orchard Street
New York, NY 10002
212-431-0233

Programs and presentations of the immigrant experience and new life in America; includes experiences of women in tenement living and sweatshop labor.

National Shrine of Blessed Kateri Tekakwitha

State Route 5
Fonda, NY 12068
518-853-3646

Honors a 17th-century Mohawk Indian who has been beatified by the Roman Catholic Church. Kateri is the first Native American to be eligible for sainthood. She was baptized at the site and made her home there. Shrine is part of a restored Native American village that includes exhibits and artifacts.

National Women's Hall of Fame

76 Fall Street
Seneca Falls, NY 13148
315-568-2936

Museum of outstanding women in American history. Includes collection of photographs, artifacts, and documents relating to women's

history and a 2,000-volume library. The Hall of Fame continues to induct women each year.

Oswego Historical Society

135 East Third Street
Oswego, NY 13126
315-343-1342

Houses collection of Dr. Mary Walker, first woman to serve as surgeon in Civil War. She was a prisoner of war and winner of the Congressional Medal of Honor. Visits by appointment only.

Narcissa Prentiss House

7275 Mill Pond Road
Prattsburgh, NY 14873
607-522-4537

Birthplace of Narcissa Prentiss, early-19th-century missionary to the Indians with her husband, Dr. Marcus Whitman. Includes furnishings as well as books about the Whitmans' work in the Pacific Northwest.

See additional listing for Whitman *under* Washington.

Eleanor Roosevelt National Historic Site

Route 9G
Hyde Park, NY 12538
914-229-9115

Val-Kill, Roosevelt's home from 1945 until her death in 1962. Includes furnishings and memorabilia.

Franklin D. Roosevelt Library and Museum

511 Albany Post Road
Hyde Park, NY 12583
914-229-8114

Home of President Franklin Roosevelt and Eleanor Roosevelt. Includes all of Eleanor Roosevelt's papers and a large collection of photos.

Marcella Sembrich Memorial Studio

State Route 9N
Bolton Landing, NY 12814
518-644-9839

Restored home and studio of Sembrich, an opera star of the early 20th century; includes mementos of her career.

Elizabeth Cady Stanton Home

32 Washington Street
Seneca Falls, NY 13148
315-568-2991

Restored home (built 1836) of Stanton, one of the major figures in the drive for woman suffrage; part of Women's Rights National Historical Park (see below).

The Strong Museum

One Manhattan Square
Rochester, NY 14607
716-263-2700

Commemorates and houses vast collection of philanthropist Margaret Woodbury Strong. Important collections on home life, toys, and dolls of 19th and early 20th centuries.

Harriet Tubman Home
180 South Street
Auburn, NY 13021
315-252-2081

Restored home of the former slave and abolitionist; includes furnishings and memorabilia.

See additional listing for Tubman *under* Georgia.

Women's Rights National Historical Park
116 Fall Street
Seneca Falls, NY 13148
315-568-2991

Commemorates site of first women's rights convention in 1848. Visitor Center at this site features exhibits on the history of the women's rights movement. The center administers the Elizabeth Cady Stanton Home (see above).

North Carolina

Charlotte Hawkins Brown Memorial State Historic Site
Sedalia, NC 27342
919-449-4846

Site of Palmer Memorial Institute, a school for blacks founded by African-American educator Brown in 1902. Exhibit includes audiovisual presentation of school's history and Brown's contribution to education in the South.

Virginia Dare Memorial
Fort Raleigh National Historic Site
Manteo, NC 27954
919-473-5772

Honors the first English child born in the New World (1587). Fort Raleigh, on Roanoke Island, is the site of the first English colony (established 1585) in what is now the eastern United States.

Ohio

International Women's Air and Space Museum
26 North Main Street
Centerville, OH 45459
513-433-6766

Includes clothing and uniforms, photographs, and memorabilia relating to women in aviation.

Oklahoma

Pioneer Woman Statue and Museum
701 Monument Road
Ponca City, OK 74601
405-765-6108

Seventeen-foot bronze statue commemorates pioneer women of Oklahoma; adjacent museum contains artifacts from lives of these women.

Oregon

Pioneer Mothers' Memorial Cabin
Champoeg State Park
Newberg, OR 97132
503-633-2237

Built in 1931 as a tribute to pioneer mothers; furnished with 19th-century artifacts.

Pennsylvania

Pearl S. Buck House
Green Hills Farm
520 Dublin Road
Perkasic, PA 18944
215-249-0100

Furnishings, books, and personal belongings of novelist Buck, the first American woman to win the Nobel Prize for literature.

See additional listing for Buck *under* West Virginia.

Rachel Carson Homestead
613 Marion Avenue
Springdale, PA 15144
412-274-5459

Childhood home of naturalist Carson; includes furnishings, memorabilia, and photographs.

Betsy Ross House
239 Arch Street
Philadelphia, PA 19106
215-627-5343

Restored home of the colonial seamstress who in 1776 made the first American flag.

South Dakota

Surveyors' House and Ingalls Home
De Smet, SD 57231
605-854-3383

Surveyors' House was the first South Dakota home (1870s) of Laura Ingalls Wilder, author of the *Little House* series. Later the Ingalls family moved into a new house nearby, built by Laura's father. Both sites include period furnishings and family memorabilia.

See additional listings for Wilder *under* Iowa, Minnesota, *and* Missouri.

Annie Tallent Monument
Custer State Park
Custer, SD 57730
605-255-4464

Honors the first white woman to enter the Black Hills, in the 1870s.

Tennessee

Civil Rights Museum
450 Mulberry Street
Memphis, TN 38103
901-521-9699

History and displays on civil rights movement, including women's role in the movement. Located in the former Lorraine Motel, where Martin Luther King, Jr. was assassinated.

Country Music Hall of Fame
4 Music Square East
Nashville, TN 37203
615-256-1639

Displays memorabilia of country music stars, including many women singers and musicians.

Dollywood
Pigeon Forge, TN 37863
615-428-9620/9630

Eighty-eight-acre theme park conceived and operated by country-western singer Dolly Parton. The Dolly Parton Museum at the site traces the development of her career.

Loretta Lynn's Ranch, Museum, and Home
Hurricane Mills, TN 37078
615-296-7700

Memorabilia and costumes of country-western singer Lynn are exhibited at the museum; visitors can tour ranch and home.

Texas

Lyndon Baines Johnson Library
2313 Red River Street
Austin, TX 78705
512-482-5137

Houses papers and manuscripts of Lady Bird Johnson as First Lady, including her extensive work on behalf on environmental awareness and wildflower preservation.

National Cowgirl Hall of Fame and Western Heritage Center
515 Avenue B
Hereford, TX 79045
806-364-5252

Memorabilia honoring rodeo performers and other women of the American West; also includes western art and a research library.

Elisabet Ney Museum
304 E. 44th Street
Austin, TX 78751
512-458-2255

Home and studio of 19th-century sculptor Ney. Displays a collection of her sculpture, including models and casts. Library at site includes related documents and letters.

Babe Didrikson Zaharias Memorial
1750 East I-10
Beaumont, TX 77703

Exhibits trace the life and career of a 20th-century Olympic athlete and golf champion.

Utah

Daughters of Utah Pioneers Museum

300 North Main Street
Salt Lake City, UT 84103
801-538-1050

Farm wagons, artwork, crafts, relics, and manuscripts of men and women who pioneered in the creation of Utah, 1847–1900. The Daughters of Utah Pioneers organization also maintains similar museums at the following locations:

160 North Main Street
Logan, UT 84321
801-752-5139

2141 Grant Avenue
Ogden, UT 84401
801-621-5224

143 North 100 East Street
St. George, UT 84770
801-628-7274

Vermont

Electra Havemeyer Webb Memorial

Shelburne Museum
Shelburne, VT 05482
802-985-3346

Webb was a New York heiress and prominent art connoisseur. The Shelburne Museum, a grouping of 37 buildings—many of them restored historic structures—on 45 acres, includes her collections of American art and artifacts. The

Webb Memorial houses major European paintings as well as works by American artist Mary Cassatt.

Virginia

Belle Boyd Cottage

101 Chester Street
Front Royal, VA 22630
703-636-1446

Mid-19th century home of Boyd, a Confederate spy. Includes period furnishings and Civil War memorabilia.

Custis-Lee Mansion

Arlington National Cemetery
Arlington, VA 22101
703-557-0613

The home of Robert E. Lee and his wife, Mary Parke Custis Lee, granddaughter of Martha Washington. On display are domestic furnishings and examples of pre–Civil War life.

Mount Vernon

George Washington Parkway
Mount Vernon, VA 22121
703-780-2000

Home of George and Martha Washington. Collections of domestic artifacts, papers, and exhibits about plantation life of 18th-century women.

Maggie L. Walker National Historic Site

110 ½ E. Leigh Street
Richmond, VA 23223
804-780-1380

Walker (1867–1934), an African-American entrepreneur and publisher, was the first woman to found a bank in the United States. Her home, restored to look as it did in the 1930s, includes period furnishings, clothing, photographs, and memorabilia.

Mary Ball Washington Museum and Library

Route 3
Lancaster, VA 22503
804-462-7280

Honors George Washington's mother, who was born in Lancaster County. Includes large library on colonial history as well as 18th-century memorabilia and clothing.

Mary Washington House

1200 Charles Street
Fredericksburg, VA 22401
703-373-1569

Home (1772–89) and gardens of Mary Ball Washington, mother of George Washington. Includes 18th-century furnishings and artifacts.

Washington

Hilda Klager Lilac Gardens

Woodland, WA 98674
206-225-8996

Former estate of Klager, world-renowned for her hybrids of apples and lilacs. House includes memorabilia and furnishings.

Sacajawea Interpretive Center

Sacajawea State Park
Road 40 East
Pasco, WA 99301
509-545-2361

Honors the Native American woman who guided Meriwether Lewis and William Clark on their western expedition (1803–6). Center includes artifacts of area Indians.

See additional listing for Sacajawea *under* North Dakota.

Whitman Mission National Historic Site

Walla Walla, WA 99362
509-522-6360; 509-529-2761

Memorial to Narcissa Prentiss Whitman and her husband, missionaries to Indians in the Northwest (1836–47). Site includes museum that offers demonstrations of pioneer crafts during the summer.

See additional listing for Prentiss *under* New York.

West Virginia

Pearl S. Buck Birthplace Foundation

Box 126
Hillsboro, WV 24946
304-653-4430

Memorabilia and family furnishings of novelist Buck, first American woman to win a Nobel Prize for literature. Buck's manuscripts are housed nearby at West Virginia Wesleyan College.

See additional listing for Buck *under* Pennsylvania.

Wisconsin

Caddie Woodlawn Memorial Park

State Route 25
Menomonie, WI 54751

Honors the pioneer girl who inspired the children's book *Caddie Woodlawn*, by Carol Ryrie Brink; site includes Woodlawn's family home with memorabilia.

Wyoming

The Lockhart Home

109 West Yellowstone
Cody, WY 82414
307-587-6074; 800-377-7055

Restored residence, including furnishings and memorabilia, of Caroline Lockhart, first woman newspaper reporter in Boston and later owner and editor of the newspaper the *Cody Enterprise* from 1904 until her death in 1962. Although the home is now a bed-and-breakfast inn, free tours are available.

Esther Morris Statue

Capitol Avenue
Cheyenne, WY 82001

Statue honors a local resident who was both a pioneer activist for women's rights (she played a crucial role in securing voting rights for women in Wyoming) and a noted justice of the peace in South Pass City, a 19th-century mining town in western Wyoming.

A Note on Resources for the Study of Women's History

State and local historical societies throughout the country are excellent sources for materials on women's history.

A more extensive listing of women's historical sites may be found in: Sherr, Lynn, and Jurate Kazickas. *Susan B. Anthony Slept Here.* New York: Times Books, 1994.

SERIES INDEX

References to illustrations are indicated by page numbers in *italics*.

A

Abbott, Edith, **7**:96; **11**:9-10
Abbott, Grace, **7**:96; **8**:111; **11**:10-11
Abolitionism, **3**:103-5; **4**:62, 63-64, 111-12, 116-27; **5**:29, 42-46, 49, 62, 92-95, 121-22; **6**:37-38
Abortion, **3**:26, 46; **5**:58; **6**:44, 126; **9**:109-10; **10**:*8, 78, 93-94,* 104, 112, 125-26, 133-34
Abridgment of Universal Geography, Together with Sketches of History, An (Rowson), **3**:89
Abry, Phillis, **9**:44, *94*
Abzug, Bella, **10**:93; **11**:11
  activist role of, **8**:13-14
Adam (biblical character), **2**:74
Adams, Abigail, **2**:148-49; **3**:82, 130, 132; **11**:11-12, 198
Adams, John, **2**:148; **3**:82

Addams, Jane, **6**:122, *124;* **7**:17, *75,* 92-97, 125, 126; **8**:64; **10**:66; **11**:12-13; 188
Adkins, Jesse, **8**:27
Adkins v. *Children's Hospital* (1923,) **8**:28, 31
Advertising, **4**:*32;* **7**:*58, 59;* **8**:59-62, *65;* **9**:*92, 103*
Advocate of Moral Reform, **7**:98, 99
African Americans,
  during American Revolution, **3**:61-63
  childbirth, **3**:36
  child care, **3**:44-46
  clubs of, **4**:102-3; **6**:24; **7**:33, 86-88, 90; **8**:106-8
  as domestics, **6**:68-69; **7**:42-44, 64-65, 67-68
  education of, **2**:54; **4**:41-42; **6**:31-32, 72-73; **7**:*27, 84,* 91-92
  as nurses, **6**:74-76; **8**:44-45
  as physicians, **6**:79
  post–World War II era, **9**:11, 14-16, 30-34, 57-58, 80-87, 110-15, 121-26
  religious beliefs of, **2**:93-94; **4**:65-66; **6**:24

  as teachers, **6**:30-32, 77; **7**:80
  in tobacco factories, **6**:69, 72; **7**:69
  as westward pioneers, **6**:97-98
  See also Civil rights movement; Discrimination; Exodusters; Free blacks; Slavery
African-American women,
  as artists, **8**:72-79
  in Communist party, **8**:130
  as domestic servants, **6**:68-69; **7**:60, 65-67; **8**:*15,* 47-48, 75, 114, 116; **9**:80-81
  education of, **2**:54; **4**:41-42; **6**:31-32; **7**:91-92
  male suffrage, **6**:39-40
  marriage among, **2**:58-59; **3**:*113;* **4**:24-26
  as nurses, **6**:74-76; **8**:44-45
  as professionals, **8**:44
  religious beliefs of, **2**:93-94; **4**:65-66; **6**:24
  as slaves, **2**:38-43, 93-94, 112-14, 133-34; **3**:40-41, 112-15; **4**:41-42; **5**:12-15, 17-26
  as teachers, **6**:31

Acknowledgments

Many thanks are due to Professor Nancy Cott, who read and astutely critiqued each biography in this volume; Nancy Toff, executive editor at Oxford University Press, who polished my prose and cheered my flagging spirits throughout the long writing process; Paul McCarthy, assistant project editor, who skillfully coordinated the editorial production needs of this book and patiently dealt with numerous rounds of revisions and corrections; and my husband, Jay Banks, who cheerfully spent the last two years living with more than 250 women.

Picture Credits

Harriet Sigerman is a historian and free-lance writer who has contributed to *European Immigrant Women in the United States: A Biographical Dictionary* and *The Young Reader's Companion to American History*. She has been a research assistant to Henry Steele Commager at Amherst College and for the Stanton-Anthony Papers at the University of Massachusetts at Amherst. A graduate of the University of California at Irvine, she holds an M.A. and Ph.D. in American history from the University of Massachusetts at Amherst.

Nancy F. Cott is Stanley Woodward Professor of history and American studies at Yale University. She is the author of *The Bonds of Womanhood: "Woman's Sphere" in New England 1780–1835*, *The Grounding of Modern Feminism*, and *A Woman Making History: Mary Ritter Beard Through Her Letters*; editor of *Root of Bitterness: Documents of the Social History of American Women*; and co-editor of *A Heritage of Her Own: Toward a New Social History of American Women*.